DATE DUE			

KOU

4092

Praise for the Fifth Edition of
The Leadership Challenge
NAMED A BEST BUSINESS BOOK OF 2012 BY *FAST COMPANY*

"My heart goes out to Jim Kouzes and Barry Posner with the deepest gratitude for this book, the most powerful leadership resource available. It is providential that at a time of the lowest level of trust and the highest level of cynicism, *The Leadership Challenge* arrives with its message of hope. When there are dark days in our lives, Kouzes and Posner will shine a light."
 —**Frances Hesselbein,** former CEO, Girl Scouts of the USA;
 author, *My Life in Leadership*

"Jim Kouzes and Barry Posner have taken one of the true leadership classics of the late twentieth century and made it freshly relevant for today's twenty-first century leaders. It is a must-read for today's leaders who aspire to contribute in a more significant way tomorrow."
 —**Douglas R. Conant,** *New York Times* bestselling author, *TouchPoints;*
 retired CEO, Campbell Soup Company

"For twenty-five years, the names Jim Kouzes and Barry Posner have been synonymous with leadership. There is a reason for that. This book, in its new and updated form, demonstrates that leadership is a challenge you must win every day. It shows that every leader is unique, with his or her own style, and it helps you find your style. But the real beauty of this book is that it does not just *tell* you about leadership. It takes you by the hand, and walks you through the steps necessary to be better at what you do. It also gives you the confidence to take the kinds of risks every leader needs to take to succeed. I loved this book twenty-five years ago, and I love it today."
 —**Joel Kurtzman,** author, *Common Purpose*; editor-in-chief,
 Korn/Ferry Institute's *Briefings on Talent & Leadership*

"We consider this twenty-fifth anniversary, fifth edition, *the* best leadership book out there because it combines solid research, marvelous stories, and highly usable advice. It struck us, as readers of prior editions, that Jim Kouzes and Barry Posner don't just write about leadership. They lead, and they continue to innovate and model the way. We're glad to be on the path behind them."
 —**Jennifer Granholm and Dan Mulhern,** coauthors, *A Governor's Story: The Fight for Jobs and America's Economic Future*

"If I could recommend only one of the tens of thousands of leadership books ever written, *The Leadership Challenge* would absolutely be my top choice, and by a wide margin. This new edition builds markedly on the last but remains characteristically Jim Kouzes and Barry Posner—a complex work in its underlying character, but brilliant in its simplicity and practical in design. *The Leadership Challenge* is the most useful leadership book ever written; I have each and every edition, and each is better than the last."
 —**Tom Kolditz,** author, *In Extremis Leadership*

"*The Leadership Challenge* has inspired and continues to inspire all those who have the will and commitment to take on the burden of responsibility entailed in leading other people. The book lightens that burden and even ennobles it. It values the humanity in us all and welcomes imagination and faith in the future. We are all grateful and better off with this book on the shelf and in our hearts."

 —**Peter Block,** author, *Flawless Consulting*

"The fifth edition of *The Leadership Challenge* is the culmination of decades of rigorous analysis of the characteristics of leadership. By modeling the behaviors described by Jim Kouzes and Barry Posner, every person can develop their leadership potential and become a more effective leader."

 —**Dan Warmenhoven,** executive chairman, board of directors, NetApp

"Developing generations of leaders for three decades, Jim Kouzes and Barry Posner are yet again at the cutting edge of leadership. Their five practices of exemplary leadership exactly put into words the characteristics of leadership that I have witnessed from many of the greatest football players to ever play the game. If you have ever aspired to be a leader, or need to take your leadership skills to the highest levels, this is the book for you—all you need to do is take the challenge!"

 —**Brent Jones,** former All-Pro football player;
 managing partner, Northgate Capital

"*The Leadership Challenge* is the best research-based practical field guide for leaders I have ever read. While the world around us has changed significantly since 1987, when I picked up the first edition of the book, the simple relevant truths of what great leaders do has not. I love the personal best leadership stories that highlight the five simple-to-understand exemplary practices that really matter. Great leaders are lifelong learners, and there is no better place to start or continue your leadership learning journey than to read this book."

 —**James Foster,** senior vice president, chief product supply officer, the Clorox
 Company

"Whether you are just beginning your leadership journey, are a seasoned CEO, or a professor of leadership, this timeless leadership classic needs to be within constant reach!"

 —**Harry Kraemer Jr.,** former chairman and CEO, Baxter
 International; professor of management and strategy,
 Northwestern University's Kellogg School of Management

"There are hundreds of leadership books on the market, and you'll probably get something out of each of them, but none are so solidly based on research as *The Leadership Challenge*. This is *the* book that goes beyond opinion and guides you to those behaviors that bring out the strength in others."

—**Janelle Barlow,** author, *A Complaint Is a Gift* and *Branded Customer Service*

"*The Leadership Challenge* is the first book I recommend to all new leaders in Kaiser Permanente. Twenty-five years after it was first written, it remains the best guide to leadership success, and in a time of global competition and economic uncertainty, the principles elucidated by Jim Kouzes and Barry Posner serve as a powerful foundation for any individual hoping to help others innovate and embrace change. Leaders should be required to re-read this book every five years of their career."

—**Robert Pearl,** MD, executive director and CEO, The Permanente Medical Group, Kaiser Permanente

"Seldom, it seems, have I been in the office of an HR professional where I did not see a copy of *The Leadership Challenge*. The book has become a go-to source for professionals looking for insight into leadership development. Now Jim Kouzes and Barry Posner have gone back to the well to create an all-new fifth edition. While The Five Practices of Exemplary Leadership are as timely as ever, the stories are fresh and the insights are just as compelling. Simple and accessible, *The Leadership Challenge* is so packed with information that people who care about leadership need to put it on their shelves—but only after reading it cover to cover."

—**John Baldoni,** president, Baldoni Consulting LLC; author, *Lead With Purpose, Lead Your Boss,* and *Lead By Example*

"It is truly laudatory that Jim and Barry are celebrating the twenty-fifth year of a book that never lost its appeal. The authors have observed, interviewed, consulted, taught, and thought for all those years, and they continually bring us the best stories, examples, and lessons to keep their work ever green. Bravo and thank you!"

—**Beverly Kaye,** founder, co-CEO, Career Systems International; coauthor, *Help Them Grow or Watch Them Go*

"Speaking from experience, it's not easy to make research findings engaging, practical, and a pleasure to read. In this new edition of *The Leadership Challenge*, Jim Kouzes and Barry Posner have once again found that elusive balance between focusing on the data and telling a great story. No other leadership book is as compelling, as comprehensive, or as effective in teaching us how to go about making the changes we must make, in order to become the kind of leaders who can move mountains. If you could read only one book about the art and science of leading, then this is without question the book you should read."

—**Heidi Grant Halvorson,** author, *Nine Things Successful People Do Differently*

"*The Leadership Challenge* is a proven, data-driven model for leadership that has stood the test of time. The simple, effective framework works across industries and cultures, helping leaders engage their organizations and deliver superior performance; this has never been more important than in today's interconnected, fast-moving world."

—**Mike Splinter,** CEO, Applied Materials

"*The Leadership Challenge* has re-energized leadership at Applied Materials. The Five Practices of Exemplary Leadership provide a commonsense approach that is within the reach of anybody who needs to get work done through others."

—**Mary Humiston,** senior vice president, global
human resources, Applied Materials

"Kouzes and Posner have given us a handbook of hope: leadership can be learned at any level in an organization. The book provides identifiable skills, practices, and abilities available to anyone willing to develop themselves—not just those charismatic personalities at the top. Research-based, conversationally written, and practically applied, *The Leadership Challenge* is absolutely the most comprehensive and credible book on leadership to date."

—**Dianna Booher,** author, *Creating Personal Presence*

"*The Leadership Challenge* has gone from being a revelation to a standard to a classic. It is now the defining book on leadership for our time, and there is not a business, government, academic, or military leader in the developed world who, consciously or not, has not been taught its lessons."

—**Mike Malone,** associate fellow at Said Business
School (Oxford); author, *Bill & Dave*

"When Jim Kouzes and Barry Posner write on leadership, all of us had better pay attention. The fifth edition of *The Leadership Challenge* will quickly become a classic. Stop what you are doing and start reading, leading, and achieving."

—**Pat Williams,** senior vice president, Orlando Magic;
author, *Leadership Excellence*

"*The Leadership Challenge* includes real-life stories of globally diverse and inclusive people sharing their personal leadership challenges and learnings. From these real-life stories and the authors' extensive fact-based research, Jim and Barry challenge each of us to continually improve our leadership skills and inspire others to do the same, and give us the formula to do just that. This book is as close to the bible on leadership as you will find. From business person to family person anywhere in the world, it has lessons on leadership for all."

—**Stephen Almassy,** global vice chair, OCA/Industry,
Ernst & Young Global Limited

"For the last twenty years, I have been lucky enough to have worked with some of the world's best mentors in the field of leadership development. Very few, I have discovered, are equally comfortable in both the ivory tower and corporate boardroom. Jim and Barry have found the sweet spot and showcase it brilliantly in *The Leadership Challenge*. It's hard to think of a book that has had more of an influence on my own writing, as well as my own practice advising corporate boards on CEO succession, than this landmark book. Although I could continue gushing for pages about the contributions that Jim and Barry have made to the field of leadership, I can boil down my thoughts into just two words: thank you!"

—**Jeffrey Cohn,** coauthor, *Why Are We Bad at Picking Good Leaders?*

"Nobody knows leadership better than Jim Kouzes and Barry Posner. They use real, current, and practical illustrations of what leadership looks like and then demonstrate how to improve its practice. A must-read for every leader, *The Leadership Challenge* should be a part of every entrepreneur and intrapreneur's business plan!"

—**Carol Sands,** managing member, The Angels' Forum

"Jim Kouzes and Barry Posner know how to draw upon what we know (the evidence) to describe and teach what we need to do (through examples and reflection exercises) in order to be more effective health care leaders. The book is as appropriate, accessible, and helpful for new leaders as it is for those with years of experience. I have personally observed current and future leaders using this book to strengthen their leadership and personal effectiveness."

—**Christy Harris Lemak,** director, the Griffith Leadership Center in Health Management and Policy; associate professor, health management and policy, University of Michigan School of Public Health

"Jim and Barry start from the most basic aspect of leadership: that human beings need purpose, values, and respect to be motivated. Given their starting point, it is perhaps not surprising that they hit the mark. Still the best book out there on leadership."

—**Ken Wilcox,** chairman, Silicon Valley Bank

"For twenty-five years *The Leadership Challenge* has been a source of inspiration and insight for some of the best educators I know. In this latest edition, Kouzes and Posner have added important wisdom and updated thinking to their work. *The Leadership Challenge* is indispensable reading for those who take on the leadership of our schools."

—**Kevin Skelly,** superintendent, Palo Alto Unified School District

"The nation's health care system is in transition with significant system and economic changes. Physician leadership will be necessary to make this transformation successful, while maintaining the focus on our patients. *The Leadership Challenge* gives present and future physician leaders the leadership practices that will make them both better leaders and physicians."

—**Fernando Mendoza,** MD, MPH; professor and chief, Division of General Pediatrics; service chief, general pediatrics, Lucile Packard Children's Hospital; associate dean of Minority Advising and Programs, School of Medicine, Stanford University

"Up-to-date, superbly compelling, and full of heart, the fifth edition of Jim Kouzes and Barry Posner's classic draws on an unmatched trove of new data to offer fresh context to the fundamentals of great leadership. *The Leadership Challenge* remains the essential text for leaders who want to achieve the extraordinary in today's hypercompetitive environment."

—**Sally Helgesen,** author, *The Female Advantage*

"Peter Drucker would probably have called the publishing of Jim Kouzes and Barry Posner's book *The Leadership Challenge* 'a distinguished public service.' There is no doubt that it was that and that the twenty-fifth anniversary edition of this wonderful book continues to show organizations how to get extraordinary things done."

—**William A. Cohen,** Major General, USAFR, Ret; author of *Drucker on Leadership* and *Heroic Leadership*

"This fifth edition of *The Leadership Challenge* is Jim Kouzes and Barry Posner's gift to leaders in the twenty-first century. Join them and hundreds of thousands of others using this guide to extraordinary leadership."

— **Geoff Bellman,** consultant; author, *Extraordinary Groups: How Ordinary Teams Achieve Amazing Results*

"The twenty-fifth anniversary edition of *The Leadership Challenge* is another great reference for leaders and would-be leaders globally. Over the years, the Kouzes and Posner five leadership practices have crossed borders, cultures, and generations."

—**Joe Hage,** associate CIO, American University of Beirut

"This fifth edition of *The Leadership Challenge* continues as a must-read for any global leader or aspiring leader. *The Leadership Challenge* has been my compass in guiding and developing as a leader, developing other leaders, and in engaging future leaders. Barry and Jim's research reinforces that active learning and unending practice are foundational for leaders. To be a compelling leader, mastery of the principles of *The Leadership Challenge* is absolutely essential."

—**Bill Maxwell,** former senior vice president, human resources, Oakwood Temporary Housing

"In the midst of great change, sometimes it is important to return to timeless ideas. In their twenty-fifth anniversary edition, Jim Kouzes and Barry Posner reframe their leadership principles for global challenges in the twenty-first century. If you read it before, it's time to read it again. If you haven't read it, expect a master class on leadership in these turbulent times."

—**Joel Barker,** author, *Paradigms: The Business of Discovering the Future*

"The precious message of this insightful and important book is that leadership does not attach to a job or any position. It is seized, by a combination of credibility and courage. In a world where too many are simply milling around, here is a primer for taking charge."

—**Irwin Federman,** general partner, US Venture Partners

"As the entire economy undergoes a fundamental phase change, in which both the organization and the workplace are being reinvented before our very eyes, a new generation of leaders will find in the deep insights and engaging stories of this updated edition of *The Leadership Challenge* the guidance they require."

—**Stephen Denning,** author, *The Leader's Guide to Radical Management*

"This classic has improved with age. Fresh examples and global cases make the fifth edition of *The Leadership Challenge* more relevant to more relationships than ever."

—**Tim Scudder and Michael Patterson,** coauthors, *Have a Nice Conflict*

"Few leadership books stand the test of time, but *The Leadership Challenge* continues to show the path to being a leader of substance. Filled with great examples and rooted in rock solid research, it is a must-read for every leader."

—**John B. Izzo,** author, *Stepping Up*

"*The Leadership Challenge* is the bible of leadership research and application. This 5th edition of this masterful body of work will uplift your business and your life, and—more important—help you to get extraordinary things done every day. I'd swear on it."

—**Steve Farber,** author, *The Radical Leap Re-Energized;* founder, The Extreme Leadership Institute

THE LEADERSHIP CHALLENGE MOBILE TOOL

Download *The Leadership Challenge Mobile Tool Lite* app designed to enable you to apply the concepts and practices described in *The Leadership Challenge, Fifth Edition*. Use it daily to make progress on your leadership and development path. *The Leadership Challenge Mobile Tool Lite* app is free and works with the Take Action sections at the ends of chapters Two through Eleven, adding utility and functionality to the activities suggested there. The app allows you to immediately integrate some of the Take Action activities into your daily life, making them an ongoing and natural part of your leadership repertoire. Features include the ability to:

- Create and track your own personal Take Action plan
- Create reminders
- Share via social media

The complete *Leadership Challenge Mobile Tool* is available for purchase and is even more robust with everything in the lite version plus additional features such as the ability to seamlessly request-and-receive feedback, email activities, and use calendar reminders. It also includes:

- Videos of the authors
- A concise overview of *The Leadership Challenge* model
- Daily inspirational quotes
- A news feed

These valuable tools are currently available in the Apple App Store. On an ongoing basis, these apps will be developed to fit your needs, so let us know how we can help you liberate and develop the leader within.

Visit www.leadershipchallenge.com/go/tlcapp to learn more.

THE
LEADERSHIP
CHALLENGE

FIFTH EDITION

How to Make Extraordinary Things
Happen in Organizations

JAMES M. KOUZES
BARRY Z. POSNER

THE
LEADERSHIP
CHALLENGE
A Wiley Brand

Published by The Leadership Challenge®
A Wiley Brand
One Montgomery Street, Suite 1200, San Francisco, CA 94104-4594
www.leadershipchallenge.com

Author photo by John Brennan

Limit of Liability/Disclaimer of Warranty: While the publisher and author have used their best efforts in preparing this book, they make no representations or warranties with respect to the accuracy or completeness of the contents of this book and specifically disclaim any implied warranties of merchantability or fitness for a particular purpose. No warranty may be created or extended by sales representatives or written sales materials. The advice and strategies contained herein may not be suitable for your situation. You should consult with a professional where appropriate. Neither the publisher nor author shall be liable for any loss of profit or any other commercial damages, including but not limited to special, incidental, consequential, or other damages. Readers should be aware that Internet Web sites offered as citations and/or sources for further information may have changed or disappeared between the time this was written and when it is read.

For additional copies or bulk purchases of this book or to learn more about The Leadership Challenge®, please contact us toll free at 1-866-888-5159 or by email at leadership@wiley.com.

Wiley also publishes its books in a variety of electronic formats and by print-on-demand. Some material included with standard print versions of this book may not be included in e-books or in print-on-demand. If the version of this book that you purchased references media such as a CD or DVD that was not included in your purchase, you may download this material at http://booksupport.wiley.com.

For more information about Wiley products, visit www.wiley.com.

Library of Congress Cataloging-in-Publication Data
Kouzes, James M.
  The leadership challenge : how to make extraordinary things happen in organizations / James M. Kouzes, Barry Z. Posner.—5th ed.
      p. cm.
  Includes bibliographical references and index.
  ISBN 978-0-470-65172-8 (cloth); ISBN 978-1-118-28196-3 (ebk); ISBN 978-1-118-28248-9 (ebk); ISBN 978-1-118-28431-5 (ebk)
  1. Leadership.   2. Executive ability.   3. Management.   I. Posner, Barry Z.   II. Title.
  HD57.7.K68 2012
  658.4'092—dc23

                                                    2012005728

Printed in the United States of America
FIFTH EDITION
HB Printing 10 9 8 7 6

Contents

CONTENTS

For Tae and Jackie
with all our love.
Thank you for all you do and
all that you have given us.

Making Extraordinary Things Happen in Organizations

LEADERS GET PEOPLE MOVING. They energize and mobilize. They take people and organizations to places they have never been before. Leadership is not a fad, and the leadership challenge never goes away.

In uncertain and turbulent times, accepting that challenge is the only antidote to chaos, stagnation, and disintegration. Times change, problems change, technologies change, and people change. Leadership endures. Teams, organizations, and communities need people to step up and take charge. That is why we first wrote *The Leadership Challenge,* and why we found it imperative to write this fifth edition.

Change is the province of leaders. It is the work of leaders to inspire people to do things differently, to struggle against uncertain odds, and to persevere toward a misty image of a better future. Without leadership there would not be the extraordinary efforts necessary to solve existing problems and realize unimagined opportunities. We have today, at best, only faint clues of what the future may hold, but we are confident that without leadership the possibilities will neither be envisioned nor attained.

THE LEADERSHIP CHALLENGE

The Leadership Challenge is about how leaders mobilize others to want to make extraordinary things happen in organizations. It's about the practices leaders use to transform values into actions, visions into realities, obstacles into innovations, separateness into solidarity, and risks into rewards. It's about leadership that creates the climate in which people turn challenging opportunities into remarkable successes.

The publication of this edition of *The Leadership Challenge* marks twenty-five years since the book was first released. We've spent more than three decades together researching, consulting, teaching, and writing about what leaders do and how everyone can learn to be a better leader. We're honored by the reception we've received in the professional and business marketplace. Although we and other authors regularly contribute new works, we are blessed that students, educators, and practitioners continue to find that *The Leadership Challenge* is still useful to them, both conceptually and practically, and that it stands the test of time.

We persist in asking today the same basic question we asked in 1982 when we started our journey into understanding exemplary leadership: *What did you do when you were at your personal best as a leader?* We've talked to men and women, young and old, representing just about every type of organization there is, at all levels, in all functions, from many different places around the world. Their stories, and the behaviors and actions they've described, have resulted in the creation of The Five Practices of Exemplary Leadership® framework described in this book. When leaders do their best, they Model the Way, Inspire a Shared Vision, Challenge the Process, Enable Others to Act, and Encourage the Heart.

The Leadership Challenge is evidence based. The Five Practices are derived from research and we illustrate them with examples from real people doing real things. With each edition of the book, we update the research—both our own findings and those from other scholars around the globe. And we continue to update the stories, cases, and examples of exactly what people do when they are at their best as leaders.

With each new edition, we become clearer ourselves about what really makes a difference. We get the chance to reiterate what's still important, to discard what's not, and to add what's new. We get the chance to contemporize the framework and freshen up the language and point of view so that the book is highly relevant to current circumstances and conditions. We get the chance to let go of tangents—those important but smaller points that can be distracting or make things more complicated than they need to be. We get the chance to be more prescriptive about the best practices of leaders. The more we research and the more we write about leadership, the more confident we become that leadership is within the grasp of everyone and that the opportunities for leadership are boundless and boundaryless.

Of course, with each edition, we also get to address a new audience, and sometimes even a new generation of emerging leaders. That opportunity motivates us to collect new cases, examine new research findings, and talk with people we haven't heard from. It encourages us to perform a litmus test of relevance on our results: Does this model of leadership make sense? If we started out all over again, would we find new leadership practices? Would we eliminate any of the practices? In this regard, we are aided by the ongoing empirical data provided by the online version of the Leadership Practices Inventory (LPI). This inventory, which assesses The Five Practices, provides 500,000 to 750,000 responses annually and keeps us on guard and on target in identifying the behaviors that make a difference—and the ones that don't seem to matter.

And, with each new edition, we get a chance to speak again with those of you who have read earlier editions of *The Leadership Challenge* in school or in the workplace. If you're reading this book for the first time, welcome. If you are returning to it again, welcome back. Join us in reading this new edition so that you can learn about and be reminded of The Five Practices and what they look like in action today. Learn more about how you can continue to grow and to develop yourself as leader.

We expect that all of you face vexing issues that not only make leadership more urgent but also require you to be more conscious and conscientious about being a leader. Others are looking to you to help them figure out what they should be doing and how they can develop themselves to be leaders. You don't just owe it to yourself to become the best leader you can possibly be. You're even more responsible to others. You may not know it, but they're expecting you to do your best.

A FIELD GUIDE FOR LEADERS

How do you get other people to want to follow you? How do you get other people, by free will and free choice, to move forward together on a common purpose? How do you mobilize others to want to struggle to achieve shared aspirations? These are the important questions we address in *The Leadership Challenge*. Think of it as a field guide to take along on your leadership journey. Think of it as a manual you can consult when you want advice and counsel on how to get extraordinary things done in your organization.

In Chapter One, we establish our point of view about leadership by sharing a *Personal-Best Leadership Experience*—a case study about how one leader helped turn her organization around and develop it into an award-winning venture. We provide an overview of The Five Practices, summarize the findings from our more than three decades of empirical studies about what leaders do when they are at their best, and show that these leadership practices make a difference.

Asking leaders about their personal bests is only half the story. Leadership is a relationship between leaders and followers. A complete picture of leadership can be developed only if you ask followers what they look for and admire in a leader. In the second part of Chapter One, we reveal what characteristics people value most in their leaders, and demonstrate that credibility is the foundation of the relationship between leaders and their constituents.

The ten chapters that follow describe The Ten Commitments of Leadership—the essential behaviors that leaders employ to make extraordinary things happen—and explain the fundamental principles that support each of The Five Practices. We offer evidence from our research, and that of others, to support the principles, provide actual case examples of real people who demonstrate each practice, and prescribe specific recommendations of what you can do to make each practice your own and to continue your development as a leader. A *Take Action* section concludes each of these chapters—here's what you need to do to make this leadership practice an ongoing and natural part of your behavioral and attitudinal repertoire. Whether the focus is your own learning or the development of your constituents—your direct reports, team, peers, manager, community members, and the like—you can take immediate action on every one of our recommendations. They don't require a budget or approval from top management—or anyone else. They just require your personal commitment and discipline. If you'd like a mobile partner or tool to help you take action along your leadership journey and development path, download *The Leadership Challenge Mobile Tool* app, which has been designed to work with these sections, the activities within, and the practices in general.

In Chapter Twelve, we offer a call to everyone to accept personal responsibility to be a role model for leadership. Through five editions now of *The Leadership Challenge*, we keep relearning and reminding ourselves and others that leadership is everyone's business. The first place to look for leadership is within yourself. Accepting the leadership challenge requires practice, reflection, humility, and commitment to making a difference. And, in the end, we conclude that leadership is not an affair of the head. Leadership is an affair of the heart.

We recommend that you first read Chapter One, but please note that after that there is no sacred order to proceeding through the rest of this book. Go wherever your interests take you. We wrote this material to support you in your leadership development. Just remember that each practice is essential. Although you might skip around in the book, you can't skip any of the fundamentals of leadership.

Finally, technology allows us to offer you insights beyond those in this book. On our Web site www.theleadershipchallenge.com, you can find out more about how we conducted our research, look at detailed information on our methodology, review statistical data, read highlights of validation studies by other scholars of our leadership paradigm, and sign up for our monthly newsletter.

The domain of leaders is the future. The leader's unique legacy is the creation of valued institutions that survive over time. The most significant contribution leaders make is not simply to today's bottom line; it is to the long-term development of people and institutions so they can adapt, change, prosper, and grow. We hope this book contributes to the revitalization of organizations, to the creation of new enterprises, to the renewal of healthy communities, and to greater respect and understanding in the world. We also fervently hope that it enriches your life and that of your community and your family.

Leadership is important, not just in your career and within your organization, but in every sector, in every community, and in every country. We need more exemplary leaders, and we need them more than ever. There is so much extraordinary work that needs to be done. We need leaders who can unite us and ignite us.

In the end, we realize that leadership development is self-development. Meeting the leadership challenge is a personal—and daily—challenge for everyone. We know that if you have the will and the way to lead, you can. You have to supply the will. We'll do our best to keep supplying the way.

May 2012

James M. Kouzes
Orinda, California

Barry Z. Posner
Santa Clara, California

CHAPTER 1

When Leaders Are at Their Best

"FEARLESS." That's what it says in bold white letters on a black bracelet that Barby Siegel wears.[1] She borrowed it from her teenage daughter to serve as a daily reminder of the spirit she likes to bring to her role as CEO of Zeno Group, an award-winning, multidisciplinary public relations firm. And it's exactly that kind of spirit that fueled the extraordinary growth and willingness to take risks that *PRWeek* cited in 2011 when it awarded Zeno two of its top honors—Agency of the Year and Midsize Agency of the Year.

But Zeno wasn't always at the head of its class. When Richard Edelman, president and CEO of Zeno's parent company, Daniel J. Edelman, Inc., called Barby and asked her to lead Zeno to the next level, the agency was languishing. Barby, who had honed her craft over eleven years at Edelman and then for eight years at Ogilvy PR, where she restarted their global consumer marketing practice, was ready for a new opportunity and challenge.

Barby knew Zeno had a great team and a solid client base, but for them to grow to the next level, she believed that they had to get some early game-changing wins. And to do that they'd need some of that fearlessness that she proudly advocates for with her bracelet. She would tell them, "We need to stand on our own two feet and not be afraid because we're Zeno that we can't go after this piece of business or that we're not going to be taken seriously." She talked about it as "playing ahead of the game—ahead of where we really were." It didn't take long for this focused determination and can-do spirit to spread.

One of Barby's early actions was to hold a day-and-a-half leadership team meeting with her direct reports. Together they talked about such basic questions as "Who are we? What are we focusing on?" The conversations and sharing of ideas were galvanizing, and during that meeting they came up with the words that they envisioned as describing themselves. These words—*fearless, collaborative, creative, decidedly different,* and *nimble*—are their values and their promise to their clients.

Zeno describes itself as providing "senior level strategy and day-to-day engagement" and as having "no silos," and you can see this in Barby's actions. For example, she has spent many a night in the conference room with team members preparing decks for client presentations. And if she's not working on a presentation, she might be at the local grocer buying snacks to take back to the room. She's present at client pitches. She also spends as much time as she can with staff. Barby takes this responsibility seriously. "I often say, 'I am privileged to lead this team.' I am. Without them we'd be nothing. I need all these people to bring their best game every day. I wake up every day and say, What can I do to make sure these people are happy and energetic, that they're going to stay and continue to give our clients their best work every day?"

These sentiments are reciprocated by her associates. Alison Walsh, account supervisor, affirms that "when you have a CEO who is so ingrained in the agency, staff, and each and every one of the clients, you only want to push yourself further." Because Barby is so transparent about her values and vision for the organization, "There's no question," according to Alison, "that people want to follow her."

Barby describes the Zeno corporate culture as one that promotes hard work and continued success while also encouraging work-life balance and individualism. "I'm sure many companies describe themselves as a family," says Barby. "We take it seriously." For example, there are a lot of women in the firm, and Barby takes her role as a woman CEO very seriously. "I want them to see that it's possible to have a really great career and have a family and do all the things that that entails." She talks a lot about her own kids, her husband, her two older sisters, and her elderly parents. She'll tell her staff when she goes out to have lunch with her parents. "I want them to know that it's okay to get out of the office for a couple of hours and tend to their families." She has a photo gallery in her office with lots of family pictures displayed along with photos of agency get-togethers and some of the staff and their babies. "I'm very mindful," says Barby, "that the staff is like me. We all have mortgages to pay. Many have children to raise. When I make decisions about what the firm is going to do, I am mindful that at the end of the day there are hundreds of families depending on our doing right for our clients."

Unlike traditional agencies, Zeno is an organization without walls, where everyone, regardless of level, routinely works together on all aspects of a client engagement. "Everyone is treated with great respect," said Cheryl Pellegrino, senior vice president. "There is a strong sense of collaboration and teamwork. People genuinely like one another and work well together. It's all for one and one for all." Barby has structured the organization and assignments so that people literally have to work with one another, learn from one another, and celebrate together. Marcie Kohenak, account supervisor, adds that whereas many agencies may say they're one team, "Zeno walks the walk. Never before have I worked in an office where colleagues are so collaborative, looking out for clients and the teams before them- selves, and where individuals from different offices and fields are always working together. Not only does this attitude benefit our clients, who are always being served by a subject matter expert, but as employees we have the opportunity to constantly grow, working with and learning from colleagues across the country."

Zeno is also unique in the PR business in how it manages its books: all offices operate under one P&L. If a client in Chicago needs the expertise of someone in Los Angeles, New York, Toronto, or São Paulo, there's no conflict or conversation about it. Barby said that this means that "the staff can just do their best work, and don't need to feel pulled by one P&L or another. Everyone is focusing on our client's success."

Collaborating across offices to get the job done also facilitates innovation and experimentation. Creativity is hugely important to Barby. "We want to be creative in everything we do, even in the most mundane tasks," she said. This is what, in large part, keeps Jessica Vitale, vice president, with Zeno. "You get countless opportunities to work on exciting projects for clients who are leaders in their field, and the chance to work alongside incredibly smart, passionate people across multiple offices who provide great support and encourage, even push, you to grow," she said. This learning environment, Barby explained, "helps all of us to think differently, to be unafraid to experiment and try some things that have not been done before."

There are many celebrations over the year, such as the Friday after-work sing-alongs and other informal get-togethers and recognitions. Barby established an annual New Year's Eve party every June 30, the end of Zeno's fiscal year. On that day, all the offices connect by teleconference. They pop champagne and raise a virtual toast. Barby reflects on what they've accomplished and talks about what's ahead in the future. Then all the offices continue with their own celebrations.

In an end-of-year email to her staff, Barby summed up Zeno's achievements and culture:

> Each of you played a major role in the success of our firm, and each of you are key to the journey that continues.... [Words of praise] should be aimed squarely at you for the amazing work you and your teams have delivered and the ever-deepening client partnerships you are forging.... As we close out the year, I am more excited than ever for what's to come, and there isn't a group of professionals I would rather do it with day in and day out.
>
> We have much to look forward to. Some days will be harder than others but we are on a mission to take this firm to greater heights on the shoulders of client trust and partnership, game-changing work and a talented and highly motivated staff. I think we have seen that when we band together we can really do it.

Barby is not one to rest on her laurels, though. The recognition Zeno has earned is just the beginning. "I can't just live in the present," she said. "I've got to always be thinking about the next thing we should be working on and where we're headed, whether geographically or with innovation or talent." No doubt that the next thing is likely to require more of that same fearlessness that got Barby and her colleagues to where they are today.

THE FIVE PRACTICES OF EXEMPLARY LEADERSHIP

In undertaking the transformation at Zeno, Barby Siegel seized the opportunity to change business as usual. And although Barby's story is exceptional, it is not singular. We've been conducting original global research for more than thirty years, and we've discovered that such achievements are actually commonplace. When we ask people to tell us about their personal-best leadership experiences—experiences that they believe are their individual standards of excellence—there are thousands of success stories just like Barby's.[2] We've found them in profit-based firms and nonprofits, agriculture and mining, manufacturing and utilities, banking and health care, government and education, the arts and community service, and many, many others. These leaders are employees and volunteers, young and old, women and men. Leadership knows no racial or religious bounds, no ethnic or cultural borders. Leaders reside in every city and every country, in every function and every organization. We find exemplary leadership everywhere we look.

And we've also found that in the best organizations, everyone, regardless of title or position, is encouraged to act like a leader. That's because in these places, people don't just believe that everyone can make a difference; they act in ways to develop and grow people's talents, including their leadership capabilities. Joon Chin Fum-Ko, director of people development and engagement at Infocomm Development Authority of Singapore, underscores this thinking when she explains how they are "working to build an organization and culture where everyone feels that they are leaders, regardless of what they do, and appreciates that what each one of us does has an impact, even a legacy."

We first asked people in the early 1980s to tell us what they did when they were at their "personal best" in leading others, and we continue to ask this question of people around the world. After analyzing thousands of these leadership experiences, we discovered, and continue to find, that regardless of the times or setting, people who guide others along pioneering journeys follow surprisingly similar paths. Although each experience was unique in its individual expression, there were clearly identifiable behaviors and actions that made a difference. When making extraordinary things happen in organizations, leaders engage in what we call The Five Practices of Exemplary Leadership. They

- Model the Way
- Inspire a Shared Vision
- Challenge the Process
- Enable Others to Act
- Encourage the Heart

These leadership practices are not the private property of the people we studied. Nor do they belong to a few select shining stars. Leadership is not about who you are; it's about what you do. The Five Practices are available to anyone who accepts the leadership challenge—the challenge of taking people and organizations to places they have never been before, of doing something that has never been done before, and of moving beyond the ordinary to the extraordinary.

Although the *context* of leadership has changed dramatically since we first began our research thirty years ago, the *content* of leadership has not changed much at all. The Five Practices framework has passed the test of time. Our research tells us that the fundamental behaviors and actions of leaders have remained essentially the same and are as relevant today as they were when we first began our study of exemplary leadership.

You've already learned how one leader (Barby Siegel) used The Five Practices to lead her colleagues and organization to greatness, and how she and they are not ready to rest on their laurels. In the remainder of this chapter, we briefly introduce each of The Five Practices and provide short examples that demonstrate how leaders across a variety of circumstances use them to make the extraordinary happen. When you explore The Five Practices in depth in Chapters Two through Eleven, you'll find over a hundred more examples from the real-life experiences of people who have taken the leadership challenge.

Model the Way

Titles are granted, but it's your behavior that earns you respect. This sentiment was shared across all the cases we collected. David Kim, senior operations manager with Siemens Ultrasound, reflecting on his personal-best leadership experience, remarked that "Everybody is a leader whether you supervise a group of people or not. Even as an individual contributor when I transitioned into the corporate world from the army, I continued to display leadership and take initiative to get the job done. Titles don't make you a leader. It's how you behave that makes a difference." Exemplary leaders know that if they want to gain commitment and achieve the highest standards, they must be models of the behavior they expect of others.

To effectively Model the Way, you must first be clear about your own guiding principles. You must *clarify values by finding your voice.* Dave Halvorson, staff engineer with Intel, observed that "you do not need to be a manager with direct reports to be a leader, but you do have to know what your values and guiding principles are." Alan

Spiegelman, veteran wealth management adviser with Northwestern Mutual, reinforced Dave's point when he told us, "Before you can be a leader of others, you need to know clearly who you are and what your core values are. Once you know that, then you can give those values a voice and feel comfortable sharing them with others." But *your* values aren't the only values. On every team, and in every organization and community, others also feel strongly about matters of principle. As a leader, you also must *affirm the shared values* of the group.

Eloquent speeches about common values aren't nearly enough, however. Leaders' deeds are far more important than their words when constituents want to determine how serious leaders really are about what they say. Words and deeds must be consistent. Exemplary leaders *set the example by aligning actions with shared values.* Through their daily actions, they demonstrate their deep commitment to their beliefs and those of the organization. Dr. Jiangwan Majeti's experience as research project manager at Amgen underscores this observation: "Leading by example is more effective than leading by command. If people see that you work hard while preaching hard work, they are more likely to follow you." One of the best ways to prove that something is important is by doing it yourself and setting an example. Jiangwan's actions spoke volumes about how the team needed to "take ownership of things they believed in and valued," because there wasn't anything that she asked others to do that she wasn't willing to do herself.

Inspire a Shared Vision

People describe their personal-best leadership experiences as times when they imagined an exciting, highly attractive future for their organizations. They had visions and dreams of what *could* be. They had absolute and total personal belief in those dreams, and they were confident in their abilities to make extraordinary things happen. Every organization, every social movement, begins with a dream. The dream, or vision, is the force that creates the future. For Taryn Walker, product manager at Kaiser Permanente, this meant "remaining focused on the long-term vision and constantly reminding others (often when they became discouraged) of the ultimate outcome and how important this was."

Leaders *envision the future by imagining exciting and ennobling possibilities.* You need to make something happen, to change the way things are, to create something that no one else has ever created before. Much as an architect draws a blueprint or an engineer builds a model, you need to have a clear vision of what the results should look like before starting any project. You also have to be able to connect it to the past, to the history that got you to where you are. In starting the "Thinker's Club" at Juniper Networks, for example, Vittal Krishnamurthy imagined "that one day it would be a hub for innovative thinking, where people brainstorm on some of the most difficult issues and seek innovative solutions, and the go-to place where creative solutions emerge." He wanted to improve the quality of people's lives by making them creative thinkers, but he also realized that however noble this aspiration, visions seen only by leaders are insufficient to create an organized movement or a significant change in a company.

You can't command commitment; you have to inspire it. You have to *enlist others in a common vision by appealing to shared aspirations.* This means, as Rajan Prajapat, strategic partner manager at Google, pointed out, "that you have to have a vision in mind and be clear about why it's important to you. And you need to be equally clear about why it should matter to those you're sharing your vision with." Rupessh Roy, project manager at NetLogic Microsystems, realized in his personal-best leadership experience that people have to believe that you understand their needs and have their interests at heart. "You need to have clear goals and a vision to make a positive difference," he said, "and you have to be able to share that vision with others and get them to believe in it." Unity of purpose is forged when you show your constituents how the dream is a shared dream and how it fulfills the common good. When you express your enthusiasm and excitement for the vision, you ignite that passion in others.

Challenge the Process

Challenge is the crucible for greatness. Every single personal-best leadership case involved a change from the status quo. Not one person claimed to have achieved a personal best by keeping things the same. The challenge might have been an innovative new product, a cutting-edge service, a groundbreaking piece of legislation, an invigorating campaign to get adolescents to join an environmental program, a revolutionary turnaround of a bureaucratic military program, or the start-up of a new plant or business. It could also be dealing with unexpected economic downturns, personal betrayal, loss of physical ability, natural disasters, civil unrest, and technological disruptions. When Katherine Winkel, marketing operations manager at Seattle Genetics, reflected on her personal best and listened to those of her colleagues, she was struck by "how similar the stories were and how each person had to overcome uncertainty and fear in order to achieve his or her best."

Leaders venture out; they don't sit idly by waiting for fate to smile on them. This was exactly what Rob Pearson, now senior director of R&D at Maquet Cardiovascular, experienced in his first job after college at Medtronic Corporate Ventures: "Change was thrust upon me when I had to choose between being passive (guaranteed to fail) or seizing the initiative and bending the rules to suit my needs (increasing the possibility of success). I decided to rise up and meet the challenge head on." By making something happen, Rob was able to move his project forward.

Leaders are pioneers, willing to step out into the unknown. But leaders aren't the only creators or originators of new products, services, or processes. In fact, it's more likely that they're not. Innovation comes more from listening than from telling. You have to constantly be looking outside yourself and your organization for new and innovative products, processes, and services. You need to *search for opportunities by seizing the initiative and by looking outward for innovative ways to improve.*

Because innovation and change involve *experimenting and taking risks,* your major contribution will be to create a climate for experimentation in which there is recognition of good ideas, support of those ideas, and the willingness to challenge the system. Taking risks, says Ryan Diemer, business planner and purchasing analyst at Stryker Endoscopy, "is never easy and sometimes scary." But what he learned from his personal-best leadership experience is "that taking risks is necessary because it requires you and those you are working with to challenge not only what you are working on but how you work. Sometimes the risks pay off and sometimes they do not, but what is always true is that if you do not take a risk, you won't get any gain."

When you take risks, mistakes and failures are inevitable. Proceed anyway. One way of dealing with the potential failures of experimentation is *by constantly generating small wins and learning from experience.* Pierfrancesco Ronzi, associate with McKinsey & Company in Italy, recalled how, in successfully turning around the credit process for a banking client in North Africa, it was necessary to break the project down into parts so that people in the organization could find a place to start, to determine what would work and how they could learn from one another in the process of moving forward. "Showing them that we were able to make something happen," he said, "was a great boost for their confidence in the project and their willingness to stay involved." As Pierfrancesco suggests, leaders are constantly learning from their errors and failures as they experiment, try new things, and incrementally move projects forward. The best leaders are the simply the best learners, and life is their laboratory.[3]

Enable Others to Act

A grand dream doesn't become a significant reality through the actions of a single person. It requires a team effort. It requires solid trust and strong relationships. It requires deep competence and cool confidence. It requires group collaboration and individual accountability.[4] Sushma Bhope, program manager at Biomass NPL, appreciated how she had to "lead by empowering those around you." In consolidating a customer relationship management system across a globally dispersed company, she realized clearly that "no one could have done this alone." As other leaders have experienced, Sushma found that "it was essential to be open to all ideas and to give everyone a voice in the decision-making process.... The one guiding principle on the project was that the team was larger than any individual on the team." Sushma clearly understands that no leader has ever gotten anything extraordinary done by working solo.

Leaders *foster collaboration by building trust and facilitating relationships*. This sense of teamwork extends far beyond a few direct reports or close confidants. You have to engage all who must make the project work—and, in some way, all who must live with the results. Early in her career, Lorena Compeán, founder of Co-Creating Hong Kong, discovered that she needed to trust that other people on the project team could and would do their jobs. As the project manager, she found herself, at the beginning, "checking every single analysis they did, but I noticed how they got angry with me because I didn't let them conclude anything by themselves." She discovered that she needed to "show my trust in others in order to build their trust in me."

Constituents neither perform at their best nor stick around for very long if you make them feel weak, dependent, or alienated. Giving your power away and fostering their personal power and ownership will make them stronger and more capable. When you *strengthen others by increasing self-determination and developing competence,* they are more likely to give it their all and exceed their own expectations. Heidi Winkler, attorney-at-law with Pihl, a privately held construction company in Denmark, learned from reflecting on her personal-best leadership experience "how much easier it is to achieve shared goals (or even make goals shared) when you involve people in the decisions to be made, trust them to handle the execution, and give them responsibilities and credit along the way."

Focusing on serving the needs of others, and not one's own, builds trust in a leader. And the more that people trust their leaders and each other, the more they take risks, make changes, and keep organizations and movements alive. Derek Rupnow, business development manager at Broadcom, points out that "you develop trust and respect by building personal relationships, as well as treating everyone with respect, and making sure to keep everyone up to speed on what is going on." He seeks out the opinions of others and uses the ensuing discussions not only to build up their capabilities but also to educate and update his own information and perspective. Derek realizes that when people are trusted and have more discretion, more authority, and more information, they're much more likely to use their energies to produce extraordinary results. Through that relationship, leaders turn their constituents into leaders themselves.

Encourage the Heart

The climb to the top is arduous and steep. People become exhausted, frustrated, and disenchanted, and are often tempted to give up. Genuine acts of caring draw people forward. "Recognition is the most powerful currency you have, and it costs you nothing," says Jessica Herrin, CEO and founder of Stella & Dot, who oversees ten thousand mostly part-time stylists, who sell the jewelry line through private parties. She personally contacts at least ten stylists each day and makes it part of her regular to-do list to find and celebrate successes.[5] Right after Mark Hassin's company won the MSN-Microsoft Israel's Interactive Agencies Creative Competition, he sent a picture of the award to everyone on his team along with a note that said, "This is YOUR prize. Go tell your family, your friends—that YOU did this."

Leaders like Jessica and Mark *recognize contributions by showing appreciation for individual excellence.* Such recognition can be one-to-one or with many people. It can come from dramatic gestures or simple actions. Jennifer Dirking, associate director at Foothill–De Anza Community Colleges Foundation, is always on the lookout for ways to create a climate in which, she says, "people feel cared about and genuinely appreciated." When her team gets together to debrief an event, they start by acknowledging the aspects that were successful and giving positive feedback to the team members who deserved credit. Then, Jennifer explains, "as we evaluate those aspects that we want to improve, it is within this context of overall success. This approach improves morale and contributes to a more cooperative work environment."

It's part of your job as a leader to show appreciation for people's contributions and to create a culture of *celebrating the values and victories by creating a spirit of community.* Recognition and celebration aren't necessarily about fun and games, though there is a lot of fun and there are a lot of games when people encourage the hearts of their constituents. Neither are they about pretentious ceremonies designed to create some phony sense of camaraderie. Encouragement is, curiously, serious business because it's how you visibly and behaviorally link rewards with performance. Make sure that people see the benefit of behavior that's aligned with cherished values. Celebrations and rituals, when they are authentic and from the heart, build a strong sense of collective identity and community spirit that can carry a group through extraordinarily tough times.

The Five Practices of Exemplary Leadership are the core leadership competencies that emerged from our analysis of thousands of Personal-Best Leadership Experience cases. When leaders are doing their best, they Model the Way, Inspire a Shared Vision, Challenge the Process, Enable Others to Act, and Encourage the Heart.

These are the practices that people use when they are at their personal best as leaders. But what's the evidence that they really matter? Do these practices truly make a difference in the engagement and performance of people and organizations? Over the years, we've been challenged to answer these questions and to test the assertion that The Five Practices explain how leaders get extraordinary things done in organizations. The research and empirical evidence make the case that they do.

The Five Practices Make a Difference

The truth is that exemplary leader behavior makes a profoundly positive difference in people's commitment and performance at work. Those leaders who more frequently use The Five Practices of Exemplary Leadership are considerably more effective than their counterparts who use them infrequently.

That is the conclusion we draw after analyzing responses from nearly two million people around the world to the Leadership Practices Inventory (LPI), our 360-degree instrument assessing how frequently leaders engage in The Five Practices.[6] In addition to completing the LPI, respondents answer ten demographic questions ranging from their age and gender to their functional field, industry, and organization size.[7] They also respond to ten statements about how they feel about their leaders and their workplaces.[8]

The data show that workplace engagement and commitment are significantly explained by how the leader behaves and not at all by any particular characteristic of the constituents.

Statistical analyses revealed that a leader's behavior explains the vast majority of constituents' workplace engagement. A leader's actions contribute more to such factors as commitment, loyalty, motivation, pride, and productivity than does any other single variable.[9] Personal and organizational characteristics of constituents, in contrast, explain less than 1 percent of constituents' engagement in, commitment to, and pride in their workplaces. Workplace engagement and commitment are independent of who the constituents are (as related to factors like age, gender, ethnicity, or education) or their

FIGURE 1.1 Explaining Workplace Engagement and Commitment

position, job, discipline, industry, or nationality or country of origin. Figure 1.1 illustrates our findings.

In other words, the more you engage in The Five Practices of Exemplary Leadership, the more likely you are to have a positive influence on others and on the organization. As Caroline Wang—at one time the highest-ranking Asian female executive at IBM globally—reflected on her experiences with the Five Practices framework, "It is really not about the leader's personality; it is all about how that individual behaves as a leader." That's what all the data add up to: if you want to have a significant impact on people, on organizations, and on communities, you'd be wise to invest in learning the behaviors that enable you to become the very best leader you can.

Many other scholars have documented how leaders who engage in The Five Practices are more effective than those who don't. It doesn't matter whether the context is inside or outside the United

States, the public or private sector, or within schools, health care organizations, business firms, prisons, churches, and the like.[10] Leaders who use The Five Practices more frequently than their counterparts, for example,

- Create higher-performing teams
- Generate increased sales and customer satisfaction levels
- Foster renewed loyalty and greater organizational commitment
- Enhance motivation and the willingness to work hard
- More successfully represent their units to upper management
- Facilitate high patient-satisfaction scores and more effectively meet family member needs
- Promote high degrees of involvement in schools
- Enlarge the size of their religious congregations
- Increase fundraising results and expand gift-giving levels
- Extend the range of their agency's services
- Increase retention, reducing absenteeism and turnover
- Positively influence recruitment rates

Over a five-year period, the financial performance of organizations where senior leaders were identified by their constituents as "strongly" engaged in using The Five Practices were compared with those organizations whose leadership was significantly less engaged in The Five Practices.[11] The bottom line? Net income growth was nearly eighteen times higher, and stock price growth nearly three times higher, than their counterparts for those publicly traded organizations whose leadership was highly engaged in The Five Practices.

Although The Five Practices of Exemplary Leadership don't completely explain why leaders and their organizations are successful, it's very clear that engaging in them makes quite a difference no matter who you are or where you are located. How you behave as a leader matters, and it matters a lot.

Embedded in The Five Practices of Exemplary Leadership are behaviors that can serve as the basis for learning to lead. We call these The Ten Commitments of Leadership (Table 1.1). They focus on actions that you need to apply to yourself and that you need to take with others. These Ten Commitments serve as the template for explaining, understanding, appreciating, and learning how leaders get extraordinary things done in organizations, and we discuss each of them in depth in Chapters Two through Eleven.

Before delving into The Five Practices and The Ten Commitments further, however, we'd be remiss if we didn't consider leadership from the standpoint of the constituent. So, what do people look for in a leader? What do people want from someone whose direction they'd be willing to follow?

TABLE 1.1 THE FIVE PRACTICES AND TEN COMMITMENTS OF EXEMPLARY LEADERSHIP		
Model the Way		1. Clarify values by finding your voice and affirming shared values. 2. Set the example by aligning actions with shared values.
Inspire a Shared Vision		3. Envision the future by imagining exciting and ennobling possibilities. 4. Enlist others in a common vision by appealing to shared aspirations.
Challenge the Process		5. Search for opportunities by seizing the initiative and looking outward for innovative ways to improve. 6. Experiment and take risks by constantly generating small wins and learning from experience.
Enable Others to Act		7. Foster collaboration by building trust and facilitating relationships. 8. Strengthen others by increasing self-determination and developing competence.
Encourage the Heart		9. Recognize contributions by showing appreciation for individual excellence. 10. Celebrate the values and victories by creating a spirit of community.

LEADERSHIP IS A RELATIONSHIP

The inescapable conclusion from analyzing thousands of personal-best leadership experiences is that *everyone* has a story to tell. And these stories are much more similar in terms of actions, behaviors, and processes than they are different. The data clearly challenge the myths that leadership is something that you find only at the highest levels of organizations and society or that it's something reserved for only a handful of charismatic men and women. The notion that there are only a few great people who can lead others to greatness is just plain wrong. Likewise, it is plain wrong to believe that leaders come only from large or great or small or new organizations, or from established economies or from start-up companies. The truth is, leadership is an identifiable set of skills and abilities that are available to anyone. It is because there are so many leaders—not so few—that extraordinary things get done on a regular basis in organizations, especially in times of great uncertainty.

There was another crucial truth that wove itself throughout every situation and every action we've analyzed. Personal-best leadership experiences are never stories about solo performances. Leaders never get extraordinary things accomplished all by themselves. Leaders mobilize *others* to want to struggle for shared aspirations, and this means that, fundamentally, *leadership is a relationship*. Leadership is a relationship between those who aspire to lead and those who choose to follow. It's the quality of this relationship that matters most when engaged in getting extraordinary things done. A leader-constituent relationship that's characterized by fear and distrust will never produce anything of lasting value. A relationship characterized by mutual respect and confidence will overcome the greatest adversities and leave a legacy of significance.[12]

That is precisely what Yamin Durrani told us about his relationship with Bobby Matinpour, marketing manager at National Semiconductor, who came aboard just after the company had gone through a massive reorganization followed by a huge layoff. According to Yamin, "Company-wide there was a general lack of motivation, a sense of mistrust, insecurity, and everyone was looking after their own interest. Our group in particular was suffering from low motivation as we didn't trust each other. I dreaded going to the office, and there was too much internal competition leading to breakdowns in communication."

Bobby realized that he was going to have to get people to trust one another. His very first initiative was to sit with individual team members to understand their desires, needs, and future plans. For the first month, he spent most of the time learning and trying to understand what each person aspired to and enjoyed doing. He held weekly one-on-one meetings with individual team members, asking questions and listening attentively to what they had to say. "His friendly style and honest, straightforward approach," said Yamin, "led team members to open up and feel secure. He never acted as if he knew everything, and was open to learning new things from the team. Bobby understood that he couldn't gain the respect of the team without respecting them and allowing them the freedom to take ownership of their projects. Bobby opened up lines of communication within the team, especially by encouraging greater face-to-face interactions."

In management meetings when a question was asked, even though he could have provided the answer himself, Bobby typically referred it to one of his team members, stating, for example, "Yamin is an expert on this topic; I will let him answer this question." During the annual sales conference, attended by hundreds of company employees, he let the most junior team member deliver the group presentation, while the whole team stood behind the presenter to answer questions. Yamin observed,

> Being new to the group, Bobby could have easily fallen into the trap of trying to prove himself by individually contributing in projects, or acting as a gatekeeper for information flow; however, he opted to trust his team members on projects and took advice from them about the approach to take on a particular project. He never forced his ideas. In other words, "my way or the highway" was not his style. He encouraged team members to take initiative and acted as an adviser on projects, and let the ownership remain with the individual team member.

The results of Bobby's leadership were significant. The unit's revenue increased by 25 percent, and the product pipeline over-flowed with ideas. Team spirit soared, people felt engaged, and a general sense of collaboration and teamwork developed. Said Yamin, "I personally had not felt more empowered and trusted ever before. From this experience, I've realized that great leaders grow their fol-lowers into leaders themselves."

In the way he focused on others and not on himself, Bobby demonstrated that success in leadership, success in work, and success in life are a function of how well people work and play together. Success in leading is wholly dependent on the capacity to build and sustain those relationships. Because leadership is a reciprocal process between leaders and their constituents, any discussion of leadership must attend to the dynamics of this relationship. Strategies, tactics, skills, and practices are empty without an understanding of the fundamental human aspirations that connect leaders and constitu-ents. What are the ingredients for building such relationships?

What People Look For and Want from Their Leaders

To better understand leadership as a relationship, we investigated the expectations that constituents have of leaders. We asked people to tell us the personal traits, characteristics, and attributes they look for and admire in a person whom they would be *willing* to follow. The responses both affirm and enrich the picture that emerged from studies of personal leadership bests.

We began this research on what constituents expect of leaders more than thirty years ago by surveying thousands of business and government executives. Several hundred different values, traits, and characteristics were identified in response to the *open-ended* question about what they looked for in a person they would be willing to follow.[13] Subsequent content analysis by several independent judges, followed by further empirical analyses, reduced these items to a list of twenty characteristics (each grouped with several synonyms for clarification and completeness).

From this list of twenty characteristics, we developed the Characteristics of Admired Leaders checklist. It has been administered to well over one hundred thousand people around the globe, and the results are continuously updated. This one-page survey asks respondents to select the seven qualities, out of twenty, that they "most look for and admire in a leader, someone whose direction they would willingly follow." The key word in this statement is *willingly*. What do they expect from a leader they would follow, not because they have to, but because they want to?

The results have been striking in their regularity. Over the years, wherever this question is asked, it's clear, as the data in Table 1.2 illustrate, that there are some essential "character tests" an individual must pass before others are willing to grant the designation *leader*.

THE LEADERSHIP CHALLENGE

TABLE 1.2 Characteristics of Admired Leaders

Characteristic	Percentage of Respondents Selecting Each Characteristic				
	1987	1995	2002	2007	2012
HONEST	83	88	88	89	89
FORWARD-LOOKING	62	75	71	71	71
COMPETENT	67	63	66	68	69
INSPIRING	58	68	65	69	69
Intelligent	43	40	47	48	45
Broad-minded	37	40	40	35	38
Fair-minded	40	49	42	39	37
Dependable	33	32	33	34	35
Supportive	32	41	35	35	35
Straightforward	34	33	34	36	32
Cooperative	25	28	28	25	27
Determined	17	17	23	25	26
Courageous	27	29	20	25	22
Ambitious	21	13	17	16	21
Caring	26	23	20	22	21
Loyal	11	11	14	18	19
Imaginative	34	28	23	17	16
Mature	23	13	21	5	14
Self-Controlled	13	5	8	10	11
Independent	10	5	6	4	5

Note: These percentages represent respondents from six continents: Africa, North America, South America, Asia, Europe, and Australia. The majority of respondents are from the United States. Because we asked people to select seven characteristics, the total adds up to more than 100 percent.

Although every characteristic receives some votes, meaning that each is important to some people, what is most evident and striking is that over time, four, and only four, have always received more than 60 percent of the votes (with the exception of Inspiring in 1987). And these same four have consistently been ranked at the top *across different countries.*[14]

What people most look for in a leader (a person whom they would be willing to follow) has been constant over time. And our research documents that this pattern does not vary across countries, cultures, ethnicities, organizational functions and hierarchies, genders, levels of education, and age groups. For people to follow someone willingly, the majority of constituents believe the leader must be

- Honest
- Forward-looking
- Competent
- Inspiring

These investigations of desired leader attributes demonstrate consistent and clear relationships with what people say and write about their personal-best leadership experiences. The Five Practices of Exemplary Leadership and the behaviors of people whom others think of as exemplary leaders are complementary perspectives on the same subject. When they're performing at their peak, leaders are doing more than just getting results. They're also responding to the expectations of their constituents.[15]

As the themes of being honest, forward-looking, competent, and inspiring, are woven into the subsequent chapters on The Five Practices, you'll see in more detail how exemplary leaders respond to the expectations of their constituents. For example, leaders cannot

Model the Way without being seen as honest. The leadership practice Inspire a Shared Vision involves being forward-looking and inspiring. When leaders Challenge the Process, they also enhance the perception that they're dynamic and competent. Trustworthiness, often a synonym for honesty, plays a major role in how leaders Enable Others to Act, as does the leader's own competency. Likewise, leaders who recognize and celebrate significant accomplishments—who Encourage the Heart—show inspiration and positive energy, which increases their constituents' understanding of the commitment to the vision and values. When leaders demonstrate capacity in all of The Five Practices, they show others they have the competence to make extraordinary things happen.

PUTTING IT ALL TOGETHER: CREDIBILITY IS THE FOUNDATION

The top four characteristics—honest, forward-looking, competent, and inspiring—have remained constant in the ever-changing and turbulent social, political, and economic environment of the past thirty years. The relative importance of each has varied somewhat over time, but there has been no change in the fact that these are the four qualities people want most in their leaders. Whether they believe that their leaders are true to these values is another matter, but what they would like from them has remained the same.

These four consistent characteristics are descriptively useful in and of themselves—but there's a more profound implication revealed by these data. Three of these four key characteristics make up what communications experts refer to as "source credibility." In assessing the believability of sources of communication—whether news reporters, salespeople, physicians, or priests; whether business managers, military officers, politicians, or civic leaders—researchers typically evaluate them on three criteria: their perceived *trustworthiness,* their *expertise,* and their *dynamism.* People who are rated more highly on these dimensions are considered by others to be more credible sources of information.[16]

Notice how remarkably similar these three characteristics are to the essential leader qualities of being honest, competent, and inspiring—three of the top four items continually selected in surveys. Link the theory to the data about admired leader qualities, and the striking conclusion is that people want to follow leaders who are, more than anything, credible. *Credibility is the foundation of leadership.* Constituents must be able, above all else, to believe in their leaders. For them to willingly follow someone else, they must believe that the leader's word can be trusted, that she is personally passionate and enthusiastic about the work, and that she has the knowledge and skill to lead.

Constituents also must believe that their leader knows where they're headed and has a vision for the future. An expectation that their leaders be *forward-looking* is what sets leaders apart from other credible individuals. Compared to other sources of information (for example, journalists and TV news anchors), leaders must do more than be reliable reporters of the news. Leaders make the news, interpret the news, and make sense of the news. Leaders are expected to have a point of view about the future and to articulate exciting possibilities. Constituents want to be confident that their leaders know where they're going.

Even so, although compelling visions are necessary for leadership, if you as a leader are not credible, the message rests on a weak and precarious foundation. You must therefore be ever diligent in guarding your credibility. Your ability to take strong stands, challenge the status quo, and point to new directions depends on your being highly credible. You can never take your credibility for granted, regardless of the times or of your expertise or authority. If you ask others to follow you to some uncertain future—a future that may not be realized in their lifetime—and if the journey is going to require sacrifice, isn't it reasonable that constituents should believe in you?

The consistency and pervasiveness of these findings about the characteristics of admired leaders—people who would be willingly followed—are the rationale for **The Kouzes-Posner First Law of Leadership:**

If you don't believe in the messenger, you won't believe the message.

When we've surveyed people about the extent to which their immediate manager exhibited credibility-enhancing behaviors, the results strongly supported this "law."[17] When people perceive their immediate manager to have high credibility, they're significantly more likely to feel proud about their organization, feel a high degree of team spirit, feel a strong sense of ownership and commitment to the organization, and be motivated by shared values and intrinsic factors. What happens when people don't feel that their immediate manager has much credibility is that they start looking for other jobs, they feel unsupported and underappreciated, and they express being motivated primarily by external factors like money and benefits (which are never enough). Clearly, credibility makes a difference, and leaders must take this personally. Loyalty, commitment, energy, and productivity depend on it. Consider for a moment what researchers studying soldiers serving in "hot-combat" zones discovered about what it takes to influence people to risk injury and even death to achieve the organization's objectives. Soldiers' perceptions of their leader's credibility, the evidence shows, determines the actual extent of influence that leader can exercise.[18]

The data confirm that credibility is the foundation of leadership. But what is credibility behaviorally? In other words, how do you know it when you see it?

We've asked this question of tens of thousands of people around the globe, and the response is essentially the same, regardless of how it may be phrased in one company versus another or one country versus another. Here are some of the common phrases people use to describe credible leaders:

"They practice what they preach."
"They walk the talk."
"Their actions are consistent with their words."
"They put their money where their mouth is."
"They follow through on their promises."
"They do what they say they will do."

The last is the most frequent response. When it comes to deciding whether a leader is believable, people first listen to the words, then they watch the actions. They listen to the talk, then they watch the walk. They listen to the promises of resources to support change initiatives, then they wait to see if the money and materials follow. They hear the pledge to deliver, then they look for evidence that the commitments are met. A judgment of "credible" is handed down when words and deeds are consonant. If people don't see consistency, they conclude that the leader is, at best, not really serious or, at worst, an outright hypocrite. If leaders espouse one set of values but personally practice another, people find them to be duplicitous. If leaders practice what they preach, people are more willing to entrust them with their livelihood and even their lives.

This realization leads to a straightforward prescription for the most significant way to establish credibility. We refer to it as **The Kouzes-Posner Second Law of Leadership**:

You build a credible foundation of leadership foundation when you DWYSYWD—Do What You Say You Will Do.

DWYSYWD has two essential parts: say and do. The practice of Model the Way links directly to these two dimensions of the behavioral definition of credibility. Modeling is about clarifying values and setting an example for others based on those values. The consistent living out of values is the way leaders demonstrate their honesty and trustworthiness. It's what gives them the moral authority to lead. And that's where we begin our discussion of The Five Practices. In the next two chapters, we examine the principles and behaviors that bring Model the Way to life.

MODEL
THE WAY

The first step a leader must take along the path to becoming an exemplary leader is inward. It's a step toward discovering personal values and beliefs. Leaders must find their voice. They must discover a set of principles that guide decisions and actions. They must find a way to express a leadership philosophy in their own words and not in someone else's.

Yet leaders don't just speak for themselves. They also speak for their team and organization. Leadership is a dialogue, not a monologue. Therefore, leaders must reach out to others. They must understand and appreciate the values of their constituents and find a way to affirm shared values. Leaders forge unity. They don't force it. They give people reasons to care, not simply orders to follow.

Leaders stand up for their beliefs. They practice what they preach. They show others by their actions that they live by the values they profess. They also ensure that others adhere to the values that have been agreed on. It is consistency between words and actions that builds credibility.

In the next two chapters, we will take a look at how you must

- **Clarify Values by finding your voice and affirming shared values.**
- **Set the Example by aligning actions with shared values.**

CHAPTER 2

Clarify Values

WHO ARE YOU? This is the first question your constituents want you to answer. Finding that answer is where every leadership journey begins.

When Alex Anwar was hired as director of a new business unit at Labo America, he faced resentment from many within the company because they felt that he was too young and inexperienced to manage such a diverse group and product portfolio.[1] Because many of the units were siloed and polarized, a widespread question was whether he would be the kind of leader who would bring people together toward a common goal. Alex's first step was to communicate his values to the team. He circulated an email introducing himself, not as a manager, but as a fellow employee of the company charged with a difficult task. Instead of telling everyone what he wanted out of them, he stated clearly what values and performance criteria he demanded of himself every day. In teaching his value set, Alex ensured that people would be better prepared to understand his actions and the reasoning behind certain decisions. They were able to connect the outcome with a value (for example, hard work).

In an all-hands meeting later that week, Alex provided a few examples of cases in which he exercised his core values of honesty and sincerity, discussing how he handled a particular problem with a customer. He took his constituents through the issue as though narrating a story. He subsequently used this style of storytelling every time he made a case for how certain company situations were to be handled. By making these lessons easy to relate to, values centered, and personal, he helped people both understand and retain the intended lesson. As one of his direct reports explained, "Alex made his values understood through clearly communicating and providing contexts that would aid in their retention. He put all the values into his own words, and thus gave us a clear idea about the kind of person he was."

The Personal-Best Leadership Experience cases we've collected are, at their core, the stories of individuals who, like Alex, were clear about their personal values and understood how this clarity gave them the courage to navigate difficult situations and make tough choices. People expect their leaders to speak out on matters of values and conscience. But to speak out, you have to know what to speak about. To stand up for your beliefs, you have to know the beliefs you stand for. To walk the talk, you have to have a talk to walk. To do what you say, you have to know what you want to say. To earn and sustain personal credibility, you must first be able to clearly articulate deeply held beliefs.

Model the Way is the first of The Five Practices of Exemplary Leadership we discuss in this book, and one of the commitments you have to make in order to effectively Model the Way is to *Clarify Values.* In beginning your leadership journey, it's essential that you

- **FIND YOUR VOICE**
- **AFFIRM SHARED VALUES**

To become a credible leader, you first have to comprehend fully the deeply held beliefs—the values, standards, ethics, and ideals—that drive you. You have to freely and honestly choose the principles you will use to guide your decisions and actions. Then you have to genuinely express yourself. You have to authentically communicate your beliefs in ways that uniquely represent who you are.

However, leaders aren't just speaking for themselves when they talk about the values that should guide decisions and actions. When leaders passionately express a commitment to quality or innovation or service or some other core value, those leaders aren't just saying, "*I* believe in this." They're also making a commitment for an entire organization. They're saying, "We *all* believe in this." Therefore, leaders must not only be clear about their personal guiding principles but also make sure that there's agreement on a set of shared values among everyone they lead. And they must hold others accountable to those values and standards.

FIND YOUR VOICE

"What is your leadership philosophy?" What would you say if someone asked you this question? Are you prepared right now to say what it is? If you aren't, you should be. And if you are, you need to reflect on it daily.

Before you can become a credible leader—one who connects what you say with what you do—you first have to find your voice. If you can't find your voice, you'll end up with a vocabulary that belongs to someone else, mouthing words that were written by some speechwriter or mimicking the language of some other leader who's nothing like you at all. If the words you speak are not your words but someone else's, you will not, in the long term, be able to be consistent in word and deed. You will not have the integrity to lead.

To find your voice, you have to explore your inner self. You have to discover what you care about, what defines you, and what makes you who you are. You can be authentic only when you lead according to the principles that matter most to you. Otherwise you're just putting on an act. Consider Casey Mork's experience with an internal start-up business that never got off the ground:

> First, our manager never had a true voice, as he never had the courage to pronounce solutions or suggestions beyond what our three (never agreeing) directors input into each decision. Oftentimes it felt like he acted as a simple conduit for mixed messages from above . . . without his own personal voice defining a clear road for us to travel. This made it very difficult for the group to focus on a defined set of tasks connected to goals.
>
> Second, an outcome of the above was that we had no specific organizational values to live by. Sure we all knew the company mission, and transferred in corporate values from our previous groups (inside the same company), but he never went beyond the ordinary in defining values for *our* business. Our customers were different, and so how should we treat them differently than the rest of the company? We spent a lot of money pampering our customers; how would this apply to managing our expense accounts? Seemingly simple values went undefined and as a result were exploited by some team members.

As could have been predicted, Casey says, this lack of clarity and consistency in values at the top resulted in little internal cohesion and focus, and the company failed to generate a favorable customer experience or positive business results. In contrast, Josh Fradenburg, founder of Mindful Measures says that it was his values that drove the products that he brought to market. "It was really the values that formed the organization, rather than the organization forming the values," he recounts.

When we ask leaders how clear they are about their leadership philosophy, those who fall into the top 10 percent on this leadership behavior have quite different work attitudes than their counterparts in the bottom 10 percent. Their overall attitudes toward the workplace are significantly more positive. When asked to rate their own effectiveness as a leader, the scores of those who are clear about their leadership philosophy are 25 percent higher than those who report being not very clear about their leadership philosophy.

The impact that the leader's clarity of leadership philosophy has on his or her constituents is even more dramatic, as shown in Figure 2.1. When asked how effective the leader is, the scores from those working with leaders who are seen as being clear about their leadership philosophy are more than 40 percent higher than those scores received from constituents who view leaders as not very clear about their leadership philosophy. There are statistically significant differences between these two groups of constituents on a variety of important dimensions. For example, feeling a sense of team spirit, feeling proud about the organization, feeling committed to the organization's success, being willing to work extra hard to meet organizational objectives, and levels of trust all differ significantly. Leaders who have a clear leadership philosophy are nearly 30 percent more likely to be trusted by their constituents than those unclear about their leadership philosophy.

The evidence is clear: to be the most effective, every leader must learn to find the voice that represents who he or she is. When you have clarified your values and found your voice, you will also find

FIGURE 2.1 The Impact of Leadership Philosophy Clarity on Constituent Work Attitudes and Engagement

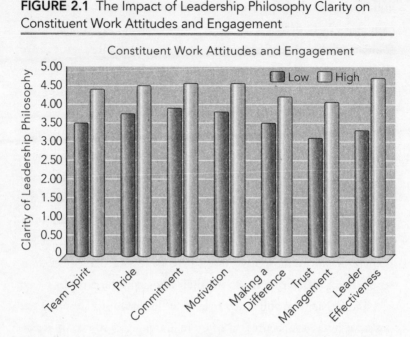

the inner confidence necessary to express ideas, chose a direction, make tough decisions, act with determination, and be able to take charge of your life rather than impersonating others.

Let Your Values Guide You

Milton Rokeach, one of the leading scholars in the field of human values, referred to a value as an enduring belief. He noted that values are organized into two sets: means and ends.[2] In the context of our work on leadership, we use the term *values* to refer to here-and-now beliefs about how things should be accomplished—what Milt calls *means* values. We will use *vision* in Chapters Four and Five when we refer to the long-term *ends* values that leaders and constituents aspire to attain. Leadership requires both. When sailing through the turbulent seas of change and uncertainty, crew members need a vision of the destination that lies beyond the horizon; they also need to understand the principles by which they must navigate their course. If either of these is absent, the journey is likely to end with the crew lost at sea.

Values influence every aspect of your life: your moral judgments, your responses to others, your commitments to personal and organizational goals. Values set the parameters for the hundreds of decisions you make every day, consciously and subconsciously. Options that run counter to your value system are seldom considered or acted on; and if they are, it's done with a sense of compliance rather than commitment.

Values constitute your personal "bottom line." They serve as guides to action. They inform the priorities you set and the decisions you make. They tell you when to say yes and when to say no. They also help you explain the choices you make and why you made them. If you believe, for instance, that diversity enriches innovation and service, then you should know what to do if people with differing views keep getting cut off when they offer fresh ideas. If you value collaboration over individualistic achievement, then you'll know what to do when your best salesperson skips team meetings and refuses to share information with colleagues. If you value independence and initiative over conformity and obedience, you'll be more likely to challenge something your manager says if you think it's wrong.

All of the most critical decisions a leader makes involve values. For example, values determine how much emphasis to place on the immediate interests of the customer or the long-term interests of the company, how to apportion time between family and organizational responsibilities, and what behaviors to reward or discourage. In turn, these decisions have critical organizational impact. Indeed, in these turbulent times, having a set of deeply held values allows leaders to focus and make choices among a plethora of competing beliefs, paradigms, and interests.

Paul di Bari's operations section within the engineering services group took on the new responsibility for the physical security of the VA Palo Alto Health Care System's 2.2-million-square-foot facility. Along with the responsibility of hiring a new technician to manage this system, Paul was also taking on a new contractor relationship. Before starting any more projects, Paul called a meeting with the new technician and contractor to figure out the status of the current access system, any open projects, and any projects on the horizon. Paul used this meeting to vocalize his intentions about how the newly developed team would work, his vision moving forward, and his expectations for all parties. His values on project timelines, preparations, submittals, and execution would require more detailed attention than in the past and would also, he hoped, create a new sense of accountability. Paul explained,

> If I was going to pay large sums of money for parts and
> services, then I had expectations for the quality of the deliver-
> able, which were far higher than the previous regime. These
> higher standards of quality were necessary to fix the system
> and to make it operate at a high level. I began to personally
> inspect the work of the contractor as we completed six open
> projects. During this time, I was also training our new techni-
> cian and establishing expectations of project management
> (for example, statements of work, pricing quotes, communica-
> tion, workmanship, and the final product) that he would need
> to carry forth. It was imperative to the long-term success of
> this program and this new team that I clearly explained what
> my values were, my project management style and
> expectations.

Paul had to find his voice as a leader by clearly stating his leadership principles and the accompanying management goals and objectives. At the beginning of the project, Paul met with the contractor and his new technician to communicate these in the context of the security access system. By clearly defining his standards, he was establishing a baseline for future performance and also a measuring block on which to base accountability. "It would have been very easy for me," Paul said, "to sit back and supervise the program from afar, but in order to earn the trust and respect of both people involved, I had to establish a sense of trust through my work ethic." Because Paul was clear about his own values, he found it relatively easy to talk about values and subsequently to use them in setting standards and expectations. This tone at the top from Paul provided guidelines for how his constituents would subsequently act and make decisions.

As Paul's experience illustrates, values are guides. They supply you with a compass by which to navigate the course of your daily life. Clarity of values is essential to knowing which way is north, south, east, and west. The clearer you are about your values, the easier it is for you and for everyone else to stay on the chosen path and commit to it. This kind of guidance is especially needed in difficult and uncertain times. When there are daily challenges that can throw you off course, it's crucial that you have some signposts that tell you where you are.

Say It in Your Own Words

People can speak the truth only when speaking in their own true voice. The techniques and tools that fill the pages of management and leadership books—including this one—are not substitutes for who and what you are. Once you have the words you want to say, you must also give voice to those words. You must be able to express yourself so that everyone knows that you are the one who's speaking.

You'll find a lot of scientific data in this book to support our assertions about each of The Five Practices of Exemplary Leadership. But keep in mind that leadership is also an art. And just as with any other art form, leadership is a means of personal expression. To become a credible leader, you have to learn to express yourself in ways that are uniquely your own. Which is exactly what Andrew Levine did, and in the process helped his colleague Pranav Sharma be able to do the same.

Andrew is a head mentor at the Young Storytellers Foundation (YSF), a nonprofit organization in the United States that provides a creative outlet to fifth-graders whose public schools do not have the budget for creative arts programs. He is passionate about and committed to providing a classroom atmosphere that pushes the imaginations of the kids they mentor, and he cares deeply for all the YSF volunteers. According to one of those volunteers, Pranav Sharma, Andrew's personal values fit comfortably with the values articulated in YSF's mission statement. Pranav told us how Andrew influenced him: "He had a unique voice among the mentors. His example led me to exhibit values he shared with the organization. He helped me understand what it meant to the kids to have a unique voice."

Pranav was paired with a fifth-grader named Rachel, and was tasked to guide her in writing an original story in a ten-page screen-play format, but he was having trouble getting Rachel to focus on her story. Whereas other mentors were making progress on their kids' stories, Pranav felt that Rachel was not very motivated. The fact that Pranav was absent a couple of times over the eight-week program because of the demands from his workplace didn't help the situation. Andrew was noticeably frustrated with Pranav and a few other mentors' seeming lack of interest in the program. He took two steps to remedy the situation. First, he reminded the delinquent mentors why they had joined the program. He talked about why he was loyal to the program. He asked them to leave the program if they were not making YSF a priority, which would be evidenced by future absences. Second, he asked the volunteers to look at the program through the perspective of the fifth-grader. What are the kids looking for from their mentors? He suggested that the volunteers stop worrying about whether they were qualified to mentor or whether the kids would like them. All that was required, Andrew explained, was to be present and to talk to them. Pranav got the point.

> Andrew was right. He was asking us to affirm our shared values
> and find our voice. What Andrew was doing was asking us to
> reexamine the reasons we joined YSF. He wanted us to be
> vested in YSF's values, which included words like *loyalty,*
> *commitment, passion,* and *patience.* He wanted us to build a
> relationship with the kids by talking to them. The only way to
> make a unique difference in a kid's life was to find my own
> voice. I had to find my voice if I was to make an indelible
> impression on my mentee.

So Pranav gave it a shot. He reflected on the reasons he had originally wanted to join YSF, which involved giving back creatively to the community. He had wanted to join a nonprofit organization that valued loyalty. He said,

> Finding my voice was not easy. I talked without pretense,
> allowing Rachel to guide the conversation. It was difficult at

first, but the enthusiasm in Rachel's eyes encouraged me to continue to establish my own voice and my own words. The result was a happy child who was proud of her original story. At the end of the program, she gave me a very creative thank-you card highlighting me as the best mentor she had had. I was proud of her.

The lesson here is that Andrew gave Pranav, and all the other mentors, time to discover how their personal values meshed with those of YSF. By telling them his own story of why he was passionate about becoming a mentor at YSF, he helped them find the words to express their own reasons for caring about YSF, its mission, and especially the children. Andrew didn't tell them what to believe; he told them about his own beliefs and asked them to find in their own values their reasons for being involved with the organization. Through this reflection, they discovered their own voice and found the words necessary to reach kids like Rachel and help them find their way.

Leaders like Andrew and Pranav understand that you cannot lead through someone else's values or someone else's words. You cannot lead out of someone else's experience. You can lead only out of your own. Unless it's your style and your words, it's not you—it's just an act. People don't follow your position or your technique. They follow *you*. If you're not the genuine article, can you really expect others to want to follow? To be a leader, you've got to awaken to the fact that you don't have to copy someone else, you don't have to read a script written by someone else, and you don't have to wear someone else's style. Instead, you are free to choose what you want to express and the way you want to express it. In fact, you have a responsibility to your constituents to express yourself in an authentic manner, in a way they would immediately recognize as yours.

Find Commitment Through Clarifying Values

It's one thing to expect leaders to be clear about their values and beliefs, but it's another to prove that it really matters that they are. What's the evidence for this assertion? How much difference does being clear about values really make? We set out to empirically investigate the relationship between personal values clarity, organizational values clarity, and a variety of outcomes, such as commitment and job satisfaction. Surveying a large sample of managers in the early 1980s, and another sample of managers nearly two decades later, revealed few differences in the findings.[3] The results of our research clearly indicate that clarity of personal values makes a significant difference in behavior at work.

Managers were asked about the extent of their clarity around their personal values as well as the values of their organization. They were also asked about their level of commitment to their organization, how proud they were to tell others they worked in their organization, their level of motivation and productivity, their job satisfaction, and the like. As you can see in Figure 2.2, the highest levels of commitment are found where personal values are the clearest. Clarity about personal values was consistently more significant in accounting for positive workplace attitudes and levels of engagement than was clarity around organizational values.[4]

The people who are clear about their personal beliefs but can't recite the corporate credo are significantly more likely to stick around and work hard than those people who've heard the organizational litany but have never listened to their own inner voice. In other words, personal values drive commitment. Personal values are the route to motivation and productivity.

How can this be? How can people who are very clear about their own values be committed to a place that has never affirmed or

THE LEADERSHIP CHALLENGE

FIGURE 2.2 The Impact of Values Clarity on Commitment

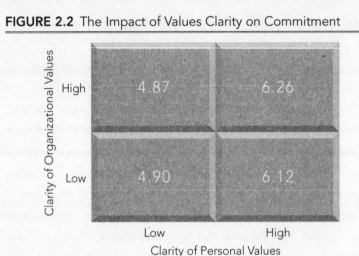

posted its organizational values? Think about it. Have you ever had the feeling, "This place is not for me?" Have you ever walked into a place, immediately gotten the sense, "I don't belong here," and just walked right out? In contrast, have you ever just known that you belong, that you can be yourself, and felt "This is the right place for me"? Of course you have. Everyone has had those experiences.

It's the same in the workplace. There comes a point when you just know whether it is or isn't a good fit with your values and beliefs, even if there was no lecture on the organization's values. You won't stick around a place for very long when you feel in your heart and in your soul that you don't belong. This is why people's years of managerial experience and hierarchical level help explain differences in the extent of personal values clarity, whereas such factors as gender, educational level, and functional discipline do not.[5] The most talented people, no matter their age or background, gravitate to companies where they can look forward to going to work each day because their values "work" in that organizational setting. Julie

Sedlock, group vice president for operations at Aéropostale, a global specialty retailer of casual apparel and accessories, echoes this observation: "I love to come to work here. I can't think of a day in twenty years that I didn't want to wake up and go to work." She explains that when you share the company's values, you "want to come to work, work hard, and achieve the goals that the organization has set."

Workplace and organizational commitment are based on alignment with personal values and who you are and what you are about. People who are clearest about personal values are better prepared to make choices based on principle—including deciding whether the principles of the organization fit with their own!

AFFIRM SHARED VALUES

Leadership is not simply about your own values. It's also about the values of your constituents. Just as your own values drive your commitment to the organization, their personal values drive their commitment. Your constituents will be significantly more engaged in a place where they believe they can stay true to their beliefs. Although clarifying your own values is essential, understanding the values of others and building alignment around values that everyone can share are equally critical.

Shared values are the foundational pillars for building productive and genuine working relationships. Credible leaders honor the diversity of their many constituencies, but they also stress their common values. Leaders build on agreement. They don't try to get everyone to be in accord on everything. This goal is unrealistic, perhaps even impossible. Moreover, to achieve it would negate the very advantages of diversity. But to take the first step and then a second and then a third, people must have some common core of understanding. After all, if there's no agreement about values, then what exactly are the leader and everyone else going to model? If disagreements over fundamental values continue, the result is intense conflict, false expectations, and diminished capacity.[6] Leaders ensure that everyone is aligned through the process of affirming shared values—uncovering, reinforcing, and holding one another accountable to what "we" value.

Hilary Hall told us about how her manager helped people examine their own values and how this built a foundation of shared values that resulted in a spirit of camaraderie and common purpose. At General Electric, Hilary was on a multinational internal audit team, which consisted of a German, two Americans, a Belarusian, and an Indian:

> At the beginning of the audit, before we even began work, our manager had us all complete a questionnaire, which included topics such as where we grew up, favorite food, hobbies, and so on. There were also questions that dug a little deeper and asked us about the type of work we liked and did not like, how we liked to work, the role we usually played on teams, and what we respected in managers and teammates. After completing the questionnaires individually, we gathered as a group and shared our responses.
>
> At the time, I thought of the exercise as a team icebreaker, a chance for us to get to know one another and build a sense of camaraderie, especially since we came from different corners of the globe. Why else would I need to know that Matt enjoys eating Mexican food, or likes to kick around ideas before having to make a decision? Reflecting on the experience now, I understand that the exercise was more than just an icebreaker; our manager was aligning the team around a common set of

values—both personal and professional—and showing the team what was important to him, too. This was especially imperative since internal audit work was often stressful, extremely deadline oriented, and required us to be at the work site for two weeks at a time. It was a demanding work environment, and I believe our success as individual auditors was contingent on our success as a team, which begins with mutual respect and trust.

Hilary was clear that if the team members had not aligned themselves around common values, their effectiveness as a team, as well as their manager's credibility, would have suffered. They could have easily lost touch with one another and worked according to their own individual standards, which would have resulted in uneven motivation and commitment toward common work goals. "From this experience," says Hilary,

> I have learned that a good leader takes the time to break the ice and know his or her team on a personal level, but a great leader goes one step further and learns about each person's values, how they build trust, and what is core to their motivation and drive. They then share the team's values, as well as their own, and align the team around a strong focal point for working together toward a shared goal (or goals).

Research confirms Hilary's experience. Organizations with a strong corporate culture based on a foundation of shared values outperform other firms by a huge margin. Their revenue and rate of job creation grow faster, and their profit performance and stock price are significantly higher. Furthermore, studies of public sector organizations support the importance of shared values to organizational effectiveness. Within successful agencies and departments, considerable agreement, as well as intense feeling, is found among employees and managers about the importance of their values and about how those values should best be implemented.[7]

In our own research, we've found that shared values make a significant and positive difference in work attitudes and commitment.[8] For instance, shared values

- Foster strong feelings of personal effectiveness
- Promote high levels of company loyalty
- Facilitate consensus about key organizational goals and stakeholders
- Encourage ethical behavior
- Promote strong norms about working hard and caring
- Reduce levels of job stress and tension
- Foster pride in the company
- Facilitate understanding about job expectations
- Foster teamwork and esprit de corps

Periodically taking the organization's pulse to check for values clarity and consensus is well worthwhile. It renews commitment. It engages the institution in discussing values (such as diversity, accessibility, sustainability, and so on) that are more relevant to a changing constituency. Once people are clear about the leader's values, about their own values, and about shared values, they know what's expected of them and how they can count on others. With this clarity, they can manage higher levels of stress and better handle the often conflicting demands of work and their personal lives.

Give People Reasons to Care

Important as it is that leaders forthrightly articulate the principles for which they stand, the values leaders espouse must be consistent with the aspirations of their constituents. Leaders who advocate values that aren't representative of the collective won't be able to mobilize people to act as one. There has to be a shared understanding of what's expected. Leaders must be able to gain consensus on a common cause and a common set of principles. They must be able to build and affirm a community of shared values.

It's vitally important that leaders and constituents arrive at consensus on shared values, because once they are articulated, those values become a pledge to employees, customers, clients, business partners, and other constituents. They are a promise to people that everyone in the organization will do what the values prescribe. Regardless of whether the organization is a team of two, an agency of two hundred, a school of two thousand, a company of twenty thousand, or a community of two hundred thousand, shared values are the ground rules for making decisions and taking action. Unless there's agreement on these principles, leaders, constituents, and their organizations risk losing credibility.

Recognition of shared values provides people with a common language. Tremendous energy is generated when individual, group, and organizational values are in synch. Commitment, enthusiasm, and drive are intensified. People have reasons for caring about their work. When individuals care about what they are doing, they are more effective and satisfied. They experience less stress and tension. Shared values are the internal compasses that enable people to act both independently and interdependently.

Nicole Matouk was a student records analyst at Stanford Law School when the school implemented a major transition from the semester to the quarter system. Because of all the preparations that needed to be made in advance of the transition (such as overhauling the computer systems) and because of the quarter system itself, which required an additional term of work, by the end of the school year, everyone was exhausted and in need of encouragement. The associate dean sent an email to the people working in the registrar's office, asking for their feedback about the transition and inviting them to meet with her over coffee and talk informally about the transition process.

Everyone had the opportunity to speak about the topics he or she felt strongly about, and all were given equal and ample time to express themselves. No one felt pressured, and the staff felt free to express their opinions without any fear of retribution. The dean asked questions about how they could make their jobs more efficient and which new systems could be implemented to make procedures easier for both the students and the staff. Nicole went on to explain that

> The dean's questions kept us from taking a bath in the negative emotions we were feeling, and they helped us refocus on our goals as an office. She used these questions to affirm our shared values. The dean didn't have to struggle to think of the questions she wanted to ask, or how she would connect what we were discussing to our goals; her values were guiding her questions. As we talked, I could tell she was leading me in a certain direction, but it didn't seem manipulative. This was so much more powerful to me than reading about the values in the handbook. I was generating the answers to her questions, so I felt this is what I believe, not just what I am supposed to agree with.
>
> Not only did this meeting help our team to individually generate answers that were in line with our values and the office's values, it helped us to affirm our shared values as an office. We came out of that meeting more united and with the knowledge that we were all working to achieve the same thing, instead of pulling against each other for time and attention.

Nicole's experience reaffirms that people are more loyal when they believe that their values and those of the organization are aligned. The quality and accuracy of communication, and the integrity of the decision-making process, increase when people feel part of the same team. They are more creative because they become immersed in what they are doing. Our research, along with the findings of others, clearly reveals that when there's congruence between individual values and organizational values, there's significant payoff for leaders and their organizations.[9]

We found that nearly two-thirds of people surveyed felt that organizations, and their leaders, should be spending more time talking about values.[10] The Trustmark Companies take this message seriously. They put their entire organization (twenty-five hundred employees) through an internal leader-led "Values Experience" during which people had the chance to think about their values and reflect on how their values guided their actions.[11] Feedback from this experience was so positive that Trustmark continues to give people the opportunity to share their values in unique ways. For example, on each floor of the company atrium, they post yards and yards of white paper for employees to write about, draw, and otherwise depict their values. Trustmark also instituted a "WeekEND Message" in which senior leaders throughout the organization volunteer to write an article to share. Each Friday, via email, they convey their thoughts and ideas, focused on their top five values. Leaders at every level are reaching out to others with stories that speak to their values.

Through conversations and discussions, like those at Trustmark, leaders renew commitment by reminding people why they care about what they are doing, and these exchanges reinforce feelings that everyone is on the same team (especially critical in distributed workplaces). Once people are clear about the leader's values, about their own values, and about shared values, they know what's expected of them. This clarity enriches their ability to make choices, enables them to better handle stressful situations, and enhances understanding and appreciation of the choices made by others.

Forge Unity, Don't Force It

When leaders seek consensus around shared values, constituents are more positive. People who report that their senior managers engage in dialogue regarding common values feel a significantly stronger sense of personal effectiveness than individuals who feel that they're wasting energy trying to figure out what they're supposed to be doing.

Erika Long, HR manager for Procter & Gamble (P&G), started with the company as an intern and was immediately impressed with how leaders demonstrated their values and the core principles of the company in every decision they made. She says,

> Leaders at P&G are constantly affirming these values. Anytime they are faced with a difficult decision, they will look to the PVP [the company's Purpose, Values, and Principles] to guide their actions. I met with the director of sales for the Hong Kong and Taiwan regions. I asked him, how does he make sure he is always making the right business decisions? He said, simply, "I look to the PVP. It guides the way I do business. If I am put in a position that is in conflict with those guidelines, I simply don't do it."

Erika says that "people who work at P&G are proud to say so, and everyone feels they are part of something special. Their core values align with those of the organization." When people are unsure or confused about how they should operate, they tend to drift, turn off, and depart. The energy that goes into coping with, and possibly fighting about, incompatible values takes its toll on both personal effectiveness and organizational productivity.

"What are our basic principles?" and "What do we believe in?" are far from simple questions. One study reported 185 different behavioral expectations about the value of integrity alone.[12] Even with commonly identified values, there may be little agreement on the meaning of values statements. The lesson here is that leaders must engage their constituents in a dialogue about values. A common understanding of values emerges from a process, not a pronouncement.

This is precisely the experience of Charles Law, who at American Express was assigned to lead the launch of a marketing campaign with a team of six colleagues of different ethnicities and business functions. At first, progress was slow, as frequent conflicts drove down team morale. Each team member was focused on his or her own goals, without considering the interests of others. Differences between them led to mistrust, and worse yet, according to Charles, he had the least experience of anyone in the group, so team members were skeptical about his leadership competency.

Charles saw that the team needed to agree on a shared set of values in order to function well. He noted that it was not so important what the particular value was called or labeled but that everyone agreed on the importance and meaning of the values. One of his initial actions was to bring people together just for that purpose, so that they could arrive at shared understandings of what their key priorities and values were and what these meant in action. He sat down and listened to each team member individually, and reported about everyone's opinions at their next group meeting. He encouraged open discussions and worked through any misunderstandings.

The last thing Charles wanted them to feel was that his values were being imposed on them. So each person talked about his or her own values and the reasoning behind them. In this manner, they were able to identify as a group the common values that were important. "With a set of shared values, created with everyone's consent," Charles explained, "everyone strived to work together as a team toward success. Shared values created a positive difference in work attitudes and performance. My action made my colleagues work harder, emphasized teamwork and respect of each other, and resulted in better understanding of each other's capabilities to meet appropriately set mutual expectations."

Charles understood that leaders can't impose their values on organization members. Instead they must be proactive in involving people in the process of creating shared values. Imagine how much ownership of values there can be when leaders actively engage a wide range of people in their development. Shared values are the result of listening, appreciating, building consensus, and resolving conflicts. For people to understand the values and come to agree with them, they must participate in the process: unity is forged, not forced.

For values to be truly shared, they must be more than advertising slogans. They must be deeply supported and broadly endorsed beliefs about what's important to the people who hold them. Constituents must be able to enumerate the values and have common interpretations of how those values will be put into practice. They must know how their values influence the way they do their own jobs and how they directly contribute to organizational success.

Jade Lui described an incident early in her career in which the managing director, in Jade's words, "taught us to model the company's values." When someone discovered that an applicant had withheld critical information from a client, although it was not information that the client had requested, the question arose whether to share that information and possibly lose the deal. Although the situation occurred during a particularly difficult financial time for their company, the response from their leader about what to do didn't come as a surprise to Jade because it embodied the "core values espoused by the company." He told them that

> first and foremost, we should be *honest* with our clients. If we concealed the truth from the client, we would tarnish our reputation of *service excellence*. Further, we are *committed to long-term partnerships* with our clients. Sacrificing revenue for the short term in exchange for the client's appreciation of our integrity, excellence, and commitment would bring more business in the long run. He continued to reassure that everyone in the company would *work together* to survive the temporary business downturn.

Having everyone on the same page when it comes to operating principles (values) ensures consistency in words and deeds for everyone, boosting in turn not just individual credibility but organizational reputation. Jade notes that not only is that client still one of their company's most loyal partners, but "the lessons learned from my managing director's decision are still firmly engraved in my mind." She has subsequently "taught the next generation of staff the same shared values."

A unified voice on values results from discovery and dialogue. Leaders must provide a chance for individuals to engage in a discussion of what the values mean and how their personal beliefs and behaviors are influenced by what the organization stands for. Leaders must also be prepared to discuss values and expectations in the recruitment, selection, and orientation of new members. Better to explore early the fit between individuals and their organization than to have members find out at some key juncture that they're in serious disagreement over matters of principle.

TAKE ACTION

Clarify Values

The very first step on the journey to credible leadership is clarifying your values—discovering those fundamental beliefs that will guide your decisions and actions along the path to success and significance. That involves an exploration of the inner territory where your true voice resides. It's essential that you take yourself on this journey because it's the only route to authenticity and because your personal values drive your commitment to the organization and to the cause. You can't do what you say if you can't say what you believe. And you can't do what you say if you don't believe in what you're saying.

Although personal values clarity is essential for all leaders, it's insufficient alone. That's because leaders don't just speak for themselves; they speak for their constituents as well. There must be agreement on the shared values that everyone will commit to upholding. These give people reasons for caring about what they do, which in turn makes a significant and positive difference in work attitudes and performance. A common understanding of shared values emerges from a process, not a pronouncement; unity comes about through dialogue and debate, followed by understanding and commitment. Leaders must hold themselves and others accountable to a set of shared values, which is a topic explored more fully in the next chapter.

Model the Way begins with clarifying values by *finding your voice and affirming shared values.* This means you have to

- Examine your past experiences to identify the values you use to make choices and decisions.
- Answer the question, What is my leadership philosophy?
- Articulate the values that guide your current decisions, priorities, and actions.
- Find your own words for talking about what is important to you.
- Discuss values in various recruitment, hiring, and on-boarding experiences.
- Help others articulate why they do what they do, and what they care about.
- Provide opportunities for people to talk about their values with others on the team.
- Build consensus around values, principles, and standards.
- Make sure that people are adhering to the values and standards that have been agreed on.

Use *The Leadership Challenge Mobile Tool* app to immediately integrate these activities into your life and make this practice an ongoing part of your behavioral repertoire.

CHAPTER 3

Set the Example

KANEKA TEXAS IS A specialty polymer manufacturing company in Pasadena, Texas. In operation since 1984, the plant had been through a number of growth spurts when Steve Skarke suddenly found himself tapped to be the plant manager in 2002. Steve readily admits that he was unprepared for the job, but after a few years of "trial-and-error leadership," he started honing in on his own style of leading, which usually included some rather unorthodox ideas—at least for the mostly conservative crew at Kaneka.[1]

Steve wanted to make a real change in the state of housekeeping around the site. For a couple of years, the manufacturing management team had been discussing the vision of becoming a "World Class Plant." They debated the defining characteristics of a world-class plant and agreed that a strong culture of safety and good housekeeping should be at the top of the list. Looking around, Steve could clearly see that the housekeeping conditions at Kaneka did not meet the company's shared vision. In fact, whenever they had a pending customer visit, Steve would have to remind everyone to

71

make an extra effort to clean up. This included sending people out to pick up trash in the plant, on the roads, and in the parking lot. It was a disruption to daily activities. Steve knew there had to be a way to make cleaning a part of their daily routine. It would take a cultural shift.

One day while Steve was out at lunch, he stopped into a hardware store and bought a two-gallon plastic bucket. He put the words "World Class Plant" on the side of the bucket. "That afternoon," Steve said, "I walked through the plant and picked up as much trash as I could fit into my bucket, and it was overflowing. I then walked through the main control room with my bucket of trash and, with everyone intently watching, emptied it into a trashcan and simply walked out the other door, saying nothing. Word spread that I was in the plant with a bucket picking up trash."

Each time Steve ventured out with his bucket in hand, he made sure that he would be seen. It didn't take long for more buckets to appear. Other managers went out into the plant to pick up trash each day, setting the example for all to follow. Pretty soon Steve walked through the control room, operators would ask how much trash he was able to find. If his bucket was full, he would walk by the supervisor's office and hold it up for inspection. The process that Steve had started by his visible example soon became the norm.

"Over the course of the next few weeks or so," Steve reported, "trash disappeared from the plant, and it was getting more difficult for me to put anything in my bucket. On 'empty bucket days' I would make a point to stop by the control room and thank the gang for their efforts. It became an inside joke with some of the operators."

In addition to the actual trash removal, the activity started generating lots of discussion and new ideas about how they could make the job of cleaning the plant easier. Trash cans that had been previously removed were put back in key areas where collection would be easier. The operation staff agreed to maintain these cans and came up with more ideas to better organize their work areas. The maintenance technicians began carrying buckets around to keep parts and trash contained to make cleanup quicker and easier. During this time, a new program called "My Machine" was also enacted: each operator was assigned a certain piece of equipment to clean, paint, and, to ensure proper operation, learn about its function.

"By simply deciding to venture out and start picking up trash," Steve told us, "I was modeling the way by aligning my actions with the shared value of having a clean plant. It also helped me 'find my voice' around this very important issue of housekeeping. I made it personal for everyone. In a short time, many others were setting the same example.

"I don't really remember how long it took," Steve recalled, "but one day I decided to retire my bucket. I made it clear to everyone that the team had made a real cultural shift and that I would no longer give any advance warning of customer visits.... I am proud of the team and what we accomplished, and I have been able to keep my promise of not asking for special attention in advance of visitors. I simply announce the visit and comment that 'I know the plant is ready!'"

They are still working to improve housekeeping at Kaneka Texas; it's a never-ending battle, and one that fits their shared value of continuous improvement. But the very simple action of one leader resulted in a huge cultural shift in the organization. And Steve still has his bucket in his office as a reminder that setting the example works and that his job is never finished. "What is the next shared value that needs to be reinforced?" Steve asks. "What is the next process that needs to be challenged? What else should I put in my leadership bucket?"

Steve's story illustrates the second commitment of Model the Way—leaders *Set the Example.* They take every opportunity to show others by their own example that they're deeply committed to the values and aspirations they espouse. No one will believe you're serious until they see you doing what you're asking of others. You either lead by example or don't lead at all. Leading by example is how you provide the evidence that you're personally committed. It's how you make your values tangible.

In Chapter One, we reported that our research has consistently revealed that credibility is the foundation of leadership. People want to follow a leader in whom they can believe. And what makes a leader credible? We said that when people defined credibility behaviorally, they told us it meant *do what you say you will do,* or DWYSYWD for short. This chapter on Setting the Example is all about the *do* part. It's about practicing what you preach, putting your money where your mouth is, following through on commitments, keeping promises, walking the talk, and doing what you say.

Being a credible leader means you have to *live* the values. You have to *put into action* what you and others stand for. You have to *be the example* for others to follow. And, because you're leading a group of people—not just leading yourself—you also have to make certain that the actions of your constituents are consistent with the shared values of the organization. An important part of your job is to educate others on what the organization stands for, why those things matter, and how others can authentically serve the organization. As the leader, you teach, coach, and guide others to align their actions with the shared values because you're held accountable for their actions too, not just your own.

In order to Set the Example, you need to

- **LIVE THE SHARED VALUES**
- **TEACH OTHERS TO MODEL THE VALUES**

In practicing these essentials, you become an exemplary role model for what the organization stands for, and you create a culture in which everyone commits to aligning himself or herself with shared values.

LIVE THE SHARED VALUES

Leaders are their organizations' ambassadors of shared values. Their mission is to represent the values and standards to the rest of the world, and it's their solemn duty to serve the values to the best of their ability. People watch your every action, and they're trying to determine if you're serious about what you say. You need to be conscious about the choices you make and the actions you take, because other people use these signals to determine whether you're doing what you say.

The power of the leader's personal example can't be stressed enough. Researchers Tal Yaffe of Ben-Gurion University and Ronit Kark of Bar-Ilan University have found that leaders who model the behaviors of a "good organizational citizen"—that is, who persist in attaining organizational goals, promote the organization to outsiders and insiders, and initiate constructive change in the workplace—are much more likely to have direct reports who exhibit the same behaviors than those leaders who don't set that kind of example. This effect is strongest when the leader is most visible to direct reports and is considered by them to be a worthy role model.[2] Being credible and close to your constituents pays off.

Cornell University professor Tony Simons offers even more telling evidence of this. In his research on behavioral integrity, he found that organizations "where employees strongly believed [that] their managers followed through on promises and demonstrated the values they preached were substantially more profitable than those whose managers scored average or lower [on follow-through]."[3] In other words, if you want to get better results, make sure you practice what you preach. What you do speaks more loudly than what you say.

Some of the most significant signal-sending actions have to do with how leaders spend their time and what they pay attention to, the language (words and phrases) they use, how they address critical incidents, and their openness to feedback.[4] Each of these actions gives you a chance to make visible and tangible your personal commitment to a shared way of being. Each affords you the chance to show where you stand on matters of principle. Simple though they may appear, you should remember that sometimes the greatest distance you have to travel is the distance from your mouth to your feet.

Spend Your Time and Attention Wisely

How you spend your time is the single clearest indicator of what's important to you. Constituents use this metric to judge whether you measure up to espoused standards. Visibly spending time on what's important shows that you're putting your money where your mouth is. Whatever your values are, they have to show up on your calendar and on meeting agendas for people to believe that those values are significant. Take a look at your daily planner. What's the connection between how you schedule your time and what you say are your key values? Take a look at your agendas. When you're in meetings, what do you spend most of the time discussing?

If you value service to others, for example, and say that store operators are important, you should be meeting with them at their locations. If you say that you're focused on customers (or clients, patients, students, voters, or parishioners), then you should be spending your time where they spend theirs. If improving sales performance is critical, then you need to meet with customers and show up at sales meetings. If innovation is essential, you should be visiting the labs or participating in online open source discussions. If global diversity is a shared value, then you've got to be out in the field and around the world. Being "there" says more about what you value than any email message, tweet, or video can ever do.

And you don't have to be in a managerial position to set a leadership example. Informal peer leaders do it too. For instance, Mark Brunello, a sales representative for XO Communications for more than twelve years, in an industry where high turnover is the norm, has been described by his colleagues as "credibility personified."[5] One colleague speaks not only to Mark's behavior but to its consistency:

> Having him as a model to observe on a daily basis is incredibly inspirational. Whether Mark realizes it or not, his consistent behavior is a strong leadership model. We look up to him and respect him because he puts in the hours necessary to be successful. He doesn't take any liberties with the freedom that some salespeople take when managing their own schedules. He seeks out technical training that is above and beyond that required for a typical sales representative. In this way, he can

answer client questions that a competitor's sales rep may not be able to, and he differentiates himself from the rest of the marketplace. Because he pays attention to internal systems and processes, he is not only well-equipped to navigate through service delivery or account problems but when he does call someone for help, his requests get sent to the top of the list because people know they are real and he's not just being lazy.

The choices that leaders make about where they spend their time and attention, as Mark demonstrates, have a tremendous influence on those around them. The behaviors and actions of leaders send clear messages to others about what's important and what's merely lip service.

Vivien Moses, project manager at Adobe Systems, knows this all too well. A new product launch was not going as smoothly as hoped for, and the team, based in China and India, told him that things could be improved if they could get faster responses to their questions. Every morning, it was common to make calls from the United States to the Asia team at 8:00 AM Pacific Standard Time. But that meant that the team members in Asia often had to dial into the conference call from home because it was very late at night there. Vivien decided to change this practice and started taking calls during his nights and early mornings: "I thought that I should hold nighttime calls myself, to show to the team that I am willing to take calls in the night just like they do. This cut down on the time to address issues, but most importantly it set an example to the team that I am willing to put in the extra effort to finish the task ahead." Vivien understood the importance of the Golden Rule of Leadership: ask others to do only what you are willing to do yourself. By changing how he used his time, he showed others that he was serious about his dedication to the group and the task.

Watch Your Language

Try talking about an organization for a day without using the words *employee, manager, boss, supervisor, subordinate,* or *hierarchy.* You may find this exercise nearly impossible unless you've been part of organizations that use other terms—such as *associates, crew, cast members, team members, partners,* or even *constituents.* Certain words have come to be accepted as the reality of organizational life. Those words can easily trap people into a particular way of thinking about roles and relationships.[6] Exemplary leaders understand this and are attentive to language. They know the power of words. Words don't just give voice to one's own mindset and beliefs; they also evoke images of what people hope to create with others and how they expect people to behave. The words people choose to use are metaphors for concepts that define attitudes, behaviors, structures, and systems. Your words can have a powerful effect on how your constituents see their world, and you should choose them intentionally and carefully.

One company that clearly understands how to consciously use a different vocabulary to reflect its unique set of values is DaVita, the largest independent provider of dialysis services in the United States for patients suffering from chronic kidney failure. The special language begins with the choice of the company name, as selected by DaVita teammates (employees). DaVita is definitely a name that fits the nature of their work. Roughly translated from the Italian, the phrase means "he or she gives life." Every day in every clinic, DaVitans—that's what they call themselves—work hard to give life to those suffering from renal disease.

At DaVita, memorable catchphrases infuse the daily conversation and reinforce the company's values and management practices. The Three Musketeers maxim "One for all, and all for one," for example, permeates the culture of the company and reinforces the idea that everyone in DaVita is in it together, looking out for each other. Corporate headquarters is called Casa DaVita (house of DaVita). Employees are all "teammates"—be prepared to put a buck in a glass on the meeting table if you should ever use the "E word." The company is called the Village, and DaVita's CEO, Kent Thiry, is its mayor, signaling that DaVita is really like the small town in Wisconsin where Kent grew up. Teammates become "citizens" of the Village when they are willing to "cross the bridge" and make a public commitment to the community. Every member of the senior leadership crossed the bridge as part of his or her symbolic rite of passage into those roles. The company's long-standing emphasis on execution and operational excellence is embodied in the slogan "GSD" (get stuff done); the highest compliment to pay a teammate is to say that he or she is "good at GSD."[7] "At a quick glance," says Javier Rodriguez, DaVita's senior vice president,

> our language can appear to be a play on words—semantics. Quite the opposite. The words we use, while simple in nature, are packed with meaning. They create imagery and communicate history, traditions, and beliefs. Since the language is so pervasive in the organization, we get the added benefit of it serving as cultural alignment and an accountability "acid test" for behaviors— as in human medicine, an organ will reject inconsistent words and actions. In addition, our vernacular serves as a filter for recruiting. That is to say, candidates feel affiliation and alignment to our words or find them "odd" if not consistent with their beliefs.

Paying attention to the way you use language isn't one of those ideas-of-the-month that's the trendy thing to do. Researchers have documented the power of language in shaping thoughts and actions. Just a few words from someone can make the difference in the beliefs that people articulate. For example, at an East Coast university where there was a publicized incident of hate mail's being sent to an African American student, researchers randomly stopped students walking across campus and asked them what they thought of the occurrence. Before the subject could respond, however, a confederate of the researchers would come up and answer. One response was something like, "Well, he must have done something to deserve it." As you might expect, the subject's response was more often than not just like the confederate's. Then the researchers would stop another student and ask the same question. This time the confederate gave an alternative response that was something like, "There's no place for that kind of behavior on our campus." The subject's response again replicated the confederate's.[8]

This study dramatically illustrates how potent language is in influencing people's responses to what's going on around them. Language helps build the frame around people's views of the world, and it's essential for leaders to be mindful of their choice of words. If you want people to act like citizens of a village, you have to talk about them that way, not as subordinates in a hierarchy. If you want people to appreciate the rich diversity in their organizations, you have to use language that's inclusive. If you want people to be innovative, you have to use words that spark exploration, discovery, and invention. The expression "Watch your language" has come a long way from the days when your teacher scolded you in school for the use of an inappropriate word. It's now about setting an example for others, demonstrating how they need to think and act.

Ask Purposeful Questions

The questions you ask are also quite powerful in focusing attention. When leaders ask questions, they send constituents on mental journeys—"quests"—in search of answers. The questions that a leader asks send messages about the focus of the organization, and they're indicators of what is of most concern to the leader. They're one more measure of how serious you are about your espoused beliefs. Questions direct attention to the values that should be attended to and how much energy should be devoted to them.

Questions develop people. They help people escape the trap of their own paradigms by broadening their perspective and forcing them to take responsibility for their own viewpoint. Asking good questions also forces you to listen attentively to your constituents and what they are saying. This action demonstrates your respect for their ideas and opinions. If you are genuinely interested in what other people have to say, then you need to ask their opinion, especially before giving your own. Asking what others think facilitates participation in whatever decision will ultimately be determined and consequently increases support for that decision. Asking good questions reduces the risk that a decision might be undermined by either inadequate consideration or unexpected opposition.

When Joshua Fradenburg was brought on to turn around a foundering sporting goods store in Northern California, he realized that all the employees needed to contribute their ideas about how to improve sales. Josh openly sought advice and asked a lot of questions: What did they think the store was doing well, and what did they need to work on? He never criticized an idea, instead choosing to ask follow-up questions that might allow for a more productive idea. Josh encouraged his staff to offer suggestions about merchandising, sales promotions, and inventory. For example, although most of his staff ranged from fifteen to eighteen years of age, he asked them each to go to the product wall and select which skis or snowboard they wanted. Then he had them pick out their bindings and boots. After giving them a couple minutes to make their decisions,

Josh asked them what they were thinking about when they were deciding. He asked them to close their eyes and envision what it would look like to use the new gear: "Feel the cold. Hear the wind whistle by. Smell the fresh mountain air." His questions got them thinking about how most people made an emotional (rather than a technical) purchase decision. Josh used questions to reframe their thinking and their approach to sales.

Think about the questions you typically ask in meetings, one-on-ones, telephone calls, and interviews. How do these questions help clarify and gain commitment to shared values? What would you like each of your constituents to pay attention to each day? Be intentional and purposeful about the questions you ask. When you are not around, what questions should others be thinking you are going to ask them when you return? What evidence do you want to ask about which will show that people are living by shared values and making decisions that are consistent with these values? What questions should you ask if you want people to focus on integrity or on trust or on customer satisfaction or on quality, innovation, growth, safety, or personal responsibility? In Table 3.1, we've

TABLE 3.1 Ask Purposeful Questions Daily

Teamwork: What did you do today to lend a hand to a colleague?

Respect: What did you do today to acknowledge the work of one of your colleagues?

Learning: What's one mistake you made in the last week, and what did you learn from it?

Continuous improvement: What have you done in the past week to improve so that you're better this week than last?

Customer focus: What is one change you made in the last week that came from a customer suggestion?

provided a few sample questions that you could purposefully ask every day to demonstrate the importance of shared values.

Whatever your shared values are, come up with a set of routine questions that will get people to reflect on the core values and what they have done each day to act on those values.

Seek Feedback

How can you know that you're doing what you say (which is the *behavioral* definition of credibility) if you never ask others for feedback on how you're doing? How can you really expect to match your words and your actions if you don't get information about how aligned they are? There's solid evidence that the best leaders are highly attuned to what's going on inside themselves as they are leading, and to what's going on with others.[9] They're very self-aware, and they're very socially aware. They can tell in short order whether they've done something that has enabled someone to perform at a higher level or whether they've sent motivation heading south.

Soliciting feedback from those with whom he works has been important to Seang Wee Lee, product quality engineer at NetApp, throughout his career. He uses feedback to "further improve my leadership skills, identify shortfalls, and open up communications with the team. This promotes trust in my leadership and creates a climate of trust within the team and with me. I almost always learn about some things I can do to help develop each individual as well as the team, and also me." Leaders realize that although they may not always like the feedback, it is the only way they can really know how they are doing as someone's leader. Seeking feedback makes a powerful statement about the value of self-improvement and how everyone can be even better than he or she is today.

Self-reflection, the willingness to seek feedback, and the ability to then engage in new behaviors based on this information have been shown to be predictive of future success in managerial jobs.[10] However, our own studies using the Leadership Practices Inventory (LPI)—our 360-degree feedback instrument for assessing the frequency with which people engage in The Five Practices of Exemplary Leadership—consistently show that the statement which receives the lowest rating, both from leaders as well as their constituents, is "Asks for feedback on how his/her actions affect other people's performance."[11] In other words, the behavior that leaders and their constituents consider to be the weakest is the behavior that most enables leaders to know how they're doing! You can't learn very much if you're unwilling to find out more about the impact of your behavior on the performance of those around you. It's your responsibility as a leader to keep asking others, "How am I doing?" If you don't ask, they're not likely to tell you.

It's not always easy to get feedback. It's not generally asked for, and most people aren't used to providing it. Skills are required to do both. You can increase the likelihood that people will accept honest feedback from you if you make it easier for people to give honest feedback to you. To be most effective, good feedback needs to be specific, not general; focused on behavior, not on the individual (personality); solicited rather than imposed; timely rather than delayed; and descriptive rather than evaluative. You have to be sincere in your desire to improve yourself, and you have to demonstrate that you are open to knowing how others see you. Table 3.2 provides some tips you might find useful for receiving good feedback.

Of course, just because someone gives you feedback doesn't necessarily mean that he or she is right or necessarily 100 percent accurate. Consider checking with other people to determine the

---
TABLE 3.2 Tips for Receiving Feedback

- *Don't be defensive.* People will be reluctant to share feedback if they are afraid of hurting your feelings or having to justify their perceptions.
- *Listen carefully.* Relax and actively listen to understand what the other person is trying to tell you; be sensitive to how your nonverbal communication is affecting the other person's willingness to share with you.
- *Suspend judgment.* Listen, don't judge. Don't worry about what you're going to say, but rather work to understand what the other person is trying to tell you. Be welcoming and assume that the information is intended to help you be better rather than anything otherwise.
- *Ask questions and ask for examples.* Make sure you understand what is being said and learn about the context as well as the content.
- *Say thank you.* Let the other person know that you appreciate his or her feedback and that you can't get any better without knowing more about yourself and how your actions affect others.

---

reliability of any feedback you receive. After all, few people see you in your totality. Sometimes the feedback may be more about the sender than it is about the receiver. But remember this: if you don't do anything with the feedback you receive, people will stop giving it to you. They're likely to believe that you are arrogant enough to think that you are smarter than everyone else or that you just don't care about what anyone else has to say. Either of these outcomes seriously undermines your credibility and effectiveness as a leader.

Everything that's been said here applies equally to your providing feedback to your constituents, which we discuss further in

Chapter Ten. The more frequently people ask for and accept feedback, the easier it will be to deliver and to hear, especially when both parties share similar values and aspirations. The more accustomed people become to giving and receiving feedback, the more comfortable they get with the process. The more you show you are open to feedback, the more others will view the process as constructive. But it's critical that you set the right climate for feedback. Reviewing past behavior can't be a search for culprits or an opportunity to fix the blame. Regularly soliciting feedback should be a routine examination of "what happened" with the intent to make sure that learning takes place and that any problems that may have occurred are not repeated.[12]

Often leaders fear the exposure and vulnerability that accompany direct and honest feedback. Those giving the feedback can often feel a bit exposed themselves and may even fear hurting someone or possible retribution. It's a risk, but the upsides of learning and growth are far greater than the downside of being nervous or embarrassed. Learning to be a better leader requires great self-awareness, and it requires making yourself vulnerable. By asking for feedback, you signal to others your openness to doing what is right, and make it easier for others to be receptive to learning about how well they are modeling the way.

TEACH OTHERS TO MODEL THE VALUES

You're not the only role model in the organization. Everyone should set the example. Words and deeds have to be aligned at all levels and in all situations. Your role is to make sure that your constituents are keeping the promises they have made. People are watching how you hold others accountable for living the shared values and how you reconcile deviations from the chosen path. They're paying attention to what others say and do, and so should you. It's not just what *you* do that demonstrates consistency between word and deed. Every team member, partner, and colleague is a sender of signals about what's valued. Therefore, you need to look for opportunities to teach not just by your example but also by taking on the role of teacher and coach.[13]

Exemplary leaders know that people learn valuable lessons from how unplanned as well as planned events are handled. They know that people learn from the stories that circulate in the hallways, in the break room, in the cafeteria, on the retail floor, and on Facebook and Twitter. Exemplary leaders know that what gets measured and reinforced gets done. People attend to metrics as well as stories. And exemplary leaders know that if they're going to create a high-performance culture, they have to pay attention to bringing on board people who share the values that are held dear.

In order to show others what's expected and ensure that they hold themselves accountable, you need to confront critical incidents, tell stories, and make sure that organizational systems reinforce the behaviors you want repeated.

Confront Critical Incidents

You can't plan everything about your day. Even the most disciplined leaders can't stop the intrusion of the unexpected. Stuff happens. Critical incidents—chance occurrences, particularly at a time of stress and challenge—are a part of the life of every leader. They also offer significant moments of learning for leaders and constituents.

Critical incidents present opportunities for leaders to teach important lessons about appropriate norms of behavior.

Abhijit Chitnis experienced just such a situation when he was working at Accenture as a team lead on an engagement for a U.S.-based storage client, with a five-person team working out of India, along with a global team of eight from the United States and Ireland. It was during the critical year-end financial reporting period for their client, and they were assigned to work on one of the business intelligence systems that the client used to report the annual and quarter-end financial numbers to Wall Street. The schedule was tight and demanding, but the team was on time and doing fine. Then they hit a patch of bad luck. They were just two days away from the critical deadline of December 31 when they ran into a slippage and some defects. They risked failure to deliver on time. That result could also have meant that they would lose part of the client's business. Team members were disappointed, of course, not only about the slippage but also about the possibility of missing their New Year's plans with friends and family. It meant they were going to have to put in extra work over the holiday in order to complete the task.

It was in this context that Abhijit witnessed something that demonstrated to him the extraordinary results that can be achieved when a team is led by someone who, he said, "truly personified the values that he stood for." The senior client engagement delivery manager, Bob, had been on a planned vacation when he heard about the problem. Says Abhijit,

> Bob cancelled all his planned commitments, and reported back
> to work, even though he was not a part of the delivery team.
> The personal commitment everyone saw from him boosted the
> entire team's morale. He stayed with the team day and night for

two days, providing motivational support, interfacing with the client, and setting the expectations for everyone in the team. As a result of this and all the hard work put in by the team, we were successful in delivering the required reports, on time and of high quality, to the client.

Bob sent a powerful message that holiday season by showing up to work when it wasn't really expected of him. It demonstrated how committed he was to his team, the project, and the client. Bob's example for his team, Abhijit told us, "in turn made me personally committed to the goal. We took each of the words from our leader very seriously, because we believed in him and trusted him more, and because he showed us that he truly means every word that he says. Every person in the team forgot about any of their grudges and got together to work efficiently as a team." All this happened because a leader put his values into practice. It is, says Abhijit, "incredibly strong evidence of the importance of the idea of modeling the way."

There are critical moments when leaders have to put values squarely on the table in order to make sure everyone understands the principles that guide how they work together. Sometimes leaders need to clearly and unambiguously point out that a particular decision or action is being taken because a core value is at stake. In doing so, leaders demonstrate the connection between actions taken and values espoused. They set an example for what it means to live the values under even the most trying of circumstances. By standing up for values, leaders demonstrate that having shared values requires a mutual commitment from everyone to align words and deeds.

Critical incidents are those events in the lives of leaders (and organizations) that offer the chance to improvise while still staying true to the script. Although these incidents can't be explicitly planned, it's useful to keep in mind, as Abhijit and Bob did, that the way you handle these events—how you link actions and decisions to shared values—speaks volumes about what really matters to you. Critical incidents create important teachable moments. They offer leaders the occasion in real time to demonstrate what's valued and what's not.

Tell Stories

Stories are another powerful tool for teaching people about what's important and what's not, what works and what doesn't, what is and what could be.[14] Through stories, leaders pass on lessons about shared values and get others to work together.

When he was program director of knowledge management for the World Bank, Steve Denning learned firsthand how stories can change the course of an organization. After trying all the more traditional ways of getting people to change their behavior, Steve found that simple stories were the most effective means of communicating the essential messages within the organization. "Nothing else worked," Steve said. "Charts left listeners bemused. Prose remained unread. Dialogue was just too laborious and slow. Time after time, when faced with the task of persuading a group of managers or frontline staff in a large organization to get enthusiastic about a major change, I found that storytelling was the only thing that worked."[15]

In a business climate obsessed with PowerPoint presentations, complex graphs and charts, and lengthy reports, storytelling may seem to some like a soft way of getting hard stuff done. It's anything but that. Steve's experience with storytelling is, in fact, supported by the data. Research shows that when leaders want to communicate standards, stories are a much more effective means of communication than are corporate policy statements, data about performance, and even a story plus the data.[16] Information is more quickly and accurately remembered when it is first presented in the form of an example or story.[17]

That's certainly been Phillip Kane's experience. Storytelling has been a part of his life since he was a kid. His dad was a great story-teller, and he used stories especially effectively to teach lessons. Phillip has carried the family tradition into his business life at Goodyear.

When Phillip was named to head up a large team with previously poor engagement scores for communication, he needed to find a way to be more proactive about connecting with employees. So he began writing to the team every Friday. He carried the practice with him when he was appointed president of Wingfoot Commercial Tire Systems, a twenty-five-hundred-person wholly owned subsidiary of Goodyear. As Phillip explained,

> The letter, simply and unoriginally titled "The Week," began as a recap of highlights from the prior week's work but soon morphed into a communication that was less about what we do than how we do it—which to me is as, or more, important. "The Week" is based on the notion that life lessons exist in unlikely places. These lessons, if we are open to them, help make us better tire sellers, parents, spouses, friends, and members of our community. When we grow and become better as individuals, the teams we belong to get better as well and will win more. That's the point of "The Week."

When we spoke to Phillip about "The Week," he'd written more than 150 issues, each one with a story and a lesson. Storytelling, Phillip says, accomplishes two things. It offers a framework for relating to the message—something that people encounter in their own lives that can bridge to the main point. It also offers him the chance to lead through an example rather than to come across simply as preaching.

Telling stories, as Phillip knows, has another lasting benefit. It forces you to pay close attention to what your constituents are doing. Peers generally make better role models for what to do at work than famous people or ones several levels up in the hierarchy. When others hear or read a story about someone with whom they can identify, they are much more likely to see themselves doing the same thing. People seldom tire of hearing stories about themselves and the people they know. These stories get repeated, and the lessons of the stories get spread far and wide. In fact, Phillip told us that folks who worked for him in his prior job asked if they could remain on his distribution list so that they'd continue to get "The Week," even though the stories and lessons didn't necessarily relate to them directly. Now that shows the power of stories!

Reinforce Through Systems and Processes

While attending a leadership course on Mount Fuji in Japan, Bert Wong, president and managing director of Fuji Xerox Singapore, was asked to reflect on the behaviors a great leader would demonstrate. He realized he didn't have the answers. That prompted Bert to seriously reflect on his own leadership and the business he led. What he realized from his self-exploration was that his team and business were heavily reliant on him. "I was leading an orchestra of people who would merely follow my lead," Bert told us. "When I was physically present, the business would see growth, but when I was absent, business would correspondingly suffer. Initiatives would be followed through with excellent execution, but the starting point and the driving force would always stem from me." This experience prompted

Bert to begin a multiyear process of creating a sustainable organization in which everyone shared in and was driven by a common set of values. Although many initially challenged Bert's approach, his persistence led to the creation of the Fuji Xerox Singapore core values: Fighting Spirit, Innovation and Learning, Collaborate to Compete, and Care and Concern.

But Bert knew that understanding and agreeing on the values were only the first steps. The next challenge was to make them a way of life. He was determined that the Fuji Xerox core values would play a key role in guiding the everyday decisions and actions of organization members. He knew that they had to be reinforced through daily actions and through all the others processes and systems that are a part of life at work. He began talking about them at every meeting, in every success story, and whenever a contract was won. He made sure that success was attributed to living the core values. And he did more than just communicate the values. Bert also ensured that the core values were reinforced through company-wide social events. Team-building activities, such as car rallies, would emphasize Fighting Spirit, Innovation and Learning, Collaborate to Compete, and Care and Concern. The Inspirational Player of the Year Award, voted by peers, was implemented to give recognition to exemplary members who demonstrated the Fuji Xerox core values.

Organizational practices were also aligned to the Fuji Xerox core values. To reinforce the value of Collaborate to Compete, different departments began to share similar key performance indicators (KPIs). Prior to this initiative, the finance and sales departments would often come into conflict as they pursued their respective departmental KPIs. Recognizing this misalignment, Bert worked with the two departments to find more compatible KPIs, and gave finance a stake in helping win a customer contract. They were no longer two separate departments. They were one team with members collaborating together to compete.

Fuji Xerox Singapore gradually began to see changes within the organization. As the core values were reinforced in their daily work activities, people began to internalize the values in everything they did. What began as Bert's personal leadership journey led to the institutionalization of a set of principles that eventually guided everyone's decisions and actions.

All exemplary leaders understand, as Bert does, that you have to reinforce the key values that are important to building and sustaining the kind of culture you want.[18] Key performance measures and reward systems are among the many methods available to you.[19] Recruitment, selection, on-boarding, training, information, retention, and promotion systems are also important means by which you can teach people how to enact values and align behavior. They all send signals about what is valued and what is not, and they must be aligned with the shared values and standards that you're trying to instill.

TAKE ACTION

Set the Example

One of the toughest aspects of being a leader is that you're always onstage. People are always watching you, always talking about you, always testing your credibility. That's why setting the *right* example is so important, and why it's essential to make use of all the tools you have available to set the example.

Leaders send signals in a variety of ways and in all kinds of settings, and constituents pay attention to those signals so that they can figure out what's okay and what's not okay to do. How you spend your time is the single best indicator of what's important to you. Time is a precious asset, because once passed, it can never be recovered. But if invested wisely, it can earn returns for years. The language you use and the questions you ask are other powerful ways that shape perceptions of what you value. You also need feedback in order to know if you're doing what you say.

But it's not just what you do that matters. You are also measured by how consistent your constituents' actions are with the shared values, so you must teach others how to set an example. Critical incidents—those chance occurrences in the lives of all organizations—offer significant teachable moments. They offer you the opportunity to pass along lessons in real time, not just in theory or in the classroom. Critical incidents often become the sources of stories, and stories are among the most influential teaching tools you have. And remember that what gets reinforced gets done. You have to bring the right people on board, orient them, develop them, and make sure that all systems strengthen the appropriate behavior that you expect to be repeated.

To Model the Way, you need to *set the example by aligning actions with shared values.* This means you have to

- Make sure your calendar, your meetings, your interviews, your emails, and all the other ways you spend your time reflect what you say is important.
- Keep your commitments; follow through on your promises.
- Repeat, repeat, and repeat phrases that evoke the feelings that you want to create in your workplace.

- Ask purposeful questions that keep people constantly focused on the values and priorities that are the most important.
- Publicly ask for feedback from others about how your actions affect them.
- Make changes and adjustments based on the feedback you receive; otherwise people will stop bothering to provide it.
- When a situation—especially an unplanned one—arises that dramatically illustrates a shared value, make sure to call attention to it.
- Broadcast examples of exemplary behavior through vivid and memorable stories that illustrate how people are and should be behaving.
- In every way you can, reinforce the behavior you want repeated.

Use *The Leadership Challenge Mobile Tool* app to immediately integrate these activities into your life and make this practice an ongoing part of your behavioral repertoire.

INSPIRE A
SHARED
VISION

The future holds little certainty. There are no guarantees or easy paths to any destination, and circumstances can change in a moment. Pioneering leaders rely on their own internal compass and a dream.

Leaders look forward to the future. They hold in their minds ideas and visions of what can be. They have a sense of what is uniquely possible if everyone works together for a common purpose. Leaders are positive about the future, and they passionately believe that people can make a difference.

But visions seen only by the leaders are insufficient for generating organized movement. Leaders must get others to see the exciting future possibilities. They breathe life into visions. They communicate hopes and dreams so that others clearly understand and share them as their own. They show others how their values and interests will be served by the long-term vision of the future.

Leaders are expressive, and they attract followers through their energy, optimism, and hope. With strong appeals and quiet persuasion, they develop enthusiastic supporters.

In the next two chapters, we will explore how you must

- **Envision the Future by imagining exciting and ennobling possibilities.**
- **Enlist Others by appealing to shared aspirations.**

CHAPTER 4

Envision the Future

JADE LUI ALWAYS HAD A PASSION for books, and followed that passion to pursue a career in publishing. At her first job with a large international publisher in Hong Kong, Jade was given responsibilities for business development throughout the East Asia region. She was particularly excited by the prospect of promoting English books into the China market.

On her first field visit, Jade surveyed the handful of bookstores with foreign books sections in Beijing and Shanghai. The shelves were bare except for a few classics and dog-eared paperbacks. Jade said she "was stupefied," but immediately realized what it meant—that there was vast untapped market potential: "Considering the increasing number of expatriates, tourists, and young Chinese students learning the English language in China, I could only imagine the exponential growth in the demand for English books. More pertinent to me, though, was my vision of introducing quality educational English books to children in China to improve their learning experience and broaden their horizons."

One year after her initial field visit, Jade received the first coprinting order from a publishing house in China for a range of educational children's books. It came, however, with a very tight target delivery date, stringent cobranding design requirements, and a large credit limit request. In accordance with her company's usual processing practice, Jade submitted the order via email to headquarters in the United Kingdom with the conditions attached. The replies were unanimously negative. "There is no way we can meet the deadline!" said one colleague. "This is not the way we do things here," said another.

Frustrated by the lack of enthusiasm, Jade decided to organize a conference call with her support team, including the order administrator, graphic designer, and credit controller. During the call, she asked probing questions to learn more about the root cause of their negativity. She listened carefully to what they had to say, and discovered that "unlike my client-facing position, as administrative staff they held a very different mentality. Working in a vacuum, they worked 'by the book' and were concerned merely with fulfilling their job requirements. They saw little direct impact of their work on overall business performance."

Jade realized that she needed to appeal to common ideals. To combat the negativity from her team, she wanted to ensure that they felt that their work mattered and that they could make a difference.

I first drew a parallel between their administrative function and my frontline client service role. I explained how they were also important customer service agents because they were providing service to internal clients, such as me. In doing so, I aligned our objectives in delivering first-class customer service—be it to external or internal clients. I also emphasized how we were a team with the ultimate goal of fulfilling this landmark order, underscoring the active parts they played in this revenue-generating opportunity. More importantly though, I asked my team to envision the many Chinese children reading and learning from our books—the availability of which would be made possible only through their hard work.

Three months following that initial conference call, the order was completed on time and at the highest standards of professionalism. Jade and her colleagues had launched their dream. And from this experience, Jade says she learned a vital leadership lesson: "I learned to appreciate the varying perspectives held by those in different work functions, to identify the source of a problem through open dialogue, and how to motivate a team by promoting a sense of comradeship in pursuit of commons goals and a shared vision."

Jade's story illustrates how organized efforts—whether those of a company, a project, or a movement—begin with one person's imagination. Call it what you will—vision, purpose, mission, legacy, dream, aspiration, calling, or personal agenda—the result is the same. If you are going to be an exemplary leader, you have to be able to imagine a positive future. When you envision the future you want for yourself and others, and when you feel passionate about the legacy you want to leave, you are much more likely to take that first step forward. But if you don't have the slightest clue about your hopes, dreams, and aspirations, then the chance that you'll take the lead is nil. In fact, you may not even see the opportunity that's right in front of you.

Exemplary leaders are forward-looking. They are able to envision the future, to gaze across the horizon and realize the greater opportunities to come. They imagine that extraordinary feats are possible and that the ordinary could be transformed into something noble. They are able to develop an ideal and unique image of the future for the common good.

But the vision can't belong only to the leader. It's a shared vision. Everyone has dreams, aspirations, and a desire that tomorrow be better than today. When visions are shared, they attract more people, sustain higher levels of motivation, and withstand more challenges than those that are singular. You have to make sure that what you can see is also something that others can see, and vice versa.

The second of The Five Practices of Exemplary Leadership is *Inspire a Shared Vision*. To do that, leaders make a commitment to Envision the Future for themselves and others by mastering these two essentials:

- **IMAGINE THE POSSIBILITIES**
- **FIND A COMMON PURPOSE**

Leaders begin with the end in mind by imagining what might be possible. Finding a common purpose inspires people to want to make that vision a reality.

IMAGINE THE POSSIBILITIES

"The human being is the only animal that thinks about the future" (italics in the original), writes Daniel Gilbert, professor of psychology at Harvard University. "The greatest achievement of the human brain is its ability to imagine objects and episodes that do not exist in the realm of the real, and it is this ability that allows us to think about the future."[1] Our data support the importance of this ability

in leaders. Being forward-looking is the second-most admired characteristic that people look for in those people they would willingly follow. In fact, it's this quality of focusing on the future that most differentiates people who are seen as leaders from those who are not. Nearly three out of four respondents expect this from their leaders, whereas less than 30 percent expect this quality in their colleagues. However, researchers who study executives' work activities have estimated that, unfortunately, only about 3 percent of the typical businessperson's time is spent thinking about the future.[2] It's something to which every leader needs to give more time and attention.

Leaders are dreamers. Leaders are idealists. Leaders are possibility thinkers. All enterprises, big or small, begin with the belief that what's merely an image today can one day be made real. It's this belief that sustains leaders through the difficult times. Turning possibility thinking into an inspiring vision—and one that is shared—is another one of your challenges as a leader.

When we ask people to tell us where their visions come from, they often have great difficulty describing the process. And when they do provide an answer, typically it's more about a feeling, a sense, even a gut reaction. Clarifying your vision, like clarifying your values, is an intuitive and emotional process of self-exploration and self-creation. There's often no logic to it. You just feel strongly about something, and that sense, that intuition has to be fully explored.[3] Visions are reflections of one's fundamental beliefs and assumptions about human nature, technology, economics, science, politics, art, and ethics.

A vision of the future is much like a literary or musical theme. It's the prominent and pervasive message that you want to convey, the frequently recurring melody that you want people to remember; and whenever it's repeated, it reminds the audience of the entire work. Every leader needs a theme, something on which he or she can structure the rest of the performance. Think about these questions:

What's your prominent message?

What's your recurring theme?

What idea, feeling, aspiration, or concern grabs hold of you and won't let you go?

What do you most want people to envision every time they think about the future?

For many leaders, the answers don't come easily—at first. Fortunately there are ways you can improve your capacity to imagine exciting possibilities and to discover the central theme for your life and the lives of others. Improvement comes when you engage in conscious introspection. This requires you to *reflect* on your past, *attend* to the present, *prospect* the future, and *feel* your passion.

Reflect on Your Past

As contradictory as it might seem, in aiming for the future you need to look back into your past. Looking backward can actually enable you to see farther than if you only stare straight ahead. Understanding the past can help you identify themes, patterns, and beliefs that both underscore why you care about certain matters now and explain why making them better into the future is such a high priority.[4]

Consider what Joanne Chan, a pharmacist with Mannings, one of the largest health and beauty retailers in Hong Kong, learned from her leader about the past that gave her and the team perspective for moving into the future. The pharmacy department was not doing as well as expected, and Joanne and her colleagues felt frustrated and discouraged at work. However, Andy, the senior pharmacist of the team, uplifted and motivated them by constantly reminding them about how the services they provided made a difference:

> Andy often told us stories about his experiences with patients in the past. One of them involved an old lady who had difficulty walking. When she came to the store to seek advice for her health-related problems, Andy offered her a chair to sit near the store entrance, so that she did not have to walk all the way to the back of the store where the pharmacy department was located. The lady appreciated Andy's customer service, and became one of Mannings' most loyal customers. Using examples like these, Andy shared with us the vision that the pharmacy team could become the best group of health care professionals providing excellent services to the general public.

Joanne explained that she and her colleagues learned from Andy's inspiration that "a leader needs to effectively communicate a shared vision to his or her followers, and show how they fit in the big picture." Andy reflected on his past experiences, using them to bring up and reinforce the point that even a small gesture could make a difference. Sharing his past experiences pointed the team to where they wanted to be in the future with all of their customers. His storytelling brought the vision to life, because Andy's past experience not only was meaningful but also could very much happen—it represented an opportunity—for any of his colleagues at work.

Looking into your past can reveal much about the future. Studies involving senior executives reveal that those who were asked to think first about things that had happened to them in the past—before they thought about future possibilities—were subsequently able to extrapolate significantly further into the future than those executives who were asked to think first about things that might happen to them in the future.[5] This phenomenon is called "the Janus Effect," named for the Roman god with two faces, one that looks backward and the other forward. Your ability to look both to your past and your future for guidance opens up lots more exciting possibilities than doing one or the other alone.[6]

The past serves as a prologue for the future. When you gaze first into your past, you essentially elongate your future. You realize how full your life has been, and you become more aware of all the possibilities that could lie ahead. You enrich your imagination about the future and give it detail as you recall the richness of your past experiences. Looking back to all those highs, and even lows, enables you to better understand that the central, recurring theme in your life didn't just materialize this morning. It's been there for a long time. Another benefit to looking back before looking ahead is that you gain a greater appreciation for how long it can take to fulfill aspirations. You also realize that there are many, many avenues to pursue.

None of this is to say that the past *is* your future. That would be like trying to drive using only the rearview mirror. When you look deeply into your entire life history, you understand things about yourself and about your world that you cannot fully comprehend by looking at the future as a blank slate. It's difficult, if not impossible, to imagine going to a place you've never experienced, either actually or vicariously. Taking a journey into your past before exploring your future makes the trip much more meaningful.

Attend to the Present

To envision the future, you have to look around and notice what's going on. Right now as you listen to your constituents, what are the hot topics of conversation? What are they saying they need and want? What are they saying that gets in the way of them doing the very best they can? What are they saying should be changed? Is there anything they have stopped talking about that seems puzzling? What does all this tell you about where things are going? What's it telling you about what lies just around the corner?

Gautam Aggarwal knew that he would need to attend to the present when he was promoted to product manager in the medical diagnostics division of Labo America. Gautam realized that he needed to "develop a clear vision of what kind of group we needed to be and how we would go about achieving our goals." He explained, "I understood that a leader's vision for the future has to be supported with facts about both the past and present."

One of the first things he did was to hold an open forum with all reports, direct and indirect, about how they perceived the product line's presence in the market at the time, and where they saw it three to five years in the future. "We would all have to be on the same page about where we were today before we could go to any place in the future," he reasoned. "I gave everyone the opportunity of providing feedback on what we had been doing right, and what needed both immediate as well as long-term improvement." These discussions provided Gautam and his colleagues with a realistic assessment of current conditions, strengths, and challenges, while also helping them identify and make choices about which of the many promising paths forward they should pursue. To be able to envision the future, you have to realize what's already going on. You have to spot the trends and patterns, and appreciate both the whole and the parts. You have to be able to see the forest *and* the trees.[7]

Imagine the future as a jigsaw puzzle. You see the pieces, and you begin to figure out how they fit together, one by one, into a whole. Similarly, with your vision, you need to rummage through the bits and bytes of data that accumulate daily, and notice how they fit together into a picture of what's ahead. Envisioning the future is not about gazing into a fortune-teller's crystal ball; it's about paying attention to the little things that are going on all around you and being able to recognize patterns that point to the future.

Prospect the Future

Even as you stop, look, and listen to messages in the present, you also need to raise your head and gaze out toward the horizon. Being forward-looking is not the same as meeting the deadline for your current project. Leaders have to prospect the future. They have to be on the lookout for emerging developments in technology, demographics, economics, politics, arts, and all aspects of life inside and outside the organization. They have to anticipate what might be coming just over the hill and around the corner.

One of the leaders we interviewed told us, "I'm my organization's futures department." All leaders should view themselves this way. Leaders need to spend considerable time reading, thinking, and talking about the long-term view, not only for their specific organizations but also for the environments in which they operate. This imperative intensifies with the leader's scope and level of responsibility. For example, when a leader's role is strategic (as it is for a CEO, president, or research director, for example), the time orientation is longer term and more future oriented than it is for a leader whose role is more tactical (for example, a production supervisor or operations manager).

There is no hard-and-fast rule as to how far into the future a leader should look, although it oftentimes varies with hierarchical level.[8] Consider our findings about the perceived importance of "forward-looking" as a key leader characteristic varies by organizational level. Eighty-eight percent of senior executives select forward-looking, as do 68 percent of middle managers, but only about 44 percent of college students consider it a preeminent leadership requirement. This is an indication that as individuals move into more senior levels in organizations, which bring with them responsibilities for longer-term projects and results, they see the value of looking farther out into the future.

Darrell Klotzbach worked at a small start-up company that was taking on the challenge of developing software titles for young children. Everyone was quite keyed up about the project because, as Darrell explained, "there were endless possibilities. We all wanted to develop a high-quality game that children would find exciting to play, that they would play again and again, and that would be an experience that they would learn from." Darrell said that he "kept people focused on the future, reminding people how much kids enjoyed what we were doing, and how much they would enjoy it when we were done. Without keeping an eye on the future, they might have become bogged down with some of the day-to-day mundane activities and become frustrated by some very difficult challenges."

Darrell appreciates how the leader's job is to keep people focused on the future so that they will be eager to meet the daily challenges, work through the inevitable conflicts, and persevere to the end. Visions are future oriented and are made real over different spans of time. It may take three years from the time you decide to climb a mountain until you actually reach the summit. It may take a decade to build a company that is one of the best places to work. It may take a lifetime to make neighborhoods safe again for children to walk alone. It may take a century to restore a forest destroyed by a wildfire. It may take generations to set a people free.

Imagination, asserted Nobel Prize–winning physicist Albert Einstein, is more important than intelligence,[9] and this is particularly true for leaders dealing with rapidly changing times. You need to give greater consideration to what you're going to do after the current problem, task, assignment, project, or program has been completed. "What's next?" should be a question you frequently ask yourself. If you're not thinking about what's happening after the completion of your longest-term project, then you're thinking only as long term as everyone else. In other words, you're redundant! The leader's job is to think about the next project, and the one after that, and the one after that.

Great football coaches, for example, aren't thinking about the current play on the field—that's the execution left up to the players, and they'll be either successful or not. What the coach is thinking about is the play after that, considering all the possibilities before even knowing the outcome of what's currently being executed.[10] Similarly, Grand Master bridge players (or chess or even poker players) aren't simply thinking about their next move. They are considering possible permutations that could emerge as the game unfolds. And that's what you should be doing—thinking about what you and your team will be undertaking after what you're currently working on has been completed. As a leader, you need to be thinking a few "moves" ahead of your team and picturing the future possibilities.

In a series of studies, researchers have shown how leaders who are focused on the future attract followers more readily, induce more effort and intrinsic motivation from group members, promote group identification, mobilize collective action, and ultimately achieve better performance on measures of both individual and organizational outcomes.[11] Leaders must spend time thinking about the future and become better at projecting themselves ahead in time.

Whether it's through reading about trends, talking with futurists, listening to podcasts, or watching documentaries, developing a deep understanding of where things are going is a significant part of your job. Your constituents expect it of you. You have to spend more of today thinking more about tomorrow if your future is going to be an improvement over the present. And throughout the process of reflecting on your past, attending to the present, and prospecting for the future, you need to keep in touch with what moves you, what you care about, where your passion is.

Feel Your Passion

Passion goes hand in hand with attention. People don't see possibilities when they don't feel any passion. Envisioning the future requires you to stay in touch with your deepest feelings. You have to find something that's so important that you're willing to put in the time, suffer the inevitable setbacks, and make the necessary sacrifices. Everyone has concerns, desires, questions, propositions, arguments, hopes, and dreams—core issues that can help organize aspirations and actions. And every individual has a few things that are much more important than other things. Whatever yours are, you need to be able to name them so that you can talk about them with others. You have to step back and ask yourself, "What is my burning passion? What gets me up in the morning? What's grabbed hold of me and won't let go?"

Leaders want to do something significant, accomplish something that no one else has yet achieved. What that something is—your sense of meaning and purpose—has to come from within. No one can impose a self-motivating vision on you. That's why, just as we said about values, you must first clarify your own vision of the future before you can expect to enlist others in a shared vision.

Researchers in human motivation have long talked about two kinds of motivation—extrinsic and intrinsic.[12] People do things either because of external controls—the possibility of a tangible reward if they succeed or punishment if they don't—or because of an internal desire. People do something because they feel forced or because they want to. People do something to please others or to please themselves. No surprises when it comes to predicting which condition is more likely to produce extraordinary results.

The research is very clear: external motivation is more likely to create conditions of compliance or defiance; self-motivation produces far superior results. There's even an added bonus. People who are self-motivated will keep working toward a result even if there's no reward.[13] In contrast, people who are externally controlled are likely to stop trying once the rewards or punishments are removed—or, as so aptly put by psychologist and motivational expert Edward Deci, "Stop the pay, and stop the play."[14]

Exemplary leaders have a passion for something other than their own fame and fortune. They care about making a difference. If you don't care deeply for and about something, how can you expect others to feel any sense of conviction? How can you expect others to feel passion if you're not energized and excited? How can you expect others to suffer through the long hours, hard work, absences from home, and personal sacrifices if you're not similarly committed? This is exactly what Andrew Rzepa discovered as part of his own personal-best leadership experience.

About a month after Andrew became chairman of a committee of trainee solicitors (lawyers) from across Manchester, England, the national Trainee Solicitors Group arranged a conference for all the trainees in the United Kingdom to take place in his city. Although not his event per se, given the close affiliation of their local with the national organization, Andrew decided that he would do all he could to make the event a success. He got his colleagues together and publicly declared that he was going to do everything in his power to ensure that there would be at least three hundred delegates at the event. (With three weeks to go, the enrollment was only at seventy-five.) "I spoke passionately about how good it would feel to be there at a packed event and to look around thinking that we had achieved that."

After sharing his own feelings, Andrew invited the committee members to indicate whether "they were willing to personally commit themselves to the realization of this goal." Andrew acknowledged that because this event was neither part of the committee's goals nor the reason members had volunteered for the committee, he wouldn't have been surprised had the majority said no. "To my pure joy," Andrew exclaimed, "sixteen out of the twenty said yes, they were willing to do all they could to make the event a success." And the fact that there were some "doubters" actually energized everyone involved. "The committee members were more passionate than I had ever seen them before," Andrew said. In the end, after a solid combined effort from all quarters, they succeeded in getting 316 attendees to the event. Andrew's passion not only fueled his own drive but also was contagious in getting others to work as hard as they could to realize a future possibility.

When you feel your passion, as Andrew did, you know you are on to something very important. Your enthusiasm and drive spread to others. Finding something you truly believe in is the key to articulating a vision in the first place. Once you're in touch with this inner feeling, you can look and think beyond the constraints of your current position and view the possibilities available in the future.

FIND A COMMON PURPOSE

All too often, leaders have come to assume that it is solely their responsibility to be the visionaries. After all, if focusing on the future sets leaders apart, it's understandable that they would get the feeling that it's their job to embark alone on a vision quest to discover the future of their organization.

This is *not* what constituents expect. Yes, leaders are expected to be forward-looking, but they aren't expected to impose their vision of the future on others. People don't really want to picture only the *leader's* vision. They want to see how their own visions and aspirations will come true, how their hopes and dreams will be fulfilled. They want to view themselves in the picture of the future that the leader is painting. The key task for leaders is inspiring a *shared* vision, not selling their own idiosyncratic view of the world. What this requires is finding common ground among those people who have to implement the vision. Your constituents want to feel part of the process.[15]

Buddy Blanton, a programs manager for strategy and development at Northrop Grumman Corporation, certainly found this to be true. Buddy wanted to learn how he could be more effective at creating a shared vision, so he asked his team for feedback. What they told him helped him understand that it's the process, not just the vision, that's critical in getting everybody on the same page:

> One of the team members that I most respect spoke first, and gave me this advice: "You would benefit by helping us, as a team, to understand how you got to your vision. We want to walk with you while you create the goals and vision so we all get to the end vision together." Another team member said that

sharing this road map would help him to feel more ready to take the initiative to resolve issues independently. A couple of other team members stated that this communication would help them to understand how the goals are realistic. One of the team members said that they would like to be a part of the vision-building process so they could learn how to better build visions for their team.

What Buddy found out is what every leader must understand: nobody really likes being told what to do or where to go, no matter how right it might be. People want to be a part of the vision development process. The vast majority of people are just like Buddy's team members. They want to walk with their leaders. They want to dream with them, invent with them, and be involved in creating their own futures.

This means that you can't adopt the view that visions come from the top down. You have to start engaging others in a collective dialogue about the future, not delivering a monologue. You can't mobilize people to willingly travel to places they don't want to go. No matter how grand the dream of an individual visionary, if others don't see in it the possibility of realizing their own hopes and desires, they won't follow voluntarily or wholeheartedly. You must show others how they, too, will be served by the long-term vision of the future, how their specific needs can be satisfied.

Listen Deeply to Others

By knowing their constituents, listening to them, and taking their advice, leaders are able to give voice to their constituents' feelings. They're able to stand before others and say with assurance, "Here's what I heard you say that you want for yourselves. Here's how your own needs and interests will be served by enlisting in a common cause." In a sense, leaders hold up a mirror and reflect back to their constituents what they say they most desire.

You need to strengthen your ability to hear what is important to others. The outlines of any vision do not appear from crystal ball gazing in the isolation of the upper levels of the organization's stratosphere. They originate from conversations with customers in the retail stores. They come from interactions with employees on the manufacturing floor, in the lab, or in the cafeteria. They're heard in the hallways, in meetings, and in people's homes.

The best leaders are great listeners. They listen carefully to what other people have to say and how they feel. They have to ask good (and often tough) questions, be open to ideas other than their own, and even lose arguments in favor of the common good. Through intense listening, leaders get a sense of what people want, what they value, and what they dream about. This sensitivity to others is no trivial skill. It is a truly precious human ability.[16]

Jacqueline Wong can testify to the power of listening deeply. Although she had received many individual achievement awards, when she was promoted to head up one of the teams at CFS, a private investment advisory firm, she realized that "team achievements became what mattered." Her personal-best leadership experience of winning the company-wide Team of the Quarter award for outstanding sales performance, she said, "began with listening to the team and finding out what they most valued and wanted in their lives."

> I asked them to draw their dreams of their future. From those
> images, I was able to understand how I could align their goals
> with the team vision. One common vision was happiness and
> providing for our families. I merely had to build the link, and

this link led us from the team's mission to their dreams in the long run. I inspired my team by explaining how the team goal would take them one step closer to their destination. By outperforming all the other teams, they would build the confidence they needed to continue in this commission-based investment-service business. Consequently, they would be able to provide a good standard of living for the people they loved. For my group, their self-motivation to reach the shared vision drove them to spectacular success in that quarter. We outperformed the first runner-up by 118 percent.

Jacqueline often sat with each team member not only to talk about progress but also to discover each person's strengths and motivations. "Knowing what my team members valued," she said, "helped me communicate with them in a common language." For example, she learned from one team member about his parents' pending retirement. She took that opportunity to tell her colleague how he would be able to significantly help his parents with their retirement fund by working hard on the project. In another instance, a team member was significantly underperforming. Jacqueline had a talk with her and found out that she was unsure of her ability to meet the objectives and therefore hadn't really bought into the "same aspiration as the rest of the team." Jacqueline started taking her along to some of her own business deals and showing her what was possible. Other members of the team started doing this as well. After a while, Jacqueline said, this team member "bought into our team goal, and her performance improved dramatically; and by the end of the target period, in fact, she had the second-best performance on the team." Through paying attention to what people told her, Jacqueline was able to identify opportunities for them and develop a winning mindset within the team.

Make It a Cause for Commitment

When you listen deeply, as Jacqueline did, you can find out what gives work its meaning to others. People stay with an organization, research finds, because they like the work they are doing and find it challenging, meaningful, and purposeful.[17] When you listen with sensitivity to the aspirations of others, you discover that there are some common values that link everyone together.[18] People want a chance to

Be tested, to make it on their own
Take part in a social experiment
Do something well
Do something good
Change the way things are

Aren't these the essence of what most leadership challenges are all about? Indeed, what people want has not changed very dramatically through the years.[19]

These findings suggest that there's more to work than making money.[20] People have a deep desire to make a difference. They want to know that they have done something on this earth, that there's a purpose to their existence. Work has become a place where people pursue meaning and identity.[21] The best organizational leaders address this human longing by communicating the significance of the organization's work so that people understand their own important role in creating and performing that work. When leaders clearly communicate a shared vision of an organization, they ennoble those who work on its behalf. They elevate the human spirit.

Although this idea may be easy enough to comprehend, Sonja Shevelyov, human resources manager at Ooyala, a leader in online video management, told us,

It can be difficult to implement. There is immense value in creating meaning to the work that is being asked of people. I've learned how important it is to take time to listen closely and connect with what is meaningful to others. In an environment with rapidly changing priorities, I find I am constantly in a reactive state. Creating time and driving any projects to completion in a proactive way is a struggle.

It can be difficult to anticipate the future, because it requires you to be proactive and be disciplined around establishing what those shared values are and not just assuming them. The payoff is huge because I can connect to the feeling that what I'm doing is bigger than myself, even noble.

People commit to causes, not to plans. How else do you explain why people volunteer to rebuild communities ravaged by a tsunami, ride a bike from San Francisco to Los Angeles to raise money to fight AIDS, or rescue people from the rubble of a collapsed building after an earthquake? How else do you explain why people toil 24/7 to create the next big thing when the probability of failure is very high? People are not committing to the plan in any of these cases. There may not even be a plan to commit to. They are committing to something much bigger, something much more compelling than goals and milestones on a piece of paper. That's not to say that plans aren't important to executing on grand dreams. They absolutely are. It's just to say that the plan isn't the thing that people are committing to.

The most successful strategies are visions.[22] McGill University professor Henry Mintzberg has observed, "Calculated strategies have no value in and of themselves. . . . Strategies take on value only as committed people infuse them with energy."[23] When people are part of something that elevates them to higher levels of motivation and morality, they develop a sense that they belong to something very special. This sense of belonging is particularly important in tumultuous times.

Look Forward in Times of Rapid Change

In this digital age when the business world is changing at warp speed, people often ask, "How can I have a vision of what's going to happen five or ten years from now, when I don't even know what's going to happen next week?" Venture capitalist Geoff Yang has taken risks on many new technology companies that are expected to move at a rapid pace. What types of innovators is he willing to back? "Men and women with great vision," he says. "They are able to recognize patterns when others see chaos in the marketplace. That's how they spot unexploited niche opportunities. And they are passionate about their ideas, which are revolutionary ways to change the way people live their lives or the way businesses operate. When they come to me they have conviction."[24]

Look at it this way. Imagine you're driving along the Pacific Coast Highway heading south from San Francisco on a bright, sunny day. The hills are on your left, the ocean on your right. On some curves, the cliffs plunge several hundred feet to the water. You can see for miles and miles. You're cruising along at the speed limit, tunes blaring, top down, wind in your hair, and not a care in the world. You come around a bend in the road, and suddenly, without warning, there's a blanket of fog as thick as you've ever seen it. What do you do?

We've asked this question many, many times, and here are some of the things people tell us:

"I slow way down."

"I turn my lights on."

"I grip the steering wheel with both hands."

"I tense up."

"I sit up straight or lean forward."

"I turn the music off."

Then you go around the next curve in the road; the fog lifts, and it's clear again. What do you do? Relax, speed up, turn the lights off, put the music back on, and enjoy the scenery.

This analogy illustrates the importance of clarity of vision. Are you able to go faster when it's foggy or when it's clear? How fast can you drive in the fog without risking your own or other people's lives? How comfortable are you riding in a car with someone else who drives fast in the fog? The answers are obvious, aren't they? You're better able to go fast when your vision is clear. You're better able to anticipate the switchbacks and bumps in the road when you can see ahead. There are times in your life, no doubt, when you find yourself driving in the fog, metaphorically speaking. When this happens, you get nervous and unsure of what's ahead. You slow down. But as you continue forward along the path, the way becomes clearer, and eventually you're able to speed up again. This is exactly the experience that Kyle Harvey described.

As a marketing specialist with a Silicon Valley semiconductor company, Kyle was given a huge project with another marketing team member to create a video and articles about the wide range of products they offered. He set up a meeting with his coworker to determine the direction that they were going to take. "At the beginning it was really confusing," Kyle said.

She seemed uninterested in the project, and you could have said we were in the densest part of the fog. There was no vision for the project, and we really had no direction. After about two weeks, we still had not accomplished anything, so I set up another meeting. This time, before going into the meeting, I developed a vision about how to approach the project. I knew that she was extremely artistic and enjoyed being creative. I found ways to incorporate her talents and what she liked doing into the project. This jump-started her and then we really got engaged. After about ten or fifteen minutes of explaining how she would be able to use her creativity, she began explaining how she wanted the video to look. The fog kept lifting and the view ahead was becoming clearer. . . . After a month of work on the project, it finally seems like we have begun driving faster and left the fog behind. Each of us has been contributing significantly, and she became extremely focused and driven to reach our goal.

The fog analogy is especially strong for me in this case. I found that when our vision was unclear, we pulled off to the side of the road and did not continue to drive. However, after finding ways to motivate and inspire her, we have been back on the road and moving through the fog. It was nice to be able to start from nothing and then build it up to what we have now. It was important for me to realize that the "shared vision" does not always come instantly or in the first meeting. The vision gets clearer the more people communicate and find ways to inspire each other.

Simply put, to become a leader, you must be able to envision the future. The speed of change doesn't alter this fundamental truth. People want to follow only those who can see beyond today's problems and visualize a brighter tomorrow.

TAKE ACTION

Envision the Future

The most important role of vision in organizational life is to give focus to human energy. To enable everyone concerned with an enterprise to see more clearly what's ahead of him or her, you must have and convey an exciting, ennobling vision of the future. The path to clarity of vision begins with reflecting on the past, moves to attending to the present, and then goes prospecting into the future. And the guardrails along this path are your passions—what it is that you care about most deeply.

Although you have to be clear about your own vision before you can expect others to follow, you need to keep in mind that you can't effectively, authentically lead others to places they personally don't want to go. If the vision is to be attractive to more than an insignificant few, it must appeal to all who have a stake in it. Only *shared* visions have the magnetic power to sustain commitment over time. Listen to the voices of all your constituents; listen for their hopes, dreams, and aspirations. And because a common vision spans years and keeps everyone focused on the future, it has to be about more than a task or job. It has to be a cause, something meaningful, and something that makes a difference in people's lives. Whether you're leading a small department of ten, a large organization of ten thousand, or a community of a hundred thousand, a shared vision sets the agenda and gives direction and purpose to the enterprise.

To Inspire a Shared Vision, you must *envision the future by imagining exciting and ennobling possibilities*. This means you have to

- Determine what you care about, what drives you, where your passions lie.
- Make a list of all the things you want to accomplish, and ask yourself "Why?"
- Use your past experiences as clues for understanding key themes in your life and understanding what you find worthwhile.
- Be curious about what is going on around you—especially things that aren't working well.
- Ask "What's next?" about every project long before it is completed.
- Spend time thinking and finding out about the future.
- Listen to your constituents about what is important to *their* future.
- Involve others in crafting what could be possible; don't make it a top-down process.
- Weave together your own hopes and dreams with those of your constituents.
- Get people on the same page, the same path, about where you all are going.
- Elevate what you and others are doing from a job to a "calling."

Use *The Leadership Challenge Mobile Tool* app to immediately integrate these activities into your life and make this practice an ongoing part of your behavioral repertoire.

CHAPTER 5

Enlist Others

SALVATORE SARNO CAME TO South Africa from Italy at the age of nineteen and eventually became chairman of MSC South Africa, a privately owned container shipping line and one of the leading carriers in the world. His leadership story, however, is not a corporate one; rather he made an entire nation excited about his dream that South Africa would be the first African team to race in the most important sailing competition in the world, the America's Cup.[1] He wanted to give people who grew up in difficult conditions the chance to represent the pride of their nation in front of the world, to show that with passion you could overcome other problems like lack of budget or experience.

His dream sounded a bit crazy to the people with whom he first shared it, but Salvatore merged his passions for sailing and for South Africa into a common purpose for the nation and for the African people. Those who'd yearned to realize a dream from the time they first sailed into Cape Town Bay and those who were raised in places like Durban were suddenly given a chance to be part of something grand—something that gave them a new reason to train, to improve, and to commit to a meaningful cause. They would have the opportunity to make history.

Salvatore did what all exemplary leaders do. He looked forward and talked about what could be. He painted a picture of the future so that others could see what was possible. He shared his passion and enthusiasm with the people around him. It was infectious, and one young man remembered how Salvatore used to tell him nearly a decade before the race: "Imagine the underdog South African boat with his mixed white and black crew sailing head to head with the strongest team of the world. This is the World Cup of sailing, and we are going to play this game sooner or later!"

The team's name, *Shosholoza,* means "go forward, make your road, forge ahead"—an acknowledgment of the dedication to pursue excellence, especially when doing so is a challenge. The spirit of the Shosholoza project was all about doing something unique. In his speeches to his team, Salvatore would stress that it was "an opportunity to show that all South Africa's citizens can work together, do well and have success together. In essence it is an opportunity to be part of the African renaissance."[2] His appeals enlisted the team in a noble endeavor to make history for their country, got them to believe in the possibility, motivated them to work even harder than they could imagine, and built their pride in being the best they could be. And for Salvatore, like all leaders who enlist others in a common vision, it all came down to something fairly simple and straightforward: having a passion for making a difference in people's lives.

In 2007, Shosholoza took part in the America's Cup Race, a remarkable achievement in itself, considering that only twelve countries were represented. Despite a significantly lower budget and less experience than the other teams, Shosholoza held its own, achieving some amazing victories in the heads-up challenges against giants like Luna Rossa and Mascalzone Latino before eventually placing sixth at the final round in Valencia.

In the personal-best leadership cases we collected, people talked about the need to get everyone on board with a vision and to *Enlist Others* in a dream, just as Salvatore did. They had to communicate and build support for the direction in which the organization was headed. These leaders knew that in order to make extraordinary things happen, everyone had to fervently believe in and commit to a common purpose.

Part of enlisting others is building common ground on which everyone can agree. But equally important is the emotion that leaders express for the vision. Our research shows that in addition to expecting leaders to be forward-looking, constituents expect their leaders to be *inspiring*. People need vast reserves of energy and excitement to sustain commitment to a distant dream. Leaders are expected to be a major source of that energy. People aren't going to follow someone who's only mildly enthusiastic about something. Leaders have to be *wildly* enthusiastic for constituents to give it their all.

Whether you're trying to mobilize a crowd in the grandstand or one person in the office, to Enlist Others you must act on these two essentials:

- **APPEAL TO COMMON IDEALS**
- **ANIMATE THE VISION**

Enlisting others is all about igniting passion for a purpose and moving people to persist against great odds. To get extraordinary things done in organizations, you have to go beyond reason, engaging the hearts as well as the minds of your constituents. You start by understanding their strongest yearnings for something meaningful and significant.

APPEAL TO COMMON IDEALS

In every personal-best case, leaders talked about ideals. They expressed a desire to make dramatic changes in the business-as-usual environment. They reached for something grand, something magnificent, something that had never been done before.

Visions are about ideals. They're about hopes, dreams, and aspirations. They're about the strong desire to achieve something great. They're ambitious. They're expressions of optimism. Can you imagine a leader enlisting others in a cause by saying, "I'd like you to join me in doing the ordinary"? Not likely. Visions stretch people to imagine exciting possibilities, breakthrough technologies, and revolutionary social change.

Ideals reveal higher-order value preferences. They represent the ultimate economic, technological, political, social, and aesthetic priorities. The ideals of world peace, freedom, justice, an exciting life, happiness, and self-respect, for example, are among the ultimate strivings of human existence. They're outcomes of the larger purpose that practical actions will enable people to attain over the long term. By focusing on ideals, people gain a sense of meaning and purpose from what they undertake.

When you communicate your vision of the future to your constituents, you need to talk about how they're going to make a difference in the world, how they're going to have a positive impact on people and events. You need to show them how their long-term interests can be realized by enlisting in a common vision. You need to speak to the higher meaning and purpose of work. You need to describe a compelling image of what the future could be like when people join together in a common cause.

Connect to What's Meaningful to Others

Exemplary leaders don't impose their visions of the future on people; they liberate the vision that's already stirring in their constituents. They awaken dreams, breathe life into them, and arouse the belief that people can achieve something grand. When they communicate a shared vision, they bring these ideals into the conversation. What truly pulls people forward, especially in more difficult and volatile times, is the exciting possibility that what they are doing can make a profound difference in the lives of their families, friends, colleagues, customers, and communities. They want to know that what they do matters.[3] Nancy Sullivan, vice president for disability benefits at the Trustmark Companies, told us, "When you know what road you should be on and are doing exactly what you should be doing, you fulfill your life purpose, personal passions, and heart's desire. When your life and career are on course and you understand your purpose, you feel full, satisfied, and ever so powerful. Nothing will stop you."

Nancy's passion for the work her division does is quite evident in these words, and she needed to draw on that energy when her group was notified that they were unlikely to meet their division objectives after consistently exceeding them for nine straight years. Nancy knew that her team could pull through, but for them to do so, she needed to connect her constituents to more than just the division plan. She needed to paint a bigger picture of what they could accomplish together and show them how their long-term interests could be realized by enlisting in a common vision.

Nancy developed a four-page vision message and posted it in the office kitchen where everyone congregated. In team meetings, division meetings, one-on-ones, and chats in the hallway, she spoke with genuine conviction about the meaning and purpose of their work and pointed out specific parts of her vision message that would help them see themselves as she saw them—as the best of the best. It was not only a message about what they could achieve in business but also a connection to the significant role they played in the lives of all their constituents. Here is part of that message:

> I dream of a place here in our office, where the sales team maintains respect and confidence in our decisions not just today but tomorrow and always; the constant challenges to our decisions just don't exist. Where our insureds trust our decisions and feel our genuine commitment to serving them well in their greatest time of need. Where our customers have confidence that your decision was contractual yes, but more importantly ethically correct and sound. Where the only title that you can think of for introducing your co-worker is respected colleague and friend.

> I dream of a place where growth and opportunities are massive because of the time and energy you invested with your commitments and therefore our opportunities and potential are endless. A place that no longer manages claims, but manages decisions on disability. A place that is no longer thought of as disability-claim experts, but disability experts. A place where our colleagues and government officials look to for disability solutions. A place where Trustmark is the number one company to serve as the assistance to all disability needs.

And day in, day out, Nancy stressed the exciting possibilities the future held: "Imagine your own career ten years out, and dream of a position that serves you well. Create ideas that get you there. Look within for strengths that you didn't even know you had. Look beyond any possibilities. Stretch yourself with ideas that seem unachievable. If the thoughts are laughable, then that is exactly what we are looking for. Create your own position. Create our future."

In time, all of Nancy's staff connected with those ideals and aspirations and united around their division objectives. Each member of the team could easily see how he or she would answer a friend's question, "So, why do you work there?" Nancy's message had lifted them up from the mechanics of disability claims and reminded them of the nobility of what they accomplish. Nancy's focus on the purpose and meaning of the division's work engaged their spirits and enabled them to surpass their targets for the tenth year in a row.

The outcomes Nancy's staff experienced are quite consistent with the extensive research on employee engagement. Michael Burchell and Jennifer Robin of the Great Places to Work Institute, for example, report that "when we ask employees in great workplaces to describe what it is like to work there, they begin to smile and talk about how they are excited to get to work, and then, at the end of the day, are surprised to discover that the day has already disappeared. . . . They share their belief that what they do matters in the organization—that their team or the organization would be less successful if it weren't for their efforts."[4] This is what Nancy accomplished at Trustmark. You have to make sure that the people on your team know that their work does, in fact, matter.

Leaders help people see that what they are doing is bigger than they are and bigger, even, than the business. Their work can be something noble. When people go to bed at night, they can sleep a little easier knowing that others are able to live a better life because of what they did that day.

Take Pride in Being Unique

Exemplary leaders also communicate what makes their constituents, work group, organization, product, or service singular and unequaled. Compelling visions differentiate and set "us" apart from "them," and they must do so in order to attract and retain employees, volunteers, customers, clients, donors, and investors.[5] There's no advantage in working for, buying from, or investing in an organization that does exactly the same thing as the one across the street or down the hall. Saying, "Welcome to our company. We're just like everyone else," doesn't exactly make the spine tingle with excitement. When people understand how they're truly distinctive and how they stand out in the crowd, they're a lot more eager to voluntarily sign up and invest their energies.

Feeling special fosters a sense of pride.[6] It boosts the self-respect and self-esteem of everyone associated with the organization. When people are proud to work for their organization and serve its purpose, and when they feel that what they are doing is meaningful, they become enthusiastic ambassadors to the outside world. When customers and clients are proud to own your products or use your services, they are more loyal and more likely to recruit their friends to do business with you. When members of the community are proud to have you as a neighbor, they're going to do everything they can to make you feel welcome.

"She made me feel proud, she made me feel that what I was doing was special and made a unique contribution," said Lina Chen when describing one of her most admired leaders. Lina worked in a research lab of renowned scientists and talented doctoral students at UCLA, but she herself was neither a scholar nor a researcher. She was responsible for computer support and making sure that all the equipment was up and running without any issues. However, she says that her leader "did not explain my job responsibility to me that way."

> She began by explaining to me the importance of the research that was being done and how it could impact the lives of many people. Furthermore, the more accurate our results from the research, the more beneficial it will be to those that are involved because we can help improve their quality of life. My job to keep the computer equipment up and running was crucial because it makes the researchers' jobs easier. I was also helping them in improving the environment and making the world a better place. It made my job very meaningful and inspiring to be part of a team that is making a difference in the world.

Leaders like Lina's at UCLA get people excited about signing on for their vision by making certain that everyone involved feels that what she does is unique and that everyone believes that she plays a crucial role regardless of job title or specific task responsibilities.

Feeling unique also makes it possible for smaller units within large organizations, or neighborhoods within large cities, to have their own visions and still serve a larger, collective vision. Although every unit within a corporation, public agency, religious institution, school, or volunteer association must be aligned with the overall organizational vision, each can express its distinctive purpose within the larger whole. Every function and every department can differentiate itself by finding its most distinctive qualities. Each can be proud of its own ideal image of its future as it works toward the common future of the larger organization.

These days, though, with the latest and greatest available in a nanosecond at the touch of a key, it's become increasingly difficult to differentiate yourself from others. Log on to any Internet search engine, type in a keyword, and up come thousands, sometimes tens or hundreds of thousands, of sites and offerings.[7] The options are overwhelming. And it's not just the speed and volume of information that create problems. Everything begins to look and sound alike. It's a sea of sameness out there. People become bored with things more quickly than ever before. Organizations, new and old, must work harder to differentiate themselves (and their products) from others around them. Business consolidations, the Internet, the information overload, the 24/7/365 always-on, everyone's-connected world demand that leaders be even more attentive to ways in which they can be the beacon that cuts through the dense mist and steers people in the right direction.

Align Your Dream with the People's Dream

In learning how to appeal to people's ideals, move their souls, and uplift their spirits—and your own—there is no better place to look than to the late Reverend Dr. Martin Luther King Jr. His "I Have a Dream" speech tops the list of the best American public addresses of the twentieth century. On the national holiday in the United States marking his birthday, this speech is replayed, and young and old alike are reminded of the power of a clear and uplifting vision of the future. If you have never listened closely to Dr. King's words, take a few moments to read or hear them.[8]

Imagine that you are there on that hot and humid day—August 28, 1963—when on the steps of the Lincoln Memorial in Washington, DC, before a throng of 250,000, Martin Luther King Jr. proclaimed his dream to the world. Imagine that you're listening to King as thousands around you clap and applaud and cry out. Now try to better understand why this speech is so powerful and how he is capable of moving so many people.

We've asked thousands of people over the years to listen to King's famous "I Have a Dream" speech and then tell us what they heard, how they felt, and why they thought this speech remains so moving even today.[9] Following is a sampling of their observations.

"He appealed to common interests."

"He talked about traditional values of family, church, and country."

"It was vivid. He used a lot of images and word pictures. You could see the examples."

"People could relate to the examples. They were familiar."

"His references were credible. It's hard to argue against the Constitution or the Bible."

"He mentioned children—something we can all relate to."

"It was personal. He mentioned his own children, but it wasn't just his kids because he also talked about everyone's children."

"He knew his audience."

"He made geographical references to places the people in the audience could relate to."

"He included everybody: different parts of the country, all ages, both sexes, major religions several times."

"He used a lot of repetition: for example, saying 'I have a dream,' and 'Let freedom ring' several times."

"He talked about the same ideas many times but in different ways."

"He began with a statement of the difficulties and then stated his
   hope for the future."

"He was positive and hopeful."

"Although positive, he didn't promise it would be easy."

"There was a cadence and a rhythm to his voice."

"He shifted from 'I' to 'we' halfway through."

"He spoke with emotion and passion. It was something he
   genuinely felt."

These reflections reveal the key to success in enlisting others. To
get others excited about your dream, you need to speak about
meaning and purpose. You have to *show them* how *their* dreams will
be realized. You have to connect your message to their values, their
aspirations, their experiences, and their own lives. You have to
show them that it's not about you, or even the organization, but
about them and their needs. King's "I Have a Dream" speech vividly
illustrates how the ability to exert an enlivening influence is rooted
in fundamental values, cultural traditions, personal conviction, and
a capacity to use words to create positive images of the future. To
enlist others, you need to bring the vision to life. You have to make
manifest the purpose so that others can see it, hear it, taste it, touch
it, feel it. You have to make the connection between an inspiring
vision of the future and the personal aspirations and passions of the
people you are addressing. You have to describe a compelling image
of how people can realize their dreams.

   Ed Fernandez took these ideas to heart when he began his new
role as general manager of WXYZ, a legacy television station owned
by Scripps in Detroit.[10] Having come from outside the organization,
Ed anticipated resistance to change and skepticism from some of the
employees, but what he found was quite the opposite. "Here was a
business, full of talented and skilled personnel," he explained, "and

they simply wanted something to believe in at a personally meaningful level. They were eager to embrace a vision (mission and purpose) that would make their community a better place."

Ed took the time to listen to their concerns, both individually and in small groups. By aligning his dreams with those of his employees, he created a shared picture of "what we wanted to be as a media organization." Taking the time to consistently communicate that vision made a remarkable difference in morale and productivity, and this process produced the concept of "Detroit 2020"—a vision to be the centerpiece of discourse that could help spark the renaissance of Detroit and the region. By utilizing the power and resources of WXYZ, this decade-long, multiplatform community impact initiative provides a shared goal for everyone to follow. Ed says, "People have a purpose for their work and know how they can contribute to the overall success." An internal survey validated the station's progress; 94 percent of the respondents agreed that "WXYZ can make things happen when committed to an idea," and more than five in six believed that "within three years WXYZ will be the market leader." By appealing to common interests as Ed did, you can get people to commit to future possibilities.

ANIMATE THE VISION

Leaders have to engage others to join in a cause and to want to move decisively forward. Part of motivating others is appealing to their ideals. Another part, as demonstrated by King's "I Have a Dream" speech, is animating the vision, essentially breathing life into it. To enlist others, you have to help them *see* and *feel* how their own interests and aspirations are aligned with the vision. You have to paint a compelling picture of the future, one that enables constituents to experience viscerally what it would be like to actually live and work in an exciting and uplifting future. That's the only way they'll become sufficiently internally motivated to commit their individual energies to the vision's realization.

"But I'm not like Martin Luther King," you say. "I can't possibly do what he did. Besides, he was a preacher, and I'm not. His constituents were on a protest march, and mine are here to get a job done." Many people initially respond this way. Most don't see themselves as personally uplifting, and certainly don't get much encouragement for behaving this way in most organizations. Despite the acknowledged potency of clearly communicated and compelling visions, our research finds people more uncomfortable with inspiring a shared vision than with any of the other leadership practices. Their discomfort comes mostly from having to actually express their emotions. That's not easy for working adults to do, but people are too quick to discount their capacity to communicate with passion and enthusiasm.

People's perception of themselves as uninspiring is in sharp contrast to their performance when they talk about their personal-best leadership experiences or when they talk about their ideal futures. When relating hopes, dreams, and successes, people are almost always emotionally expressive. Expressiveness comes naturally when talking about deep desires for the something that could be better in the future than it is today. And it doesn't matter what language they are speaking.

Most people attribute something mystical to the process of being inspirational. They seem to see it as supernatural, as a grace or charm bestowed on them—what's often referred to as charisma. This assumption inhibits people far more than any lack of natural talent for being inspirational. It's not necessary to be a charismatic person to inspire a shared vision. You have *to believe,* and you have to develop the skills to transmit your belief. It's your passion that brings the vision to life. If you're going to lead, you have to recognize that your enthusiasm and expressiveness are among your strongest allies in your efforts to generate commitment in others. Don't underestimate your talents.

Use Symbolic Language

When registered nurse Janet (McTavish) MacIntyre assumed the role of the new unit leader for the Intensive Care Unit/Cardiac Care Unit (ICU/CCU) at the Henderson Hospital in Hamilton, Ontario, she had a chance to share with others her intense passion for nursing, along with her extensive knowledge and accomplished skills.[11] The Hamilton Health Sciences at Henderson site was opening a new state-of-the-art hospital renamed the Juravinski Hospital and Cancer Centre, and Janet wanted to fully engage her colleagues in that exciting opportunity. She found some compelling ways to do that by turning to Canadian culture. "I began by creating a logo with a slogan and choosing a mascot, one that identified with our Canadian roots and symbolized the journey we were on. An Inukshuk, built by the Inuit Natives across the Canadian Arctic, is a stone landmark that denotes a spiritual resting place along a migration route to food or shelter. Most importantly, it communicates that 'you are on the path.' That was us. We were on a path. We were on a journey."

The Inukshuk mascot was built with six stones: four representing the organization's corporate values of respect, caring, innovation, and accountability; and two reflecting the ICU/CCU's values. A "passport" served as a creative education tool for getting everyone engaged—115 staff members in all, from nurses and respiratory therapists to business clerks and environmental aides. With so many diverse learning needs for the various disciplines, the passport provided a customized checklist, a site map, and information that identified a path to working safely in the new environment. A mock patient setup room, called the "sandbox," gave the staff plenty of time to "play" (and practice, hands-on) with the new technology and equipment, and lessen the anxiety on moving day.

The Inukshuk mascot, the passport, the map, and the sandbox were all ways that Janet brought the vision to life through evocative metaphors and symbols. Leaders like Janet embrace the power of symbolic language like this to communicate a shared identity and give life to visions. They use metaphors and analogies; they give examples, tell stories, and relate anecdotes; they draw word pictures; and they offer quotations and recite slogans. They enable constituents to picture the possibilities—to hear them, to sense them, to recognize them.

James Geary, a leading expert on the use of metaphorical language, found in his studies that people use a metaphor every ten to twenty-five words, or about six metaphors a minute.[12] Metaphors are everywhere—there are art metaphors, game and sports metaphors, war metaphors, science fiction metaphors, machine metaphors, and religious or spiritual metaphors. They influence what we think, what we invent, what we eat and drink, how we think, whom we vote for, and what we buy. Your ability to enlist others in a common vision of the future will be greatly enhanced by learning to use these figures of speech.

Consider, for example, the intriguing impact of language on participants in experiments in which they were told that they were either playing the Community Game or the Wall Street Game.[13] People played exactly the same game by exactly the same rules; the *only* difference was that experimenters gave the game two different names. Of those playing the Community Game, 70 percent started out playing cooperatively and continued to do so throughout. Of those told they were playing the Wall Street Game, just the opposite occurred: 70 percent did *not* cooperate, and the 30 percent who did, stopped when they saw that others weren't cooperating. Again, remember: the *name, not the game* was the only thing that was different!

You can influence people's behavior simply by giving the task or the team a name that evokes the kind of behavior implied by the name. If you want people to act like a community, use language that evokes a feeling of community. If you want them to act like traders in the financial markets, use language that cues those images. The same goes for any other vision you might have for your organization. This experiment powerfully demonstrates why you must pay close attention to the language you choose and the language you use.

Create Images of the Future

Visions are images in the mind—impressions and representations. They become real as leaders express those images in concrete terms to their constituents. Just as architects make drawings and engineers build models, leaders find ways of giving expression to collective hopes for the future.

When talking about the future, people typically speak in terms of foresight, focus, forecasts, future scenarios, points of view, and perspectives. What these words have in common is that they are visual references. The word *vision* itself has at its root the verb "to see." Statements of vision, then, should not be statements at all. They should be pictures—word pictures. They're more image than words. For a vision to be shared, it needs to be *seen* in the mind's eye.

In our workshops and classes, we often illustrate the power of images with this simple exercise. We ask people to shout out the first thing that comes to mind when they hear the words *Paris, France.* The replies that pop out—the Eiffel Tower, the Louvre, the Arc de Triomphe, the Seine, Notre Dame, good food, wine, romance—are all images of real places and real sensations. No one calls out the square kilometers, population, or gross domestic product of Paris. Why? Because most of what we recall about important places or events are those things associated with our senses—sights, sounds, tastes, smells, tactile sensations, and feelings.[14]

So what does this mean for leaders? It means that to enlist others and inspire a shared vision, you must be able to draw on that very natural mental process of creating images. When you speak about the future, you need to create pictures with words so that others form a mental image of what things will be like when you are at the end of your journey. When talking about going places you've never been, you have to be able to imagine what they'll look like. You have to picture the possibilities.[15]

Getting people to see a common future does not require some special power. Every one possesses this ability. You do it every time you return from a vacation and show the photos to your friends. If you doubt your own ability, try this exercise. Sit down with a few close friends and tell them about one of your favorite vacations. Describe the people you saw and met, the sights and sounds of the places you went, the smells and tastes of the food you ate. Show them the photos or videos if you have them. Observe their reactions—and your own. What's that experience like? We've done this activity many times, and people always report feeling energized and passionate. Those hearing about a place for the first time usually say something like, "After listening to you, I'd like to go there someday myself."

Practice Positive Communication

To foster team spirit, breed optimism, promote resilience, and renew faith and confidence, leaders look on the bright side. They keep hope alive. They strengthen their constituents' belief that life's struggles will produce a more promising future. Such faith results from an intimate and supportive relationship, a relationship based on mutual participation in the process of renewal.

Constituents look for leaders who demonstrate an enthusiastic, genuine belief in the capacity of others, who strengthen people's will, who supply the means to achieve, and who express optimism for the future. Constituents want leaders who remain passionate despite obstacles and setbacks. In today's uncertain times, leaders with a positive, confident, can-do approach to life and business are desperately needed. Naysayers only stop forward progress; they do not start it.

Indeed, consider how Ari Ashkenazi describes his contrasting experience with two supervisors. The first, he said, always tried to keep spirits up and to look on the bright side, regardless of the situation. Even when a certain project came out with less than desired results, Ari said, she would tell them that future projects would turn out better as long as they kept working hard as well as working smart. "This gave me a lot of faith in her," said Ari, "and helped me to keep from getting frustrated during my work when things didn't always go right. This also had the effect of making it easier for me to try new things as well as report negative news to her since I knew she wouldn't 'shoot the messenger' when it came to giving her news."

Ari described another supervisor who would often get easily exasperated, and when she was annoyed or angry, she'd let you know it quite plainly. All she cared about was solid numbers and results, and it felt as though she was looking down on you if things didn't go as she planned from the start. The outcome of her negative communications, Ari explained, "was to make me try to avoid her as much as possible and to hold back on giving her negative information that she needed to know, just because I feared the backlash she would give me."

Researchers working with neural networks have documented Ari's feelings in finding that when people feel rebuffed or left out, the brain activates a site for registering physical pain.[16] People actually remember downbeat comments far more often, in greater detail, and with more intensity than they do encouraging words. When negative remarks become a preoccupation, an employee's brain loses mental efficiency. This is all the more reason for leaders to be positive.

In contrast, a positive approach to life broadens people's ideas about future possibilities, and these exciting options build on each other, according to Barbara Fredrickson, professor of psychology at the University of North Carolina. Her findings indicate that being positive opens you up: "The first core truth about positive emotions is that they open our hearts and our minds, making us more receptive and more creative."[17] Her research finds that as positivity flows through people, they see more options and become more innovative. And that's not all. People who enjoy more positivity are better able to cope with adversity and are more resilient during times of high stress.[18] That's a vital capacity when dealing with challenges that people face as leaders in these uncertain and challenging times.

Express Your Emotions

In explaining why particular leaders have a magnetic effect, people often describe them as charismatic. But *charisma* has become such an overused and misused term that it's almost useless as a descriptor of leaders. Being charismatic is neither a magical nor a metaphysical quality. It has to do with how people behave.

Social scientists have indeed investigated this elusive quality in terms of observable behavior.[19] What they've found is that people who are perceived to be charismatic are simply more animated than others. They smile more, speak faster, pronounce words more clearly, and move their heads and bodies more often. Charisma, then, can be better understood as energy and expressiveness. The old saying that enthusiasm is infectious is certainly true for leaders.

Leaders are responsible for the level of genuine excitement in their organizations. According to leadership developers Belle Linda Halpren and Kathy Lubar, "emotion drives expressiveness." They explain that leaders must communicate their emotions using all means of expression—verbal and nonverbal—if they are to generate the intense enthusiasm that's required to mobilize people to struggle for shared aspirations.[20]

Another benefit of emotions for leaders is that they make things more memorable. Because as a leader you want your messages to be remembered, you have to pay attention to adding emotion to your words and your behavior. James McGaugh, professor of neurobiology at the University of California, Irvine, and a leading expert on creation of memory, has reported that "emotionally significant events create stronger, longer-lasting memories."[21] No doubt you've experienced this yourself when something emotionally significant has happened to you—a serious trauma, such as an accident, or a joyful surprise, such as winning a contest. But the events don't have to be real to be memorable. They can simply be stories. For example, in one experiment, researchers showed subjects in two groups a series of twelve slides. The slide presentation was accompanied by a story, one line for each slide. For one group in the study, the narrative was quite boring; for the other, the narrative was emotionally moving. They didn't know when they watched the slides that they would be tested, but two weeks later they returned and took a test of how well they remembered the details of each slide. Although the subjects in the two groups didn't differ in their memory of the first few and last few slides, they did differ significantly in the recollection of the slides in the middle. "The subjects who had listened to the emotionally arousing narrative remembered details in those particular slides better" than the group that listened to the neutral story. "Stronger emotional arousal," James says, "is associated with better memory; emotional arousal appears to create strong memories."[22]

You don't need a complete narrative, and you don't need slides. Just the words themselves can be equally effective, as demonstrated in another laboratory experiment. Researchers asked subjects to learn to associate pairs of words. Some of the words in the pairs were used because they elicited strong emotional responses (as indicated by changes in galvanic skin response). One week later, people remembered the emotionally arousing words better than they remembered the less arousing words.[23] Whether you're hearing a story or a word, you're more likely to remember the key messages when they're attached to something that triggers an emotional response. The reasons for this have to do with human physiology. People are wired to pay more attention to stuff that excites them or scares them.

Keep all this in mind the next time you deliver a PowerPoint presentation. It's not just the content that will make the message stick; it's also how well you tap into people's emotions. People have to feel something if they are to become willing to change. Thinking isn't nearly enough to get things moving. Your job is to get them to feel motivated to change, and expressing emotions helps do that.[24]

Showing people a concrete example is better than telling them about an abstract principle, but that still leaves them on the outside looking in. If you can get them to experience what you are trying to explain, they will understand in a deeper way. When helping volunteers in hospice care understand what it is like to be the person or family they'll be helping, trainers frequently use the following exercise.[25] The trainer hands out packets of index cards and asks volunteers to write on each of their cards something they love and would be devastated to lose—the names of family members (spouse, parents, children, siblings, pets), activities (walking, playing music, traveling), or experiences (reading, listening to music, enjoying gourmet dinners, watching sunsets).

Then the trainer walks around the room and randomly takes cards from the volunteers. One person loses two of them, another loses all of them; the person who lost two loses two more. The effect is dramatic. Volunteers clutch their cards and struggle not to let them go. When they release the cards, they are visibly upset; some even break down and cry.

This poignant exercise speaks volumes about how much more effective it is when leaders can tap into people's emotions rather than simply tell them what to do or how to feel. If the trainers had merely shared facts, the volunteers might have been able to conceptually understand the losses that the hospice residents were suffering, but not in a way that would have led to true empathy. Through this exercise, they could briefly experience the same type of losses in a deep way that they would probably never forget.

The dramatic increase in the use of electronic technology also has an impact on the way people deliver messages. More and more people are turning to their digital devices and social media—from podcasts to webcasts, Facebook to YouTube—for information and connection. Because people remember things that have strong emotional content, social media has the potential for engaging people more than do emails, memos, and PowerPoint presentations. Leadership is a performing art, and this has become even truer as new technologies hit the market. It's no longer enough to write a good script—you've also got to put on a good show. And you've got to make it a show that people will remember.

Speak Genuinely

None of these suggestions about being more expressive will be of any value whatsoever if you don't believe in what you're saying. If the vision is someone else's and you don't own it, you'll find it very difficult to enlist others in it. If you have trouble imagining yourself actually living the future described in the vision, you'll certainly not be able to convince others that they ought to enlist in making it a reality. If you're not excited about the possibilities, you can't expect others to be. *The prerequisite to enlisting others in a shared vision is genuineness.*

When Emily LoSavio walked away from a successful job in the insurance industry, she knew just where she was headed: to fulfill a lifelong desire to make a difference in the lives of young people.[26] That commitment to spend her life doing work in service to others came from her childhood. "It started early on," she recalls. "For me, my father was a powerful role model. He grew up with a single mom who raised him on welfare, and then went on to great educational success at Harvard on a scholarship. His story is a testament to the power of education and also the power of support. He always made it clear that it wasn't about him being so special or different but that every child had the potential if the community came together to invest in that child."

Incorporating the inspirational lessons learned from her father as a foundation and following her passion and bold vision for the part she could play in helping children face life's most difficult challenges, Emily founded Opportunity Impact in San Francisco. Opportunity Impact prepares young people—specifically those living in public housing—for a future of their own design. "Our goal," says Emily, "is to open doors for children to design, believe in, and create their own future. And that begins with being able to envision something outside their experience."

Although getting others in the community to see the vision of Opportunity Impact can be a daily challenge, Emily pursues it with passion. "I sometimes joke that people say, 'You're crazy!' And sometimes, when you have this passion about a vision, you do come off a little crazy," Emily said. "But if you believe it, it also becomes contagious. People will stand behind you when they know you truly believe that there is a different future ahead and they can follow you there." You can see that contagion in those who work with Emily. "That Emily walked away from success in the business world to start Opportunity Impact, I still find absolutely amazing," observed David Boyer, founder of Waystohelp.org.

There's no one more believable than a person with a deep passion for something. There's no one more fun to be around than someone who is openly excited about the magic that can happen. There's no one more determined than someone who believes fervently in an ideal. People want leaders who are upbeat, optimistic, and positive about the future. It's really the only way you can get people to willingly follow you to someplace they have never been before.

TAKE ACTION

Enlist Others

Leaders appeal to common ideals. They connect others to what is most meaningful in the shared vision. They lift people to higher levels of motivation and morality, and continuously reinforce that they can make a difference in the world. Exemplary leaders speak to what is unique and singular about the organization, making others feel proud to be a part of something extraordinary. And the best leaders understand that it's not their personal idiosyncratic view of the future that's important; it's the aspirations of all their constituents that matter most.

To be sustained over time, visions must be compelling and memorable. Leaders must breathe life into visions; they must animate them so that others can experience what it would be like to live and work in that ideal and unique future. They use a variety of modes of expression to make their abstract visions concrete. Through skillful use of metaphors, symbols, word pictures, positive language, and personal energy, leaders generate enthusiasm and excitement for the common vision. But above all, leaders must be convinced of the value of the shared vision and communicate that genuine belief to others. They must believe in what they are saying. Authenticity is the true test of conviction, and constituents will follow willingly only if they sense that the vision is genuine.

Here are some actions you can take in order to *enlist others in a common vision by appealing to shared aspirations:*

- Talk to your constituents and find out about their hopes, dreams, and aspirations for the future.
- Show that you listen to what they say by incorporating their inputs.
- Make sure that your constituents know what makes their product or service unique and special.
- Promote people's pride in what they contribute.
- Show your constituents how their long-term interests are served by enlisting in a common vision.
- Share metaphors, symbols, examples, stories, pictures, and words that represent the image of what you all aspire to become.
- Be positive, upbeat, and energetic when talking about the future of your organization.
- Express how you are feeling.
- Acknowledge the emotions of others and validate them as important.
- Have a reason for getting up in the morning, bouncing out of bed, and being jazzed about going to work.

Use *The Leadership Challenge Mobile Tool* app to immediately integrate these activities into your life and make this practice an ongoing part of your behavioral repertoire.

CHALLENGE
THE
PROCESS

C hallenge is the opportunity for greatness. People do their best when there's the chance to change the way things are. Maintaining the status quo simply breeds mediocrity. Leaders seek and accept challenging opportunities to test their abilities. They motivate others as well to exceed their self-perceived limits. They seize initiative and make something meaningful happen. Leaders treat every assignment as an adventure.

Most innovations do not come from leaders—they come from the people closest to the work. They also come from outsight. Exemplary leaders look for good ideas everywhere. They promote external communication. They listen, take advice, and learn.

Progress is not made in giant leaps; it's made incre-mentally. Exemplary leaders move forward in small steps with little victories. They turn adversity into advantage, setbacks into successes. They persevere with grit and determination.

Leaders venture out. They test and they take risks with bold ideas. And because risk-taking involves mistakes and failure, leaders accept the inevitable disappointments and treat them as opportunities for learning and growth.

In the next two chapters, we will see how you must

- **Search for Opportunities by seizing the initiative and looking outward for innovative ways to improve.**
- **Experiment and Take Risks by constantly generating small wins and learning from experience.**

CHAPTER 6

Search for Opportunities

JOE BARSI HAS A SAYING taped to his computer that reads, "If you have not endured the most difficult, you cannot become the most successful." Leaders like Joe understand that you don't get any place different if you just keep doing the same things over and over again. Getting out of routines and ruts requires treating every job and assignment as an adventure. This involves putting your head up and looking all around, and being willing to invest your time and energy in finding out about other possibilities.

Joe's personal-best leadership experience involved reviving a branch office of one of the world's leading global third-party logistics providers, and this required changing their business-as-usual environment. Joe got everyone on the team to adjust their focus, to start focusing outward rather than inward, and to spend time not just understanding customer requirements but actually getting out of the office and meeting face-to-face with them. Joe himself started looking around for areas where they could further expand their customer focus, which resulted in many little actions, such as extending the opening and closing hours of the office so that services were available over a longer time period, conducting business reviews with their top ten customers, and analyzing their competitors for best practices in their industry.

They spent considerable time and energy gathering data to learn about how they could do their jobs better and provide enhanced services. Joe also realized that many people had a lot more product and transportation experience than he had, and he challenged them to share that experience not just with one another but with him as well. "How are we going to work together to improve this business? What will we have to do differently?" Joe asked them. At the end of two years, net revenue increased by over 140 percent, and they went from one of the lowest-ranking offices in the company to a top-thirty branch.

Sometimes challenges find leaders, and sometimes leaders find the challenges; most often, it's a little of each, as in Joe's situation. What Joe did is what all exemplary leaders do. He looked outward, keeping up with changing market trends and remaining sensitive to external realities. He convinced others to take seriously the challenges and opportunities that were ahead of them in the future. He served as a catalyst for change, challenging the way things were being done and convincing others that new practices needed to be incorporated to achieve greater levels of success.

Like Joe's story, personal-best leadership cases are all about significant departures from the past, about doing things that have never been done before, and about going to places not yet discovered.

Change is the work of leaders. It's no longer business as usual, and exemplary leaders know that they have to transform the way things are done. Delivering results beyond expectations can't be achieved with good intentions. People, processes, systems, and strategies all have to change. And all change requires that leaders actively seek ways to make things better—to grow, innovate, and improve. Exemplary leaders make the commitment to *Search for Opportunities* to get extraordinary things done. They make sure they engage in these two essentials:

- **SEIZE THE INITIATIVE**
- **EXERCISE OUTSIGHT**

Sometimes leaders have to shake things up. Other times they just have to harness the uncertainty that surrounds them. Regardless, leaders make things happen. And to make new things happen, they rely on outsight to actively seek innovative ideas from outside the boundaries of familiar experience.

SEIZE THE INITIATIVE

When people recall their personal-best leadership experiences, they always think about some kind of challenge. Why? Because personal and business hardships have a way of making people come face-to-face with who they really are and what they're capable of becoming. They test people, and they require inventive ways of dealing with new situations. They tend to bring out the best in people. When times are stable and secure, however, people are not severely tested. They may perform well, get promoted, and even achieve fame and fortune. But certainty and routine breed complacency.

Meeting new challenges always requires things to be different than they currently are. You can't respond with the same old solutions. You have to change the status quo. And that's exactly what people did in their personal-best leadership experiences. They met challenge with change.

The interesting thing about this is that we didn't ask people to tell us about change. They could discuss any leadership experience they chose—past or present, unofficial or official; in any functional area; in any community, voluntary, religious, health care, educational, public sector, or private sector organization. But what people chose to discuss were the changes they made in response to the challenges they faced. Their electing to talk about times of change underscores the fact that leadership demands altering the business-as-usual environment. There is a clear connection between challenge and change.

Rosabeth Moss Kanter, a Harvard Business School professor, investigated the human resource practices and organization designs of innovation-producing organizations, seeking to learn what fostered and what hindered innovation in corporations. Our study and Rosabeth's were done independently of each other, in different regions and periods in time, and with different purposes. We were studying leadership; Rosabeth was studying innovation. Yet we arrived at similar conclusions: *leadership is inextricably connected with the process of innovation,* of bringing new ideas, methods, or solutions into use. To Rosabeth, innovation means change, and "change requires leadership . . . a 'prime mover' to push for implementation of strategic decisions."[1] Her cases and ours are evidence of that.

The study of leadership is the study of how men and women guide others through adversity, uncertainty, hardship, disruption, transformation, transition, recovery, new beginnings, and other significant challenges. It's the study of people who triumph against overwhelming odds, who take initiative when there is inertia, who confront the established order, who mobilize people and institutions in the face of strong resistance. It's also the study of how men and women, in times of constancy and complacency, actively seek to disturb the status quo and awaken others to new possibilities. Leadership, challenge, and seizing the initiative are inextricably linked. Humdrum situations simply aren't associated with award-winning performances.

That's exactly the attitude that Arvind Mohan displayed when he was hired as a new manufacturing engineer at a high-technology firm just before a major industry downturn and two rounds of layoffs. Instead of being overwhelmed by this situation, he was determined "to take initiative instead of feeling helpless." He understood that the company was trying to streamline its cost structure to mitigate the industry's cyclical nature, and he had some ideas about how they could reduce the required lead time from customer order to delivery.

When he approached his manager, he found that her attention was more focused on dealing with current, and dire, problems. Refusing to be discouraged by this crisis, Arvind told her, " 'There is not much activity on the floor right now. Besides, you've always encouraged me to think out of the box. You've seen the preliminary numbers I've put together. How about I work with the production team and see what I can come up with?' Intrigued with my initial analysis, she gave me the go-ahead."

When Arvind explained that he had some ideas about how profits could be improved by increasing production throughput, the assembly line manager shot back, "Manufacturing is not the issue! We have long lead times because sales cannot get customers to order more frequently. You need to talk to sales." Wanting to turn the manager's cynical view into a positive outlook, Arvind said, "I agree. Why don't we start, however, by looking at our production efficiency?" Intrigued by his proposal and by the opportunity to learn from what Arvind proposed, the manager gave the green light to proceed. Arvind picked one of the smaller production lines to experiment with, simulated different production scenarios, and found that they could increase throughput by nearly 50 percent.

Buoyed by this success, Arvind convinced his manager to bring sales into the mix. When he broached the possibility of reducing the window time between customer order and delivery, their sales rep thundered: "The last time I pushed my accounts to order more frequently, they ended up going to another vendor. I can't let that happen again." Again, Arvind was not dissuaded. He suggested that they visit one of Toyota's factories and learn about how they trend down on lead-time by sharing the resultant cost savings with their customers. Sales got excited about this possibility, and in the course of six months, they were able to convince all of their accounts to increase their order frequency.

This experience taught Arvind that "if you can think of ways to improve the process, you should take it." This means you have to stop simply "going through the motions" when it comes to doing your job. It's a lesson all leaders need to learn. Even if you're on the right track, you're likely to get run over if you just sit there. To do your best as a leader, you have to seize the initiative to change the way things are.

Make Something Happen

Some standard practices, policies, and procedures are critical to productivity and quality assurance. However, many are simply matters of tradition, which is what Pat Oldenburg observed when he joined McAfee, the maker of computer security software for business and home. Pat decided that some changes were needed; and rather than wait for someone else to initiate them, he took it upon himself to do something about the way his team measured their effectiveness. He got everyone together and proposed a new idea that would free up valuable time and deliver information that everyone wanted:

> I started the meeting by reflecting on my experience at my old company, and how we moved from a model of reporting on numbers of activities to a model of reporting on other value-added things like prospects served and revenue assisted. I told the team that the current method was not scalable at the company, and a change had to be made. I said that scalability and resources are the big issue, but that one thing was to implement one-to-many sales calls. These calls would move from a reactive activity to a proactive one, as our team would host two to three calls per quarter with forty to fifty prospects attending each call.

Pat could sense that the team was hesitant to take on this initiative—hosting informational calls with clients—because no one had been thinking there was any reason to do things differently. Sensing their hesitation, he proposed that they could host one call the first quarter and continue taking the sales calls as normal. The team agreed, and they hosted their first roundtable reference call several weeks later, with more than ninety separate prospects in attendance. The call was subsequently featured in the chief marketing officer's internal newsletter, saying that the team had successfully fused marketing and sales activities in a productive way. With the positive press and the rave reviews from various sales reps, the team immediately began planning the next quarter's calls, drafting new guidelines that emphasized using roundtable reference calls over one-to-one sales calls unless absolutely necessary. Pat says that as "we continue to develop the roundtable program, we are surveying participants and employees about ways to continue to change the format and content of the calls, and will continue to challenge the status quo to deliver the largest benefit to our customers that we can."

As Pat experienced, new jobs and new assignments are ideal opportunities for asking probing questions and challenging the way things are done. They are the times when you're expected to ask, "Why do we do this?" But don't just ask this when you're new to the job. Make it a routine part of your leadership. Treat today as if it were your first day. Ask yourself, "If I were just starting this job, what would I do differently?" Then do those things immediately. This is how you'll continuously uncover needed improvements.

And don't stop at what you can find on your own. Ask your colleagues and direct reports about what really bugs them about the organization. Ask what gets in the way of doing the best job possible. Promise to look into everything they bring up and get back to them with answers in ten days. Wander around the plant, the store, the branch, the halls, or the office. Look for things that don't seem right. Ask questions. Probe.

Leaders like Joe, Arvind, and Pat are fundamentally restless. They don't like the status quo. They want to make something happen. They want to change the business-as-usual environment. Research clearly shows that managers who rate high in proactivity are assessed by their immediate managers as more effective leaders.[2] MBA students who rate high on proactivity also are considered by their peers to be better leaders; in addition, they are more engaged in extracurricular and civic activities targeted toward bringing about positive change.[3] Similar results about the connection between proactivity and performance have been found among entrepreneurs, administrative staff, and even college students searching for jobs. Proactivity consistently produces better results than reactivity or inactivity.[4] In our research, we've found that proactive managers score higher than average on the leadership practice of Challenge the Process; this inclination is independent of both gender and national culture.[5] Everyone performs better when he or she takes charge of change.

Leaders at all levels work outside their job descriptions and see opportunities where others don't. They don't wait for permission or instructions before jumping in. You make something happen when you notice what isn't working, create a solution for the problem, gain buy-in from constituents, and implement the desired outcome.

Consider these two examples from Starbucks. One store manager purchased her own blender to create a drink she invented because the company (at that time) didn't want to invest in blenders. She took the initiative, created the product in her own store, and tested it with her customers. As more and more people requested the product, the company ultimately ended up being convinced to invest in the drink. Since then, the Frappuccino has brought hundreds of millions of dollars to Starbucks. Another store manager had a passion for music and began playing a variety of different types of music he liked at his store. Customers kept asking to buy the music, but it wasn't for sale. So this manager approached Starbucks executives and asked, "Why not compile our own CD or tape? Customers would snap it up." Now CDs are sold in almost every one of the coffee shop locations.[6] These store managers were not corporate executives, but they took the initiative to make something different happen. And that's what leaders do. They take the initiative.

When thinking back on his early career experiences as a financial analyst, Varun Mundra realized that "when I did question the status quo, when I did come up with innovative ideas, when I followed through with the changes I suggested, got feedback, understood my mistakes, learned from them, and was open to improvements, I won the respect of the people around me." As they say in basketball, none of the shots you *don't* take ever go in the basket. You've got to make something happen in order to score some points. That's the key insight Varun had when he took the initiative. "It did not matter as much whether the changes were as effective as hoped for," he told us, "but the fact that someone was ready to stand up and challenge what everyone else used as the norm was generally enough to get something started." As Varun's experience attests, you need to give everyone on your team the chance to search for better ways of doing things and to step forward and take initiative.

Encourage Initiative in Others

Change requires leadership, and every person, down to the most junior member of a team, can drive innovation and improvements in a team's processes. This was precisely what John Wang, senior software engineer at Visa, remembers about the environment at his job after graduating from college. His manager fostered an atmosphere that supported experimentation and innovation, which allowed him and others to find little areas where they could improve existing processes and complete their assignments faster and more efficiently. One such area was the weekly backup process for the group's main file server. John recounts,

As junior engineers, we were placed in charge of this job, under the supervision of a senior engineer. My group had a tape backup unit that would finish recording the first tape in the middle of the night. Unfortunately, the backup process required two tapes to complete the backup. We were forced to initiate the recording of the second tape after one of us got to the office the next morning, which delayed the backup process. My coworker and I wanted to change the process, and we explored various alternatives. We found a better backup tape drive; however, this unit was quite expensive!

We were a little nervous about requesting this hardware upgrade, but since we had been previously encouraged to take the initiative to improve any processes during our induction into the department, we decided to offer our suggestion to our supervisor. To our surprise, he was very pleased that we had found a way to improve the backup process and immediately placed an order for the tape drive. He also mentioned our discovery to the manager. Our manager praised our initiative in finding a better way of running backups. This encouragement gave us clear positive feedback and the courage to find other suggestions over the next few years to improve our departmental processes. Indeed, this episode gave everyone the clear signal that suggestions were truly welcomed.

The lesson that John took to heart is one that leaders deeply appreciate: "giving everyone—even junior members of a team—the opportunity to take initiative can result in unexpected positive changes." Another benefit John pointed out was that by allowing the junior engineers to work on this issue, their senior manager was able to focus his attention on other pressing issues, which benefited him individually and the group as a whole. "This principle is one that I have tried to implement in my own life," John says, "giving people I work with a chance to do things differently than I would. This means I also get a chance to focus on other things that need my attention."

As John's experience illustrates, leaders seize the initiative themselves and encourage initiative in others. They want people to speak up, offer suggestions for improvement, and be straightforward about their constructive criticism. Yet when it comes to situations that involve high uncertainty, high risk, and high challenge, many people feel reluctant to act, afraid they might make matters worse.

We asked constituents about the extent to which their leaders "seek out challenging opportunities that test his/her own skills and abilities." We also asked them about the extent to which their leaders "challenge people to try out new and innovative ways to do their work." Comparing those leaders who reported that they "almost always" challenge themselves and others to those who "almost never" or "sometimes" engaged in these behaviors yielded quite dramatic (and statistically significant) differences in how people felt about their workplaces. Those people who felt that they were challenged, and who observed that their leaders were also challenging themselves, experienced between 25 to 35 percent stronger feelings of pride, motivation, and team spirit. The biggest difference between the two groups was in how they viewed their leaders' effectiveness. The least challenging leaders earned evaluations from their constituents that were nearly 40 percent lower than those received by leaders viewed as seeking out challenges for themselves and their teams.

There are a number of ways you can create conditions so that your constituents will be ready and willing to seize the initiative in tumultuous as well as tranquil times. First, create a can-do attitude by providing opportunities for people to gain mastery on a task one step at a time. Training is crucial to building people's ability and their confidence that they can effectively respond to and improve the difficult situations they face. During periods of rapid change, it may seem as though there's no time to stop for training, but this short-term thinking is sure to doom the organization. The best leaders know that the investment in training will pay off in the long term. People can't deliver on what they don't know how to do, so you have to upgrade capabilities continuously.

Another form of preparation is mental simulation.[7] Playing a scenario through in your mind until you can picture it frame by frame is a terrific way to encourage and support initiative. Asking people to imagine the steps they will take before they enact them is a powerful heuristic strategy for giving people the confidence that they can act when the real situation requires it. It's much the same as practicing fire drills, except that you run them in your head.

In addition, find ways for people to stretch themselves. Set the bar incrementally higher, but at a level at which people feel they can succeed. Raise it too high, and people will fail; if they fail too often, they'll quit trying. Raise the bar a bit at a time, and eventually more and more people master the situation and build the self-confidence to continue moving the bar upward. You can also foster initiative by providing visibility and access to role models, especially among peers, who are successful at meeting the new challenges. Seeing one of their own succeed in doing something new and different is an effective way to encourage others to do it too.

Challenge with Purpose

Leaders don't challenge for challenge's sake. It's not about shaking things up just to keep people on their toes. Individuals who criticize new thoughts and ideas or point out problems with the ideas of others without offering any kind of alternate options are not challenging the process. They are simply complaining. Leaders challenge for meaning's sake. They challenge, often with great passion, because they want people to live life on purpose and with purpose. What gets people through the tough times, the scary times—the times when they don't think they can even get up in the morning or take another step—is a sense of meaning and purpose. The motivation to deal with the challenges and uncertainties of life and work comes from the inside, not from something that others hold out in front of you as some kind of carrot.[8] The challenges that leaders raise are always accompanied by a drive to do something themselves to resolve and improve the situation, not simply complain.

The evidence from our research, and from studies by many others, is that if people are going to do their best, they must be internally motivated.[9] Their tasks or projects must be intrinsically engaging. When it comes to excellence, it's definitely not "What gets rewarded gets done"; it's "What *is* rewarding gets done." You can never pay people enough to care—to care about their products, services, communities, families, or even the bottom line. After all, why do people push their own limits to get extraordinary things done? And for that matter, why do people do so many things for nothing? Why do they volunteer to put out fires, raise money for worthy causes, or help children in need? Why do they risk their careers to start a new business or risk their security to change the social condition? Why do they risk their lives to save others or defend liberty? How do people find satisfaction in efforts that don't pay a lot of money, options, perks, or prestige? Extrinsic rewards certainly can't explain these actions. Leaders tap into people's hearts and minds, not merely their hands and wallets.

Arlene Blum knows firsthand the importance of challenging with purpose. Arlene, who earned a doctorate in biophysical chemistry, has spent most of her adult life climbing mountains. She's completed more than three hundred successful ascents. Her most significant challenge—and the one for which she is best known— was not the highest mountain she'd ever climbed. It was the challenge of leading the first all-woman team up Annapurna I, the tenth-highest mountain in the world. "The question everyone asks mountain climbers is 'Why?' " Arlene explains, and when they learn about the lengthy and difficult preparation involved, they ask it even more insistently. For us, the answer was much more than "because it is there." We all had experienced the exhilaration, the joy, and the warm camaraderie of the heights, and now we were on our way to an ultimate objective for a climber—the world's tenth-highest peak. But as women, we faced a challenge even greater than the mountain. We had to believe in ourselves enough to make the attempt in spite of social convention and two hundred years of climbing history in which women were usually relegated to the sidelines.[10]

In talking about what separates those who make a successful ascent from those who don't, Arlene says, "The real dividing line is passion. As long as you believe what you're doing is meaningful, you can cut through fear and exhaustion and take the next step."[11]

Why concern yourself with purpose and meaning? After all, people in the workplace aren't volunteers; they're getting paid. However, it's precisely because people are getting paid—precisely because they are eligible for bonuses and other awards—that you ought to be concerned. If work is seen solely as a source of money and never as a source of fulfillment, organizations will totally ignore other human needs at work—needs involving such intangibles as learning, self-worth, pride, competence, and serving others. Employers will come to see people's enjoyment of their tasks as totally irrelevant, and they will structure work in a strictly utilitarian fashion. The results will be—and already have been—disastrous. Just take a look at the costs of recruitment and retention these days. Have big stock option plans or huge signing bonuses really done much to make organizations successful? There's very convincing evidence that reliance on extrinsic motivators can actually lower performance and create a culture of divisiveness and selfishness, precisely because it diminishes an inner sense of purpose.[12]

EXERCISE OUTSIGHT

You need only to scan the headlines to know how dramatic the changes are that influence people's lives at home and at work. The old norms are being replaced by still uncertain ground rules. Recent research on the sources of innovation clearly indicates that the most disruptive and destructive innovations can wreak havoc on even the very best companies.[13] The only effective response from leaders is to anticipate the disruptions and get ahead of the curve. For sure, they can never afford to be behind it. So where do new ideas for products, processes, and services come from?

Look Outside Your Experience

Surprisingly, researchers find that innovations come from just about anywhere.[14] According to a global study of CEOs, two of the three most significant sources of innovative ideas are actually outside the organization.[15] Sometimes ideas come from customers, sometimes from lead users, sometimes from suppliers, sometimes from business partners, and sometimes from the R&D labs. What this means is that leaders must always be actively looking for the fuzziest signs and intently listening to the weakest signals to anticipate the emergence of something new over the horizon. This means honing your "outsight"—the capacity to perceive external things—and helping your constituents develop that ability as well.

Studies into how the brain processes information suggest that in order to see things differently and hence creatively, you have to bombard your brain with things it has never encountered. This kind of novelty is vital, explains neuroscientist Gregory Berns of Emory University, because the brain, evolved for efficiency, routinely takes perceptual shortcuts to save energy. Only by forcing yourself to break free of preexisting views can you get your brain to recategorize information. Moving beyond habitual thinking patterns is the starting point to imagining truly novel alternatives.[16]

Because the human mind is surprisingly adroit at supporting its deep-seated ways of viewing the world while sifting out evidence to the contrary, Marie Capozzi, Renee Dye, and Amy Howe, with McKinsey & Company, suggest that the antidote is direct personal experience: "Seeing and experiencing something firsthand can shake people up in ways that abstract discussions around conference room tables can't. It's therefore extremely valuable to start creativity-building exercises or idea generation efforts outside the office, by engineering personal experiences that directly confront the participants' implicit or explicit assumptions."[17] Consider what one North American specialty retailer did in seeking to reinvent its store format while improving the experience of its customers:

> To jump-start creativity in its people, the company sent out several groups of three to four employees to experience retail concepts very different from its own. Some went to Sephora, a beauty product retailer that features more than 200 brands and a sales model that encourages associates to offer honest product advice, without a particular allegiance to any of them. Others went to the Blues Jean Bar, an intimate boutique retailer that aspires to turn the impersonal experience of digging through piles of jeans into a cozy occasion reminiscent of a night at a neighborhood pub. Still others visited a gourmet chocolate shop.

These experiences were transformative for the employees, who watched, shopped, chatted with sales associates, took pictures, and later shared observations with teammates in a more formal idea generation session. By visiting the other retailers and seeing firsthand how they operated, the retailer's employees were able to relax their strongly held views about their own company's operations. This transformation, in turn, led them to identify new retail concepts they hadn't thought of before, including organizing a key product by color (instead of by manufacturer) and changing the design of stores to center the shopping experience around advice from expert stylists.[18]

Of course, the process doesn't have to be quite so elaborate, and it can take place right where you are today. Consider what Heidi Castagna, director of sales initiatives at Seagate Technology, did to scan the horizon.[19] Heidi leveraged the resources within various subscription services supplied by her company to understand how other firms were reacting to the economic downturn. She attended workshops and meetings dedicated to sharing best-in-class sales enablement models and practices. She spoke with consultants who specialized in helping make sales organizations more efficient. From these activities, Heidi was able to actively learn what had become important to buyers and what was working well for other companies. She successfully looked beyond the "four walls" of Seagate to learn about ideas and perspectives that would have otherwise been unknown to her. By combining her experience with this outsight, she was able to determine the important core messages and meanings from these various sources in order to best understand how she and her group could be innovative and stay ahead of the competition.

Leaders like Heidi understand that innovation requires more listening and greater communication than routine work does. Successful innovations don't spring from the fifty-second floor of the headquarters building or the back offices of City Hall. You have to establish relationships, network, be connected, and be out and about. Changing the business-as-usual environment requires staying in touch with the world around you.

Promote External and Internal Communication

You can expect demand for change to come from both inside and outside the organization. Too often, however, managers cut themselves off from critical information sources over time because they're so busy trying to build an organization that will be operationally efficient and self-sustaining. And when the pressures for profit and efficiency are greatest, these managers may even mistakenly act to eliminate or severely limit the very things that provide the new ideas they need to weather the storms of uncertainty—by cutting the budgets for travel and training, for example. Unless external communication is actively encouraged, people interact with outsiders less and less frequently, and new ideas are cut off.

This was precisely the conclusion of classic studies by MIT Sloan School of Management professors Ralph Katz and Tom Allen.[20] They examined the relationship between how long people had been working together in a particular project area—what they called "group longevity"—and three areas of interpersonal oral communication (intraproject, organizational, and professional communication) for the project groups at various stages of their existence. Each team's technical performance was also measured by department managers and laboratory directors.

The higher-performing groups had significantly more communication with people outside their labs, whether with organizational units, such as marketing and manufacturing, or with outside professional associations. Intriguingly, however, groups that had been together the longest reported lower levels of communication in all three areas and "were significantly more isolated from external sources of new ideas and technological advances and from information within other organizational divisions, especially marketing and manufacturing."[21] The long-lived teams cut themselves off from the kind of information they needed the most to come up with new ideas, and thus reduced their performance. They'd been together so long, it appears, that they felt they didn't need to talk to outsiders; they were content just to talk to each other. It's easy to understand how some workgroups and organizations become myopic and unimaginative. The people themselves aren't dull or slow witted; they've just become too familiar with their routines and too isolated from outside influences.

Sudeep Padiyar, software development manager at Cisco, appreciates the importance of having a free flow of ideas with his team, and makes sure that no one works in a silo. He believes that "problems and their solutions are both collective team efforts, and that reduces the pressure and burden from individuals." He has removed organizational boundaries and encourages everyone on the team to take initiative. Sudeep has organized technical seminars and brainstorming sessions in which guest speakers as well as technical leaders are invited to share experiences and ideas. These internal and external communication mechanisms, he says, have substantially increased the sharing of ideas and have resulted in innovative solutions to technical challenges that the team had been dealing with previously. In addition, they use wikis for team members to pose their questions, thoughts, and solutions on an intranet site to which the engineering community has access. The stimulating and thought-provoking discussions on these online message boards have helped people solve complex problems collectively.

According to Sudeep, "The free flow of ideas and access to the best brains in the industry have created a channel that enables innovation to thrive and problems to have elegant solutions in quick time."

Just as Sudeep did, you've got to tap into the rich field of ideas that exist outside your own borders. It is imperative that you listen to the world outside. For example, P&G has moved from an internal to an external focus when it comes to looking for innovations. These days more than one-third to one-half of their new products have elements that originated from outside the company or have key elements that were discovered externally. This is quite a shift for a company that had previously developed almost all of its new products internally or had acquired other companies in order to buy the new offerings. You never know just where a great idea will come from, which means that you have to both remain connected and increase your connections.[22]

Look Out for Good Ideas

On a visit to Northern California, we stumbled across some extremely important advice for leaders. Exploring the Mendocino coast, we picked up a pamphlet describing a particular stretch of shoreline. Printed boldly across the top of the first page was this warning: "Never turn your back on the ocean." And why shouldn't you turn your back on the ocean to look inland to catch a view of the town? Because a rogue wave may come along when your back is turned and sweep you out to sea, as it has many an unsuspecting beachcomber. This warning holds lifesaving advice for travelers and leaders alike. When you take your eyes off the external realities, turning inward to admire the colorful scenery in your own organization, you may be swept away by the swirling waters of change.

You must continuously scan the external realities. To be sure, innovation requires insight—the ability to apprehend the inner nature of things—but it also requires even keener outsight. When you keep the doors to the outside world open, ideas and information can flow freely into the organization. That's the only way you can become knowledgeable about what goes on around you. Outsight is the sibling of insight, and without it innovation cannot happen. Insight without outsight is like seeing clearly with blinders on; you just can't get a complete picture.

In testing and observing three thousand executives over a six-year period, professors Clayton Christensen, Jeffrey Dyer, and Hal Gregersen noted that the important "discovery" skill relevant to innovators was *associating*. This involves making connections across "seemingly unrelated questions, problems, or ideas."[23] One powerful method for making associations is through the use of analogies, according to McKinsey & Company consultants. They suggest that by forcing comparisons between one company and a second, seemingly unrelated one, you can make considerable creative breakthroughs. Consider how you might stir the imagination by starting a discussion with your colleagues about such questions as:[24]

How would Google manage our data?
How might Disney engage with our consumers?
How could Southwest Airlines cut our costs?
How would Zappos redesign our supply chain?
How would Toyota change our production processes?
How would Starwood design our customer loyalty program?

Put yourself into new situations. Confront existing paradigms. Adopt an inquisitive attitude toward others' opinions and insights. These are methods that will keep your eyes and ears open to new ideas. Remain receptive and expose yourself to broader views.

Remove the protective covering in which organizations often seal themselves. Be willing to hear, consider, and accept ideas from sources outside the company. If you never turn your back on what is happening outside the boundaries of your organization, you will not be caught by surprise when the waves of change roll in.

Treat Every Job as an Adventure

Leaders personally seize the initiative, encourage others to do the same, and actively look everywhere for great ideas, but that doesn't mean that they can't make extraordinary things happen if they're leading a project that's been assigned to them. They don't have to wait to start their own business to change the business-as-usual environment. When we asked people to tell us who initiated the projects that they selected as their personal bests, we assumed that the majority of people would name themselves. Surprisingly, that's not what we found. Someone other than the leader—usually the person's immediate manager—initiated more than half the cases. If leaders seize the initiative, then how can we call people leaders when they're assigned the jobs and tasks they undertake? Doesn't this finding fly in the face of all that we've said about how leaders behave? No, it doesn't.

The fact that over half the cases were not self-initiated should come as a relief to anyone who thought he or she had to initiate all the change, and it should encourage everyone in the organization to accept responsibility for innovation and improvement. If the only times people reported doing their best were when they got to choose the projects themselves or when they were the CEO, the majority of leadership opportunities would evaporate—as would most social and organizational changes. The reality is that much of what people do is assigned; few get to start everything from scratch. That's just a fact of organizational life.

Stuff happens in organizations and in people's lives. It's not so important whether you find the challenges or they find you. What is important are the choices you make. What's important is the purpose you find for challenging the way things are. The question is this: When opportunity knocks, are you prepared to answer the door? Similarly, are you ready to open the door, go outside, and find an opportunity?

Even if you've been in your job for years, treat today as if it were your first day. Ask yourself, "If I were just starting this job, what would I do?" Begin doing those things now. Constantly stay alert to ways to improve your organization. Identify those projects that you've always wanted to undertake but never have. Ask your team members to do the same.

Be an adventurer, an explorer. Where in your organization have you not been? Where in the communities that you serve have you not been? Make a plan to explore those places. Take a field trip to a factory, a warehouse, a distribution center, or a retail store. If you're in an educational system, go sit in on the class that was once your favorite subject. How's it different today? If you're in city government, go to a department that really intrigues you. If you're in a professional services organization, go on a site visit with someone in a different practice.

Consider what happened when the chief executives of many large corporations got out of their offices and looked around their organizations from the ground floor, as profiled on the TV show *Undercover Boss*.[25] On the show, executives (in disguise) work the frontline jobs of their organization to see firsthand how their corporate mandates play out in the real world. Waste Management's Larry O'Donnell revealed, "In my role as COO [chief operating officer], there are many policies I create that you all have to live with. Now that I've made a connection with the people who do the hard jobs at this company, I'm going to be a better manager. I have a whole new appreciation of the impact my decisions have."[26]

You don't have to be at the top of the organization to learn about what's going on around you. Be on the lookout for new ideas, wherever you are. If you're serious about promoting innovation and getting others to listen to people outside the unit, make gathering new ideas a personal priority. Encourage others to open their eyes and ears to the world outside the boundaries of the organization. Collect ideas through focus groups, advisory boards, suggestion boxes, breakfast meetings, brainstorming sessions, customer evaluation forms, mystery shoppers, mystery guests, visits to competitors, and the like. Online chat rooms are great venues for swapping ideas with those outside your field.

Make idea gathering part of your daily, weekly, and monthly schedule. Call three customers or clients who haven't used your services in a while or who have made recent purchases, and ask them why. Sure, there's email, but the human voice is better for this sort of thing. Work the counter and ask people what they like and don't like about your organization. Shop at a competitor's store or, better yet, anonymously shop for your own product and see what the salespeople in the store say about it. Call your organization and see how the phones are answered and how questions are handled. Make sure that you devote at least 25 percent of every weekly staff meeting to listening to outside ideas for improving processes and technologies and developing new products and services. Don't let staff meetings consist merely of status reports on routine, daily, inside stuff. Invite customers, suppliers, people from other departments, and other outsiders to your meetings to offer their suggestions on how your unit can improve. Keep your antennae up, no matter where you are. You can never tell where or when you might find new ideas.

TAKE ACTION

Search for Opportunities

Leaders who are dedicated to making extraordinary things happen are open to receiving ideas from anyone and anywhere. They are adept at using their outsight to constantly survey the landscape of technology, politics, economics, demographics, art, religion, and society in search of new ideas. They are prepared to search for opportunities to address the constant shifts in their organization's environment. And because they are proactive, they don't just ride the waves of change: they make the waves that others ride. They are prepared to search for opportunities to address the constant shifts in the organization's environment.

You don't have to change history, but you do have to change "business as usual." You have to be proactive, constantly inviting and creating new initiatives. Leaders, by definition, are out in front of change, not behind it trying to catch up. Be on the lookout for anything that lulls you or your colleagues into a false sense of security. Innovation and leadership are nearly synonymous. This means that your focus is less on the routine operations and much more on the untested and untried. And when searching for opportunities to grow and improve, keep in mind that the most innovative ideas are most often not your own and not in your own organization. They're elsewhere, and the best leaders look all around them for the places in which breakthrough ideas are hiding. Exemplary leadership requires outsight, not just insight. That's where the future is.

The quest for change is an adventure. It tests your will and your skill. It's tough, but it's also stimulating. Adversity introduces you to yourself. To get the best from yourself and others, you must understand what gives meaning and purpose to your work.

To Challenge the Process, you must *search for opportunities by seizing the initiative and look outward for innovative ways to improve.* This means you have to

- Always be asking, "What's new? What's next? What's better?"
- Do something each day so that you are better than you were the day before.
- Be restless; don't let routines become ruts.
- Put yourself in new situations; take on a new project at least once a quarter.
- Find out if "the way things are done around here" still makes sense. If it doesn't, do something different.
- Ask your customers (clients, suppliers, and so on) for their ideas about what you (and your organization) can do better.
- Go on the Web each day and search for something related to what you do. Also visit sites that are totally unrelated to your business.
- Design work so that it's intrinsically interesting.
- Seek firsthand experiences outside your comfort zone and skill set.
- Talk with folks outside your organization's four walls; encourage others to do the same.

Use *The Leadership Challenge Mobile Tool* app to immediately integrate these activities into your life and make this practice an ongoing part of your behavioral repertoire.

CHAPTER 7

Experiment and Take Risks

WARD CLAPHAM BECAME the commander of the Richmond, British Columbia, detachment of the Royal Canadian Mounted Police (RCMP) at a time when the city was exploring the possibility of terminating their policing contract with the RCMP and creating their own city police force. Tens of thousands of crimes were reported each year, and youth crime was at an all-time high. Ward was charged with moving the detachment in a new direction and breaking old mindsets.

"We were definitely operating in a reactive, post-incident, corrective model of repair," said Ward. "We were putting Band-Aids on problems and not really getting at the roots of the problems. We were caught up in the status quo . . . and needed to move to a model of *prepare*, not repair." Ward also encountered low employee morale within a culture of rigid obedience and antiquated policies. Nobody was talking about the need to do things differently.

After interviewing all of his staff, meeting with many members of the community, and seeing things for himself, Ward took action.

The first thing was to reinvent and promote their primary vision—to prevent crime, with the lofty goal of ending crime. He started with the principle that a partnership with the community to prevent crime was required to achieve the end goal.

One critical issue on which Ward took immediate action was false alarms. At the beginning of his tenure, his officers were responding to over nine thousand false alarms a year. Burglar alarms have become very popular with the public, and police forces have promoted them. The problem is that 97 percent of alarms are false, diverting resources from other, more serious public safety issues. Ward challenged his team to solve this complex problem, and they came back with a comprehensive solution called "verified response to alarms" that reduced false alarms by 80 percent. "It was a huge morale boost," Ward said, "and now my officers could begin being proactive. We were able to reinvest over $310,000 in manpower every year back into our primary mission—preventing crime."

Another immediate change Ward made was to the daily morning briefings. In the past, the commander would sit at the front, and the officers would report in with their problems and wait for the commander's decisions. Ward turned this command-and-control, low-trust environment completely around. "I would challenge my leaders to think out of the box," Ward told us. "I would push the problems back to them. You know the old saying . . . no involvement, no ownership. Instead of me, the commander, making the decision, I would have them own the problem together as a team and ask them what they would do differently."

To combat youth crime, Ward doubled his community policing unit and the number of police officers dedicated to working with youth. In partnership with the school district, every grade 5 student received ten hour-long sessions taught by an RCMP officer. Ward also had his police officers reach out to the youth of Richmond in a trust-building program. In an initiative called the Onside Program, more than five hundred youth every year were taken to a professional hockey game, football game, or special event by the Richmond RCMP officers.

To change the paradigm of the police always catching kids breaking the law, Ward introduced a program called Positive Tickets. Police officers proactively went out on patrol to catch kids doing things right and reward them with a voucher or coupon to some fun, free activity. More than forty thousand Positive Tickets were given out per year, a three-to-one ratio of Positive Tickets to the traditional negative police ticket.

To institutionalize the cultural change process as well as the notion of continuous learning, Ward introduced morning training to the Richmond Detachment. "Every morning I would train all my staff for forty-five minutes—both sworn officers and civilian support staff. I would take half the officers off the street at a time. When they complained about missing their coffee break, I brought coffee and treats into the training sessions to make it up to them." Whenever possible, Ward would have his staff facilitate the training. It was not uncommon to have the constables teaching in an area of their expertise to senior police leaders.

These initiatives, and the many others Ward tried, paid off. During Ward's tenure, the Richmond Detachment enjoyed the highest morale rate in the RCMP, and his team was promoted to higher ranks or prestigious positions faster than any others in the RCMP. Overall crime was reduced by 30 percent, and youth crime was reduced by almost 50 percent—saving millions of taxpayer dollars. And in testimony to the innovativeness of Ward's efforts, fifty-three countries have studied the Richmond RCMP leadership approach.

To achieve the extraordinary, as Ward and his team demonstrated, you have to be willing to do things that have never been done before. Every single personal-best story we have heard and read speaks to the need to take risks with bold ideas. Nothing new and nothing great is achieved by doing things the way you've always done them. You have to test unproven strategies. You have to break out of the norms that box you in. You have to do the things you think you cannot. You have to venture beyond the limitations you normally place on yourself. Making extraordinary things happen in organizations demands a willingness to try new things and take chances with new ideas.

Leaders have to take this one step further. Not only do they have to be willing to test bold ideas and take calculated risks, but they also have to get others to join them on these adventures in uncertainty. It's one thing to set off alone into the unknown; it's entirely another to get others to follow you. The difference between an exemplary leader and an individual risk-taker is that leaders are able to create the conditions where people *want* to join with them in the struggle.

Leaders make risk safe, as paradoxical as that might sound. They turn experiments into learning opportunities. They don't define boldness solely in terms of go-for-broke, giant-leap projects. More often than not, they see change as starting small, using pilot projects, and gaining momentum. The vision may be grand and distant, but the way to reach it is by putting one foot in front of the other. These small, visible steps are more likely to win early victories and gain early supporters. Of course, when you experiment, not everything works out as intended. There are mistakes and false starts. They are part of the process of innovation. What's critical, therefore, is that leaders promote learning from these experiences.

Exemplary leaders make the commitment to *Experiment and Take Risks*. They know that it's essential for leaders to

- **GENERATE SMALL WINS**
- **LEARN FROM EXPERIENCE**

These essentials can help leaders transform challenge into an exploration, uncertainty into a sense of adventure, fear into resolve, and risk into reward. They are the keys to making progress that becomes unstoppable.

GENERATE SMALL WINS

While we were just beginning our work on this edition, we got a call from Don Bennett, one of the pioneering people we interviewed for the first edition of *The Leadership Challenge*. With great excitement in his voice, he told us that he'd just returned from Argentina, where he had presented the Don Bennett Golden Foot Award at the tenth World Cup of the World Amputee Football Federation, an organization he cofounded nearly thirty years ago.

Before starting his first amputee soccer team, Don was the first amputee to reach the summit of Mount Rainier. That's 14,410 feet on one leg and two crutches. In fact, he actually had to make that climb twice. On his first attempt, a howling windstorm nearly blew his climbing team off the mountain. They had to turn back 410 feet from the summit. But Don was not discouraged. For another full year, he worked out vigorously. On his second attempt, after five days of rigorous climbing, Don planted the flag.

"How did you do it?" we asked Don. "How did you make it to the top of Mount Rainier on one leg?" "One hop at a time," he said. Then he added, "I imagined myself on top of that mountain one thousand times a day. But when I started to climb it, I just said to myself, 'Anybody can hop from here to there.' And I would. And when the going got roughest, and I was really exhausted, that's when I would look down at the path ahead and say to myself, 'You just have to take one more step, and anybody can do that.' And I would."

Leaders face difficult challenges similar to Don's all the time. How do you achieve something no one has ever done before? How do you get something new started? How do you overcome a physical or competitive handicap? How do you turn around a losing business? Or start a new one? How do you solve the health care problem, or the world hunger problem, or the global climate change problem, or the global competitiveness problem? These are such daunting challenges that you get stuck before you get started. Framing the challenge as something too gigantic can actually have the effect of dampening motivation.

So how do you do it? How do you get people to want to move in a new direction, break old mindsets, or change existing behavior patterns in order to tackle big problems and attempt extraordinary performance? You climb that mountain one hop at a time. You make progress incrementally. You break the long journey down into milestones. You move people forward step-by-step, creating a sense of forward momentum by generating what University of Michigan professor Karl Weick calls "small wins."

Karl describes a small win as "a concrete, complete, implemented outcome of moderate importance."[1] Small wins form the basis for a consistent pattern of winning that attracts people who want to be allied with a successful venture. Planting one tree won't stop global warming, but planting one million trees can make a difference, and it's that first tree that gets things started. Small wins identify the place to begin. They make the project seem doable within the parameters of existing skills and resources. They minimize the cost of trying and reduce the risks of failing. What's exciting about this process is that once a small win has been accomplished, it sets in motion natural forces that favor progress over setbacks.

Consider how Alex Jukl, project manager at Seagate Technology, describes a two-year process that transformed the way the company does business with its customers.

> Because we've been focusing on small wins, it doesn't necessarily feel as though we've been overtly "challenging the process"; instead, we have been offering programs, tools, and processes that help people to do their jobs better. I believe that had we gone from 0 to 60 and commenced *all* these projects simultaneously, we would not have made much impact on the sales organization. They would have been overwhelmed and lost, unsure of what was important or what was expected of them, or worse yet, offended that we were coming in and asking them to completely rewrite their programmed behavior.
>
> Furthermore, initiating one big project to prove out these new concepts and methodologies would have carried tremendous fiscal risk for us in an uncertain economy. As a result of taking the path of small wins, our team was able to ensure that everyone was on the same page as us, and course-correct as necessary—not only did it help us to better lead and influence the sales teams in this change effort, it gave them a venue to tell *us* how we could be better leaders in our efforts as well.

As Alex's experience demonstrates, even though leaders have grand visions about the future, they get there one step at a time, building momentum as well as the strength and resolve to continue forward along the journey.

Build Psychological Hardiness

Before you can take that first hop, however, you have to take a step forward in your attitude. For example, Don Bennett didn't just leap from a hospital bed to the cliffs of Mount Rainier. His initial battle was with himself. He told us how he had to stop feeling sorry for himself and realize how lucky he really was. He realized that he had the capacity of his other leg, even though it too was badly injured. He was determined to return to an active life. He took charge and began doing things that would lead, gradually, to the summit.

The same is true for the other personal-best stories we collected. Although the circumstances weren't always as dramatic as Don's, the conditions people faced during their personal-best leadership experiences were just as uncertain and stressful as his. Although 95 percent of the cases were described as exciting, about 20 percent of leaders also called the experiences frustrating, and approximately 15 percent said that their experiences aroused fear or anxiety. Even though the emotions associated with personal-best cases are overwhelmingly positive, we can't overlook that they were also filled with tension.

But instead of being debilitated by the stress of a difficult experience, exemplary leaders said they were challenged and energized by it. That was certainly the case for Karen Slakey Hull when she assumed responsibility for Repro Graphics at the University of California, Davis.[2] The organization was in desperate straits. For three of the four previous years, they had had large operating deficits, and their reserves were now depleted. The equipment was obsolete, production volumes were low, spoilage was excessive, print quality was not up to modern standards, and customer satisfaction was suffering. Employees worked hard, but feared for their jobs and were skeptical of leadership's ability to make the required changes.

None of this deterred Karen. "I was an experienced business-woman, and not an expert in the print, copy, or graphic design business," she told us. "But I was confident," she continued, "that together with the employees of Repro Graphics, the situation could be turned around." Karen and the management staff evaluated each product and service. They looked at revenue-expense rela-tionships, customer demand, product quality, and the type and quantity of work that was being outsourced. They conducted a cus-tomer satisfaction survey and learned what was really important to customers.

When Karen asked the production manager for a proposal to modernize the equipment, he came back with a five-year plan. Karen's response to this was to ask, "What would happen if we made this investment in one year?" His eyes opened wide in an expression that said, "Wow, we really can change this place!" He returned with a one-year plan that made clear strategic and financial sense.

Upgraded equipment required new, higher-level skills. To ease the transition, production staff attended conferences on modern production equipment and processes and also received extensive training specific to the new equipment. Karen and her managers coached staff in their new roles while also recognizing employees who continued to work on traditional printing presses.

Because Repro Graphics was capable of designing and produc-ing beautiful marketing materials, Karen put significant effort into developing a brand to promote the *new* Repro Graphics. Delivery drivers started wearing Repro Graphics polo shirts. Delivery trucks proudly displayed the Repro Graphics logo and contact information.

It became very visible to both customers and staff that Repro Graphics did great work.

Throughout this time, Karen held monthly all-staff meetings so that teams could present their unit updates, which included major achievements and near-term goals. "While this created stress for many of the staff presenters," Karen reported, "it was also clear that they took great pride in telling about the accomplishments of their unit, and regular information on production and financial performance helped build confidence about the good things that were happening in Repro Graphics."

Given the difficult situation they faced, Karen, her managers, and the staff of Repro Graphics could have given up. But they didn't. They stepped up to the challenge and overcame it. It turns out that the ability to grow and thrive under stressful, risk-abundant situations, such as the one that the folks at Repro Graphics faced, is highly dependent on how you view change.

Psychologists, intrigued by people who experience a high degree of stress and yet are able to cope with it in a positive manner, have discovered that these individuals have a distinctive attitude toward stress, which they call "psychological hardiness."[3] Researchers over the last forty years have discovered that in groups as diverse as corporate managers, entrepreneurs, students, nurses, lawyers, and combat soldiers, those high in psychological hardiness are much more likely to withstand serious challenges and bounce back from failure than those low in hardiness.[4] And the good news is that hardiness is a quality that people can learn and that leaders can support.

There are three key factors to psychological hardiness: *commitment, control,* and *challenge.* To turn adversity into advantage, you need first to commit yourself to what's happening. You have to become involved, engaged, and curious. You can't sit back and wait for something to happen. When you commit, you'll find the people and the situations much more meaningful and worthwhile to you. You also have to take control of your own life. You need to make an effort to influence what is going on. Even though all your attempts may not be successful, you can't sink into powerlessness or passivity. Finally, if you are going to be psychologically hardy, you need to view challenge as an opportunity to learn from both negative and positive experiences. You can't play it safe. Personal improvement and fulfillment come through the continual process of engaging in the uncertainties of life. Easy comfort and security are not only unrealistic but also stultifying.

Your view of events contributes to your ability to cope with change and stress. For you to take that first step, to start that new project, to initiate improvement, you have to believe that you can influence the outcome of the situation. You have to be curious about whatever is going down. And you have to look for learning every step of the way. With a hardy attitude, you can transform stressful events into positive opportunities for growth and renewal. What's more, you can help your team feel the same way.

Break It Down

Leaders know they have to break down big problems into small, doable actions. They also know that when initiating something new, they have to try a lot of little things before they get it right. Not every innovation works, and the best way to ensure success is to experiment with a lot of ideas, not just one or two big ones. Successful leaders help others see how breaking the journey down into measurable milestones can move them forward. This is exactly what Tiffany Nguyen experienced while an account manager for Volt Services contingency employment services at Advanced Micro Devices (AMD).

Part of Tiffany's job was to manage requisitions, coordinate interviews, provide offer letters, and get new contractors on board. She said that she "was afraid of making drastic changes because I feared it would be too much for AMD to accept, so I made one small change at a time." First, she got permission to assist in completing the requisition form before it went through the approval process. This allowed her to be the starting point of the requisition request, ensure that all the necessary information was provided up front, and have direct access to hiring managers from the start. Next, Tiffany discovered that an email approval was as good as an actual signature on the form, and she immediately proposed an electronic signature format whereby decision makers only had to "reply all" with their approval before the form was forwarded to the next person. This new process cut at least a full week-and-a-half of processing time and showed Tiffany "how successful a larger goal can be if you break down the big problem into smaller solvable pieces."

Indeed, "big things are done by doing lots of small things," as we heard over and over in the personal-best cases we collected. When you break a big project down into pieces and try a lot of little things, you also make progress more likely. Whatever you call your experiments—model sites, pilot studies, demonstration projects, laboratory tests, field experiments, market trials—they are methods for trying lots of little things in the service of something much bigger. These are the tactics that continually generate lots of possibilities for small wins.

A small-wins approach fits especially well with the fast and fragmented pace of work in the information society. Today's manager typically spends an average of three minutes of uninterrupted time on any single event, and around twelve minutes on a "work sphere" before switching to something else.[5] That means a manager could be switching from project to project forty or more times a day. It's enough to make any leader dizzy. This kind of work pattern requires leaders to act on their dreams in brief bursts. The beauty of a small win is that it's compact, it's simple, and it can catch the attention of people who have only a few minutes to listen to an idea or read a proposal.

These little bets are limited experiments in accomplishing change. They're laboratories for trying, failing, and learning. They're also great visual aids. By showcasing some "little thing" you've experimented with, you give people a tangible sense of what success looks like. You also boost morale and confidence. People see that it's possible to do something about what might otherwise be perceived as an intractable problem. All those possibilities can add up to big results, as Justina Wang, responsible for the global sales control for a multinational company, discovered when she noticed some problems in the overseas sales process. She knew that the system needed to change, but she didn't necessarily know how, especially because this was a long and complex process, scattered across many different divisions. After asking everyone in the global sales chain for input and getting them talking, she decided to test an idea in one overseas subsidiary. It turned out well and was quickly rolled out to thirty subsidiaries on six continents. Reflecting back on her experience, Justina said, "No change can be made in one jump. Many small wins can generate big successes."

Profit from Small Wins

Small wins produce big results for a very simple reason: it's hard to argue with success. In extensive investigations into what makes knowledge workers effective, Harvard Business School professor Teresa Amabile and independent researcher Steven Kramer found that "people are more creative and productive when their inner work lives are positive—when they feel happy, are intrinsically motivated by the work itself, and have positive perceptions of their colleagues and organizations."[6] And what triggers these feelings? "The key to motivating performance is supporting progress in meaningful work."[7] Teresa and Steven go on to report that "when we think of progress, we often imagine how good it feels to achieve a long-term goal or experience a major breakthrough. These big wins are great—but they are relatively rare. The good news is that even small wins can boost inner work life tremendously."[8] Small, incremental, and consistent steps forward have a big impact on people's motivation.

The fact that small wins work isn't news to scholars of technological innovation. An extensive study involving five DuPont plants documented that minor technical changes (for example, introduction of forklift trucks)—rather than major changes (for example, introduction of new chemical processing technologies)—accounted for over two-thirds of the reductions in production costs over a thirty-year period.[9] The minor technical changes were small improvements, made by people familiar with current operations. Less time, skill, effort, and expense were required to produce them than to implement the major changes. Much of the improvement was really part of the process of learning by doing.

The scientific community has always understood that major breakthroughs are likely to be the result of the work of hundreds of researchers, as countless contributions finally begin to add up to a solution. If one looks at their sum total, all the "little" improvements in technology, regardless of the industry, likely have contributed to a greater increase in organizational productivity than all the great inventors and their inventions.[10] Indeed, researchers have found that rapid prototyping, and plenty of it, results in bringing higher-quality products to the marketplace more quickly.[11]

Small wins produce results because they attract people who want to be allied with a successful venture. Small wins build people's confidence and reinforce their natural desire to feel successful. Because additional resources tend to flow to winners, this means that slightly larger wins can be attempted next. A series of small wins therefore lays a foundation of stable building blocks. Each win preserves gains and makes it harder to return to preexisting conditions.

Small wins produce results because they make people feel like winners and make it easier for leaders to get others to want to go along with their requests. If people can see that a leader is asking them to do something that they're quite capable of doing, they feel some assurance that they can be successful at the task. If people aren't overwhelmed by a task, their energy goes into getting the job done, instead of wondering, "How will we ever solve that problem?"

Small wins produce results because they build personal and group commitment to a course of action. By working at finding all the little ways that people can succeed at doing things differently, effective leaders make people want to be involved and stay involved because they can see that what they are doing is making a difference.

LEARN FROM EXPERIENCE

Whenever you challenge the status quo, tackle demanding problems, make meaningful changes, or confront adversity, you will sometimes fail. Despite how clearly you see challenge as an opportunity, how focused you can be, or how driven you are to succeed, there will be setbacks.

People never get it right the first time—not in sports, not in games, not in school, and most certainly not in work organizations. Yes, it's something that leaders are told that they must do, but this advice is neither realistic nor useful. Sure, you should get it right *every time* once you get to production or delivery, but not when you're trying to do things you've never done before. When you engage in something new and different, you make a lot of mistakes. Everyone does. That's what experimentation is all about, and, as research scientists know very well, there's a lot of trial and error involved in testing new concepts, new methods, and new practices.

Over and over again, people in our studies tell us how important mistakes and failure have been to their success. Without mistakes, they'd be unable to know what they can and cannot do (at least at this moment). Without those experiences, respondents said, they would have been unable to achieve their aspirations. It may seem paradoxical, but many echo the thought that the overall quality of work improves when people have a chance to fail. Studies of the innovation process make the point: "Success does not breed success. It breeds failure. It is failure which breeds success."[12]

James E. West, research professor at Johns Hopkins University, has secured nearly fifty domestic and more than two hundred foreign patents. "I think I've had more failures than successes, but I don't see the failures as mistakes because I always learned something from those experiences," he says. "I see them as having not achieved the initial goal, nothing more than that."[13] Or consider how basketball hall of famer Michael Jordan explains his success. "I've missed more than nine thousand shots in my career. I've lost almost three hundred games. Twenty-six times, I've been trusted to take the game winning shot and missed. I've failed over and over again in my life. And that is why I succeed."[14]

To be sure, failure can be costly. For the individual who leads a failed project, it can mean a stalled career or even a lost job. For an adventurous leader, it can mean the loss of personal assets. For mountain climbers and other physical adventurers, it can mean injury or death. Regardless of the field, there is no success without the possibility of failure.[15]

Failure is never the objective of any endeavor. The objective is to succeed, and success always requires some amount of learning. And learning always involves mistakes, errors, miscalculations, and the like along the way. Learning happens when people can openly talk about what went wrong as well as what went right. Leaders don't look for someone to blame when the inevitable mistakes are made in the name of innovation. They ask, "What can be learned from the experience?"

Be an Active Learner

Curious about the relationship between leadership and learning, we conducted a series of empirical studies to find out if leaders could be differentiated by the range and depth of learning tactics they employ when facing new or unfamiliar experiences. First, we looked at how engaged these people were in four different approaches to learning: "taking action" (preferring to learn by trial and error), "thinking" (reading articles or books or going online to gain knowledge and background), "feeling" (confronting themselves on what they are worrying about), and "accessing others" (bouncing hopes and fears off someone they trust). We then correlated these with their leadership practices. We found that people who were more, rather than less, engaged in each of these learning tactics were also more engaged in The Five Practices of Exemplary Leadership.[16]

We're not the only ones who find a strong correlation between engagement in learning and leadership effectiveness. Researchers Bob Eichinger, Mike Lombardo, and Dave Ulrich report that in their studies, the single best predictor of future success in new and different managerial jobs is learning agility.[17] "Learning agility," as they define it, "is the ability to reflect on experience and then engage in new behaviors based on those reflections." They go on to say, "Learning agility requires self-confidence to honestly examine oneself, self-awareness to seek feedback and suggestions, and self-discipline to engage in new behaviors."[18]

Learning is the master skill. When you fully engage in learning—when you throw yourself wholeheartedly into experimenting, reflecting, reading, or getting coaching—you are going to experience the thrill of improvement and the taste of success. More is more when it comes to learning. It's clear that exemplary leaders approach each new and unfamiliar experience with a willingness to learn, an appreciation for the importance of learning, and recognition that learning necessarily involves making some mistakes.

A. G. Lafley, retired P&G chairman and CEO, has certainly accomplished a lot in his career. Yet despite his immense success, he says, "I think I learned more from my failures than from my successes in all my years as a CEO. I think of my failures as a gift. Unless you view them that way, you won't learn from failure, you won't get better—and the company won't get better."[19] It's this kind of openness and humility that is typical of people who exemplify a learning mindset.[20]

Building your capacity to be an agile learner begins with what Stanford psychologist Carol Dweck refers to as a *growth mindset*.

"The growth mindset," she says, "is based on the belief that your basic qualities are things you can cultivate through your efforts." She compares this to a *fixed mindset*—"believing that your qualities are carved in stone."[21] Individuals with a growth mindset, for example, believe that people can learn to be better leaders. Those with the fixed mindset think that leaders are born, not made, and that no amount of training is going to make you any better than you naturally are.

In study after study, researchers have found that when working on simulated business problems, those individuals with fixed mindsets gave up more quickly and performed more poorly than those with growth mindsets. The same is true for kids in school, athletes on the playing field, teachers in the classroom, and partners in relationships.[22] Mindsets and not skill sets make the critical difference in taking on challenging situations.

To develop a growth mindset and to nourish it in others, you need to embrace the challenges you face. That's where the learning is. When you encounter setbacks—and there will be many—you have to persist. You have to realize that your effort, and that of others, is your means of gaining mastery. It's neither raw talent nor good fortune that leads to becoming the best; it's hard work that gets you there. Ask for feedback about how you're doing. Learn from the constructive criticism you receive from others. And view the success of others around you as inspiration and not as a threat. When you believe that you can continuously learn, you will.

Create a Climate for Learning

To promote learning and nurture a growth mindset, you need to create a climate of inquiry and openness, of patience, and of encouragement. Studies of top performers strongly suggest that people require a supportive environment in order to become the best they can be. Researchers have found, in fact, that when there are high-quality relationships at work, people engage in more of the behaviors that lead to learning.[23] These relationships are characterized by positive regard for others and a sense of mutuality and trust. In order to create positive relationships like this, you need to offer encouraging words when people try something new, be patient and understanding when they get off track, and offer helpful suggestions as they try to learn and bounce back from mistakes.

However, a positive learning environment can't be created instantly. As Kelli Garvanian, solution consultant in the payment integrity department at Emdeon, realized, you will need to consciously adjust your own leadership behaviors.[24] Kelli has high expectations and demands a lot from herself and from others. High expectations can motivate people to stretch themselves and promote learning. However, leaders with high expectations can also become overly demanding and overly assertive. They can exhibit impatience, frustration, and anger, causing people to become defensive, less open, and less willing to take risks. That's what happened initially to Kelli.

Fortunately for Kelli and her team, she was willing to learn. She had the courage to ask for feedback about her behavior. Her team told her that sometimes she raised her voice or demanded that something be done; they felt she wasn't always respectful of them. Instead of working collaboratively, they became self-protective and focused on getting their own things done. The business results were not good, and the team members were worried about their future. Kelli knew she had to make a change.

After getting feedback and coaching, Kelli dedicated herself to working specifically on two leadership behaviors, one of which was "asking 'What can we learn?' when things don't go as expected."[25] She believed this would lead to more openness and collaboration and to increased motivation and commitment to a shared vision of the future. To remind herself how important it was to change her behavior, Kelli kept her feedback visible on the top of her desk. Then, in every meeting with her team, and whenever mistakes were made, Kelli would ask, "What can we learn?" At first, no one said anything. They didn't know what to expect or why she was asking. Kelli persisted, and after a while, her team realized that Kelli was sincere, and they began suggesting things they could do differently. In fact, at some point the team began asking "What can we learn?" in unison at the end of every meeting! That's when Kelli knew her leadership changes were beginning to have an impact on others. Her courage to learn and change created a new, very different climate for her team. And they became more willing to take risks, share new ideas, and work more collaboratively.

People know that they don't always get it right the first time they try something and that learning new things can be a bit scary. They don't want to embarrass themselves in front of peers or look stupid in front of their managers. To create a climate for learning, you have to make it safe for others to try, to fail, and to learn from their experiences. Make it a habit to ask, "What can we learn?" as often as you can.

The truth is that failures and disappointments are inevitable. How you handle them is what will ultimately determine your effectiveness and success. You have to be honest with yourself and with others. You have to own up to your mistakes and reflect on your experiences so that you gain the learning necessary to be better the next time around.

Strengthen Resilience

It takes determination and strength to deal with the adversities of life and leadership. You can't let the setbacks get you down or the roadblocks get in your way. You can't become overly discouraged when things don't go according to plan. You can't give up when the resistance builds or when the competition gets stiff. Neither can you let other tempting new projects divert your interest. You can't lose focus when there are lots of distractions all around. You have to stick with it.

This kind of determination characterizes Pat Williams, senior vice president of the Orlando Magic.[26] In his nearly fifty years as a sports executive—from managing a minor league baseball team to cofounding an elite basketball franchise, with several stops in between—Pat has had his fair share of wins and losses and career ups and downs. But he learned early on that "you don't waste those tough times."

"When the tough times hit and the setbacks and the disappointments come," he said, "you're a lot more teachable. I wouldn't be where I am today if I had not taken advantage of the disappointments and the setbacks. . . . Through those setbacks I've learned more, and made more advances, than through the good times." Pat, who's been a student of leadership throughout his career, reminded us that the greatest leaders in history all faced tremendous obstacles. He said they all should have given up about thirty times. But they didn't. They had, Pat said, what Walt Disney called "stick-to-it-ivity." "They've all battled through horribly tough times, and the reason we admire these leaders," Pat said, "was because they didn't quit. Leadership always, always, always rests on the man or woman who can finish."

Pat also told us about R. E. Littlejohn, coowner of the team and one of his early mentors when he was the general manager of a minor league baseball team in Spartanburg, South Carolina. Managing in the minor leagues is a very different experience from that in the major leagues.

> [The owners] can move the team when they want. You don't have a dome. You don't have a tarp. Rainouts are a constant problem. You've got clogged up toilets in the rest rooms. The hotdog vendor doesn't show up one night. The guy who's meant to be directing the parking lot gets sick. On any given day there are endless, endless problems. And so here I am this young baseball executive, and I would gather up my problems and go out and see Mr. Littlejohn, hoping that he would take them upon himself.
>
> But, as I presented these problems, his response would be, "Now Pat, that's going to give you a wonderful opportunity to sell yourself to the front office in Philadelphia." Or, "This issue here is going to allow you to have a whole new relationship with your manager down there in the dugout." Or, "The banker downtown who you've been having trouble selling, this could be a door opener. You've got a wonderful chance through this problem." He just kept stressing to me, "Don't run from your problems. Don't run from your problems. . . . Take advantage of those problems to go sell yourself to somebody else."

The capacity Pat describes—that ability to recover quickly from setbacks and continue to pursue a vision of the future—is often referred to as resilience. Angela Duckworth, professor of psychology at the University of Pennsylvania, calls it grit. Angela and her research colleagues define grit very simply as "perseverance and passion for long-term goals," and report that it "entails working strenuously toward challenges, maintaining effort and interest over years despite failure, adversity, and plateaus in progress."[27] Showing grit involves setting goals, being obsessed with an idea or project, maintaining focus, sticking with things that take a long time to complete, over-coming setbacks, and the like. In their empirical research, whether with kids in school, cadets in the military, working professionals, artists, academics, or others, they find convincing evidence that people with the most grit are the most likely to achieve positive outcomes. The more grit you demonstrate, the better you do.

The good news is that these qualities of resilience and grit can be developed and strengthened, much like growth mindsets. Martin Seligman, professor of psychology at the University of Pennsylvania and a leading researcher in the field, has tackled this challenge with some of the toughest populations at work—for example, active-duty soldiers in the military.[28] Seligman says that in his research, "We discovered that people who don't give up have a habit of interpreting setbacks as temporary, local, and changeable."[29] Essentially, even in times of great stress and adversity, people who are resilient remain committed to moving forward by believing that what has happened isn't going to be permanent and that they can do something about the outcome.

In light of these findings, you can do a number of things to strengthen resilience. For example, when a failure or setback occurs, don't blame yourself or the people working on the project. Instead find situational circumstances that contributed to the failure and convey a belief that this particular situation is likely to be temporary, not permanent. Emphasize that the failure or setback is a problem only in this one instance and not in every case. When success occurs and milestones are reached, to breed a growth mindset you should attribute success to the hard work and effort of the individuals in the group. Convey a belief that many more victories are at hand and be optimistic that good fortune will be with your team for a long time. You can also strengthen resilience in other ways, such as by assigning tasks that are challenging but within the person's skill level, focusing on rewards rather than punishments, and encouraging people to see change as full of possibilities.[30]

The personal-best examples involved change and stressful events in the lives of leaders; they involved significant personal and organizational change. And nearly all these cases were described in terms consistent with the conditions for hardiness and resilience. Participants experienced commitment rather than alienation, control rather than powerlessness, and challenge rather than threat. They had passion. They persevered. They didn't give up despite the failures and setbacks. Even in the toughest of times, people can experience meaningfulness and mastery. They can overcome great odds. They can make progress. They can change the way things are. It's your job as a leader to create the conditions in which all this is possible for your constituents.

TAKE ACTION

Experiment and Take Risks

Change is the work of leaders. It's what they do. They are always looking for ways to continuously improve, to grow, and to innovate. They know that the way things are done today won't get people to the tomorrow they envision. So they experiment. They tinker. They shake things up. They ask, "Where are we experimenting and how are we changing?"

But change can overwhelm, frighten, and immobilize some people. Exemplary leaders view change as a challenge that can be successfully overcome. They believe, and get others to believe, that every individual can control his or her own life and influence outcomes. They make sure that the meaning and purpose of change is clearly understood, and they create a strong sense of commitment to the mission.

Use small wins to get things moving in the right direction. Break the tasks down and set short-term goals. Take on a challenge one step at a time. Set up experiments, beta tests, and pilot projects. Taking a little-things approach gets people started, gets them moving, makes progress imaginable, builds commitment, and creates momentum.

Whenever you try new things, big or small, stuff happens so that mistakes are made and failures occur. You never get it right the first time—and may not the second or third time either. That's why exemplary leaders create a climate that's conducive to learning. People have to know that when they experiment and take risks, they won't be punished for failure. Instead failure will be treated as a learning experience. The truth is that the best leaders are the best learners. You need a growth mindset, believing that everyone can improve when he or she puts in the effort to learn. You also need to create a learning climate—one in which everyone is encouraged to share successes and failures, and one in which everyone views continuous improvement as a routine way of doing things. This entails building psychological hardiness and resilience. You have to persist despite the odds. You have to have grit. Exemplary leaders make it a practice to create a climate in which others feel strong and confident, capable of flourishing even under the most adverse circumstances.

To Challenge the Process, you must *experiment and take risks by constantly generating small wins and learning from experience*. This means you need to

- Keep people focused on what they can control in their work and in their lives.
- Assign meaningful work to people so that they can see how their efforts contribute significantly to outcomes.
- Emphasize how personal fulfillment results from constantly challenging oneself to improve.
- Set incremental goals and milestones, breaking big projects down into achievable steps.
- Continuously experiment with new ideas through model sites, pilot projects, market trials, and the like.
- Remind people of the progress they are making every day and that any setbacks are only temporary.
- When mistakes are made, always ask, "What can we learn from this experience?"
- Debrief successes and failures, recording the lessons learned and making sure that they are disseminated broadly.
- Spend time learning something relevant and new every day, and make sure you offer that opportunity to your constituents.
- Accept this mantra: Never stop experimenting.

Use *The Leadership Challenge Mobile Tool* app to immediately integrate these activities into your life and make this practice an ongoing part of your behavioral repertoire.

ENABLE
OTHERS
TO ACT

Leaders know that they can't do it alone. They need partners to make extraordinary things happen in organizations.

Leaders invest in creating trustworthy relationships. They build spirited and cohesive teams, teams that feel like family. They actively involve others in planning and give them the discretion to make their own decisions. Leaders make others feel like owners, not hired hands.

Leaders develop collaborative goals and cooperative relationships with colleagues. They are considerate of the needs and interests of others. They know that these relationships are the keys that unlock support. Leaders bring people together, creating an atmosphere where people understand that they have a shared fate and that they should treat others as they would like to be treated. Leaders make sure that everyone wins.

Mutual respect is what sustains extraordinary group efforts. Leaders nurture self-esteem in others. They make others feel strong, capable, and confident to take both initiative and responsibility. They build the skills and abilities of their constituents to deliver on commitments. They create a climate where people feel in control of their own lives.

In the next two chapters, we will explore how you must

- **Foster Collaboration by building trust and facilitating relationships.**
- **Strengthen Others by increasing self-determination and developing competence.**

CHAPTER 8

Foster Collaboration

"**WE BELIEVE THAT CULTURE** is key to preventing incidents and injuries," Cora Carmody, senior vice president of information technology at Jacobs Engineering, told us. "When we proactively look out for ourselves, our coworkers, our friends and families, then we can get closer to the reality of zero incidents and injuries."

When Cora joined the $10 billion global technical, professional, and construction services company, she found an established culture that was "amazingly positive and based on the importance of people, caring about people, and building and maintaining relationships with people." Given founder Joe Jacobs's vision of "growing globally by taking care of the company's core customers through enduring relationships" and promoting concepts like "boundaryless behavior," it's easy to see how the company's BeyondZero program takes the concept of safety beyond the norm to "a culture of caring."

To take it even further, a couple of years after Cora joined Jacobs, her team rolled out a program titled "Leadership and BeyondZero" to the global IT organization. The hour-and-a-half workshop was designed "to share leadership skills and demonstrate how they contribute to BeyondZero as well as higher levels of achievement in everything we do." Rather than leading the discussions herself or having someone in the training department do it, Cora asked everyone in the first two layers of the IT organization to lead at least one workshop, and to try to ensure that each workshop comprised attendees from a variety of IT groups. In three months, Cora's team involved over eight hundred members of global IT in more than twenty-five different sessions of the workshop. Everyone who led it agreed that he or she got as much out of facilitating the workshop as any of the participants and that the experience remained fresh even when he or she had facilitated multiple times.

It was after facilitating a couple of those discussions that Cora saw a way to address another of IT's critical concerns: strengthening relationships among a staff of eight hundred spread out in offices in more than a hundred countries. At the next workshop, she asked IT people in the room how *they* would feel about leading a fifteen-minute discussion on a leadership topic, at lunch or around a coffee table. She heard a variety of answers: "Scared," "Apprehensive," "Pretty good." Then she asked how they thought the discussion would go with a very small group of people they work with, and how people would feel to be asked for their input and listened to. "Everyone agreed that the outcome of those discussions," Cora explained, "as short as they might be, would have a tremendous positive effect on the quality of our relationships. And that they would continue to build a foundation for a safer, more caring environment." In a follow-up email to her staff summarizing the conversation that day, Cora wrote, "Even more overwhelming would be the sense of accomplishment for the leaders of these discussions. Remember our leadership premise—every last member of the IT team has the potential to be a leader—someone who can alter our attitudes of what is possible." With that opening, Cora's "Coffee Talks" were born. These are discussion questions she emails every couple of weeks to "incite some meaningful dialogue and relationship building" within small groups of IT people around the world.

Here's how it works. Anyone can initiate or host a Coffee Talk. The idea is to find one or several coworkers and ask them a simple question, such as "What do you like to do when you are not at work?" or invite conversation around a particular topic, such as silos. Coffee Talk issues have ranged from workplace safety and the future of IT to work-life balance and building trust. For example, Coffee Talk topic 4 was aimed at stimulating a two-part conversation that, Cora told us, was "all about fostering collaboration and building spirited teams—actively involving others, creating an environment of mutual trust and respect":

> First, around lunch or a coffee (or mocha), brainstorm with a
> few people: what can you do to enhance people's sense of
> contribution and self-worth? Not "What can management do to
> enhance people's sense of contribution and self-worth?"—that's
> not the question. What can *you* do—and what are you willing
> to do?
>
> Then consider a practice that supports collaboration—ask
> for volunteers. When you give people a choice about being a
> part of what's happening, they're more likely to be committed
> to a project. Is there a piece of something you are working on
> that you could open up to others? It could be a great training
> opportunity or just a way to help people feel that they are
> contributing.

As Cora demonstrates with her IT team, leadership is not a solo pursuit. It's a team effort. When talking about personal bests and about leaders they admire, people speak passionately about teamwork and cooperation as the interpersonal route to success, especially when conditions are extremely challenging and urgent. Leaders from all professions, from all economic sectors, and from around the globe continue to tell us, "You can't do it alone."

Exemplary leaders understand that to create a climate of collaboration, they must determine what the group needs in order to do their work, and build the team around common purpose and mutual respect. Leaders make trust and teamwork high priorities. By setting up the workshops and encouraging small-group Coffee Talks around leadership and safety issues, Cora was able to foster cooperation and collaboration within a large, geographically dispersed team. By giving free rein while also providing guidance on issues and topics for engaging coworkers in relationship-building conversations, she helped her team feel that they were trusted and responsible for creating the safer, more caring environment the company valued. By creating opportunities to build their skills, she strengthened their confidence and competence; by asking for regular feedback, she showed that she cared for the team and had their best interests at heart.

World-class performance isn't possible unless there's a strong sense of shared creation and shared responsibility. Exemplary leaders make the commitment to *Foster Collaboration* by engaging in these essentials:

- **CREATE A CLIMATE OF TRUST**
- **FACILITATE RELATIONSHIPS**

Collaboration is a critical competency for achieving and sustaining high performance. As organizations become increasingly diverse and globally dispersed, collaborative skills are essential to navigating the conflicting interests and natural tensions that arise. Trust is required to build collaboration and promote people working cooperatively together. And as employees and customers are more empowered than ever with the new tools of social media, relationship building is at the core of fostering collaboration.

CREATE A CLIMATE OF TRUST

The ever-increasing turbulence in the marketplace demands even more collaboration, not less.[1] The emphasis on networks, business-to-business and peer-to-peer e-commerce, strategic acquisitions, knowledge work, open source innovation, and social media, along with the surging number of global alliances and local partnerships, is testimony to the fact that in an ever more complex, wired world, the winning strategies will be based on a "We not I" philosophy.

However, "we" can't happen without trust. It's the central issue in human relationships. Without trust you cannot lead. Without trust you can't get people to believe in you or in each other. Without trust you cannot accomplish extraordinary things. Individuals who are unable to trust others fail to become leaders, precisely because they can't bear to be dependent on the words and works of others. They either end up doing all the work themselves or supervising work so closely that they become overcontrolling. Their obvious lack of trust in others results in others' lack of trust in them. To build and sustain social connections, you have to be able to trust others, and others have to trust you. Trust is not just what's in your mind; it's also what's in your heart.

Invest in Trust

Trust is a strong, significant predictor of employee satisfaction, the quality of communication, honest sharing of information, acceptance of change, acceptance of the leader's influence, and team and organizational performance.[2] Trust is also linked to profitability. High-trust organizations have been shown to outperform low-trust organizations by 286 percent.[3] And in a PricewaterhouseCoopers study on corporate innovation in companies listed on the Financial Times 100, trust was "the number one differentiator" between the top 20 percent of companies surveyed and the bottom 20 percent. The more trusted people feel, the better they innovate.[4] Simply put, the more people trust their leaders and their organizations, the more positive the outcomes—for everyone.

Psychologists have also found that people who are trusting are more likely to be happy and psychologically adjusted than are those who view the world with suspicion and distrust.[5] People who are perceived as trusting are more sought out as friends, more frequently listened to, and subsequently more influential. The most effective leadership situations are those in which each member of the team trusts the others.

In a classic research experiment, for example, several groups of business executives in a role-playing exercise were given identical factual information about a difficult manufacturing-marketing policy decision and then asked as a group to solve a problem related to that information. Half of the groups were briefed to expect trustworthy behavior ("You have learned from your past experiences that you can trust the other members of top management and can openly express feelings and differences with them"); the other half, to expect untrustworthy behavior. After thirty minutes of discussion, all team members completed a brief questionnaire about their experiences.[6]

Those who'd been told that their role-playing colleagues could be trusted reported their discussion and decisions to be significantly more positive than did the members of the low-trust group on every factor measured. The members of the high-trust group were more open about feelings, experienced greater clarity about the group's basic problems and goals, and searched more for alternative courses of action. They also reported greater levels of mutual influence on outcomes, satisfaction with the meeting, motivation to implement decisions, and closeness as a management team as a result of the meeting. In the groups whose participants were told that their management colleagues weren't to be trusted, genuine attempts to be open and honest were ignored or distorted.

The managers who experienced rejection of their attempts to be trusting and open responded in kind. "If I had my way I would have fired the entire group," said one. "What a bunch of turkeys. I was trying to be honest with them but they wouldn't cooperate. Everything I suggested they shot down; and they wouldn't give me any ideas on how to solve the problem." The responses of the other members were no less hostile: "Frankly, I was looking forward to your being fired. I was sick of working with you—and we had only been together for ten minutes." Not surprisingly, more than two-thirds of the participants in the low-trust group said that they would give serious consideration to looking for another position.[7]

Keep in mind that this was a *simulation*. These real-life executives responded as they did simply because they'd been *told* that they couldn't trust their role-playing colleagues. It shows that trust, or distrust, can come with a mere suggestion—and in mere minutes.

After this simulation, participants were asked to think about what factors might have accounted for the differences between the outcomes and feelings reported by the various groups. Not one person perceived that trust had been the overriding variable. "I never knew that a lack of trust was our problem [at work] until that exercise," reported one executive in the study. "I knew that things weren't going well, but I never really could quite understand why we couldn't work well together. After that experience, things fell into place."[8]

When you create a climate of trust, you create an environment that allows people to freely contribute and innovate. You nurture an open exchange of ideas and a truthful discussion of issues. You motivate people to go beyond compliance and inspire them to reach for the best in themselves. And you nurture the belief that people can rely on you to do what's in everyone's best interests. To get these kinds of results, you have to ante up first in the game of trust, you have to listen and learn from others, and you have to share information and resources with others. Trust comes first; following comes second.

Be the First to Trust

Building trust is a process that begins when someone (either you or the other party) is willing to risk being the first to open up, to show vulnerability, and to let go of control. Leaders go first. If you want the high levels of performance that come with trust and collaboration, you will have to demonstrate your trust in others before asking them to trust you.

Going first is a scary proposition. You're taking a chance. You're betting that others won't betray your confidence and that they'll take good care of the information you communicate, the resources you allocate, and the feelings you share. You're risking that others won't take advantage of you and that you can rely on them to do what's right. This requires considerable self-confidence. But the payoff is huge. Trust is contagious. When you trust others, they are much more likely to trust you. But should you choose not to trust, understand that distrust is equally contagious. If you exhibit distrust, others will hesitate to place their trust in you and in their colleagues. It's up to you to set the example.

Self-disclosure is one way that you go first. Letting others know what you stand for, what you value, what you want, what you hope for, and what you're willing (and not willing) to do discloses information about yourself. You can't be certain that other people will appreciate your candor, agree with your aspirations, or interpret your words and actions in the way you intend. But once you take the risk of being open, others are more likely to take a similar risk and work toward mutual understanding.

This is exactly what Masood Fakharzadeh, program manager at KLA-Tencor, experienced when he was asked to assemble an offshore product development team. In order to develop trust, he told us, "Early on I asked everyone for their help. I told them that this is the first time that I'm leading such a project, and I needed their help and expertise to make the project successful. I wanted to show them that I had full trust in them by asking them to help me." Masood reported that his demonstration of trust in them "resulted, in turn, in people opening up and sharing lots of information. This got them fully engaged, and they took ownership."

Trust can't be forced, however. If someone is bent on misunderstanding you and refuses to perceive you as either well intentioned or competent, there may be little you can do to change that perception. However, you have to remember that placing trust in others is the safer bet with most people most of the time. Humans are hardwired to trust: they have to trust in order to function effectively in the world.[9]

Show Concern for Others

The concern you show for others is one of the clearest and most unambiguous signals of your trust. When others know you will put their interests ahead of your own, they won't hesitate to trust you.[10] But this concern is something people have to see in your actions.

You have to listen to others, pay attention to their ideas and concerns, help them solve their problems, and be open to their influence. When you show your openness to their ideas and your interest in their concerns, your constituents will be more open to *yours.*

The simple act of listening to what other people have to say and appreciating their unique points of view demonstrates your respect for them and their ideas. Being sensitive to what others are going through creates bonds that make it easier to accept one another's guidance and advice. These actions build mutual empathy and understanding, and that in turn builds trust. Sinisa Ljujic, assistant production manager for manufacturing at Canada's Christie Digital, a leader in the digital cinema and digital display technology market, commented, "For the sake of the people you lead, you need to be accepting of others as they are. We are all human, and we need to treat people respectfully. I listen to what people have to say so that I know what is going on in their heads and hearts. Only then can I work with them to improve."[11]

His respectfulness and listening are evident every day on the floor with his team. You see it when he encourages people to solve problems on their own, rather than jumping in to solve them himself. You see it when he arrives early to greet everyone and inquire about how he or she is doing. You see it when he takes the time to coach people who are assuming new jobs and responsibilities. For example, when Samieh Bagheri became a new manager, she needed to learn how to motivate and inspire her new employees. She was young and dedicated, and wanted to do more in her job. At times she probably took on more than she was ready to handle. Sinisa spent considerable time with Samieh, asking her questions and listening to her thoughts about how she should approach her leadership. He worked with her on the smaller issues of communication and handling the day-to-day issues. Once she had these mastered, he began coaching on conflict management and other more difficult topics. Even when his approach might have been different from Samieh's, he supported her decisions in front of others and then coached her privately about other possible approaches.

In turn, Samieh's regard for Sinisa grew and is quite evident when she says, "He's a great leader. He has great knowledge and understanding of all of the processes in our department and is great at communicating. He has compassion for all his employees, and great personal skills. His happy attitude is contagious." Sinisa's own manager, Paul Tierney, echoes this sentiment: "He encourages his people to be independent. He coaches people respectfully in a manner that makes them feel that next time they will be able to do it on their own."

Leaders like Sinisa demonstrate how powerful listening and empathy can be in building trust.[12] You need to see the world through others' eyes and make sure that you consider alternative viewpoints. Your constituents have to feel that they can talk freely with you about their difficulties. For them to be open to sharing their ideas, their frustrations, and their dreams with you, they have to believe that you'll be caring and constructive in your responses; they have to feel that you know them.

It's interesting how these same skills of nonjudgmental listening and compassion show up in the people referred to as friends—and every successful leadership relationship has some element of friendship in it. Although it's not expected that you'll be everyone's best friend, researchers have demonstrated across a variety of settings that having a friend at work and having a friendly relationship with your supervisor contribute significantly to healthy and productive workplaces.[13] Controlled experiments also bear this out. For example, in one management simulation, whenever the person assuming the role of CEO was informed that the financial vice president was a "friend," the latter's influence was far more readily accepted than when their relationship was merely professional—even though in all cases the "information" presented was adequate to solve the company's problem.[14] When people believe that you have their interests at heart—that you care about them—they're more likely to have your interests at heart as well.

Share Knowledge and Information

Competence is a vital component of trust and confidence in a leader. People have to believe that you know what you're talking about and that you know what you're doing. One way to demonstrate your competence is to share what you know and encourage others to do the same. You can convey your insights and know-how, share lessons learned from experience, and connect team members to expertise. Leaders who play this role of knowledge builder set the example for how team members should behave toward each other. As a result, team members' trust in one another and in the leader increases, along with their performance.[15]

That was exactly the approach Darrell Klotzbach took with his unit at Adobe. When he hired a new college graduate, for example, he knew "that the work and load were going to be overwhelming, so I had to pace her adjustment into the role." He trained and coached her in the role, giving her difficult problems to solve that he had worked on in the past. "I didn't provide solutions," says Darrell, "only guidance when she got stuck." When he assigned work to her, he said,

> I did not tell her specifically what to do, but rather set out to provide direction by sharing a vision of the goal of the work. I

gave her the freedom to act how she saw fit. The main requirement was, if she got stuck, she should come to me rather than continue to be stuck, and we would work it out. I kept an open door. In addition, I had her join me in meetings with the teams I was supporting so she could see what was being requested and how I, but eventually we, would handle these. After a while, I began asking her to take on tasks to support those efforts; and, of course, I publicly gave her credit when it was her work that accomplished results.

Shortly thereafter, nearing the end of a particularly difficult release cycle, Darrell's team was loaned two people from another team to aid their efforts. What did Darrell do? Once again, he began by asking them about their interests and what they wanted to learn, and by making sure that they understood that they were contributing something valuable—and that they, too, were valuable. Darrell modeled the value of collaboration by sharing information and teaching others techniques that he knew. He connected people in his area with those outside whom he thought folks needed to know and could learn from. He also spent time, in his words, "wandering around the shop floor so that I could pick up informal pieces of information that would be valuable for the team to know." He would bring this news back and share it with everyone during meetings so that everyone could be as informed and up-to-date as he was about what was going on. Indeed, Darrell did such a good job sharing with others what he knew that when he took a sabbatical leave, despite some concerns about the timing, they managed, Darrell boasts, "to continue in my absence without needing to contact me during my time off."

The fact that trust among team members goes up when knowledge and information are shared, and the fact that performance increases as a result, underscore how important it is for leaders to stay focused on the needs of their team. If you show a willingness to trust others with information (both personal and professional), constituents will be more inclined to overcome any doubts they might have about sharing information. But if you display a reluctance to trust, and withhold information—or if you're overly concerned about protecting your turf and keeping things to yourself—you'll have a dampening effect on their trust and their performance. Managers who create distrustful environments often take self-protective postures. They're directive and hold tight to the reins of power. Those who work for such managers are likely to pass the distrust on by withholding and distorting information.[16] This just reinforces why it's so important for you to go first when it comes to sharing information.

FACILITATE RELATIONSHIPS

People work together most effectively when they trust one another. Asking for help and sharing information then come naturally. Setting a common goal becomes almost intuitive. Certainly these were the lessons Cristian Nuñez shared in analyzing his experience as deputy manager for business development at Ultramar Agencia Maritima (Chile), where he was responsible for the growth of the national logistics unit. This unit was formed by eighteen fairly independent agencies scattered along the primary ports of the country, and their main business was to assist arriving ships with their every need in terms of customs paperwork and additional services for the crew and the ship. After a number of successful years, revenues had stalled and margins were in decline. Cristian recalled,

After little less than a month in this position I realized what kept the logistics unit from growing was—itself! Evaluation purely based on bottom-line figures had generated a strong sense of competition between agencies, basically freezing cooperation between them. In fact, whenever cooperation was required, agencies would normally charge each other the market fee (sometimes even higher) that evidently left them with the highest prices in the market. Furthermore, a rather detached managerial style from the head office had generated some mistrust toward it from the agencies (and vice versa), having both parties thinking the other was not doing enough to improve business figures.

Cristian realized that the first thing he needed to do was to improve communication at all levels because without that, there could be no common goal or cooperation between units. So both he and his supervisor went to each of the agency sites to sit down and visit with the people involved. "I learned," recalls Cristian, "how much relationships can improve when people meet face-to-face, even if they'd been talking on the phone almost every day. The power and long-lasting effect of direct interaction can hardly be replaced by other means of communication."

They subsequently brought together people from each of the agencies to talk about the problem and propose solutions. Given this opportunity to work together, they quickly realized the need to align incentives to favor a collective way of doing business and came up with a profit-sharing method for collaborative deals. They also agreed to have all the agents participate in weekly telephone meetings in which they were expected to comment on business opportunities in their own as well as others' territories. Because all agencies took part in these meetings, everyone knew where the ideas came from, and it was easy to distribute profits. This action, says Cristian, boosted communication between agencies because "everyone wanted to be the first to come up with new business opportunities and get some of the credit for it." These collaborative experiences were so rewarding that after a while, agencies started sharing tips directly, without the need for any assistance from Christian and his team.

To collaborate, as Cristian discovered, people have to rely and depend on one another. They have to know that they need each other to be successful. To create conditions in which people know they can count on each other, a leader needs to develop cooperative goals and roles, support norms of reciprocity, structure projects to promote joint efforts, and support face-to-face interactions.

Develop Cooperative Goals and Roles

Whether they are in sports or health care, in education or management, or in the public or private sector, for a team of people to have a positive experience together they must have shared goals that provide a specific reason for being together. No one person can single-handedly educate a child, build a quality car, make a movie, create a world-class guest experience, connect a customer to the Internet, or eradicate a disease. The most important ingredient in every collective achievement is a common goal. Common purpose binds people into cooperative efforts.[17] It creates a sense of interdependence, a condition in which all participants know that they cannot succeed unless everyone else succeeds, or at least that they can't succeed unless they coordinate their efforts. If there's not a sense that "we're all in this together"—that the success of one depends on the success of the other—then it's virtually impossible to create the conditions for positive teamwork. If you want individuals or groups to work cooperatively, you have to give them a good reason to do so, and that good reason is generally expressed as a goal that can only be accomplished by working together.

This is exactly what Tyson Marsh recalls about his personal-best leadership experience, an effort to set up a rescue relief area in a "filthy and disorganized public school" following the horrific events of September 11, 2001. Tyson understood that to accomplish this task, he needed many people with a variety of talents and motivations to work together; he knew that this would require them all to have the same end goal in mind. Tyson wasn't anyone's boss, and he had no formal authority. He was just a volunteer like everyone else. But he saw an opportunity to make a difference.

"If I was going to get this done," Tyson said, "I would need supplies, support, and, above all, I needed other volunteers to get on board." Six young volunteers approached Tyson and asked what he would like them to do: "I took the time with each one to explain what needed to be done in order to transform this space, and each time they would listen, ask questions, and make suggestions of their own. We listened to one another's ideas, incorporating them into an overall plan which everyone felt a sense of ownership for. Within an hour, we were a team of excited and energetic volunteers ready to work hard, stretching our comfort zones to work together toward a common goal."

Tyson explained that everyone kept checking in with each other as tasks got accomplished. The team kept everything out in the open, helping maintain both a high level of trust and an appreciation for their interconnectedness. People did whatever they could do to help without being asked, and when faced with any challenges, they figured out for themselves what needed to be done. "Whether it was moving tables, removing trash, or folding blankets, every task felt important, and you could use your own creativity to solve problems." Together they turned a dirty and disheveled school cafeteria into a clean, organized oasis where weary rescue workers could get a hot meal, take a nap, and escape, even for a moment, the grim reality of their task at Ground Zero.

Tyson, like other leaders we studied, realized that keeping individuals focused on a common goal promoted a stronger sense of teamwork than emphasizing individual objectives. For cooperation to succeed, roles must also be designed so that every person's contributions are both additive and cumulative to the final outcome. Individuals must clearly understand that unless they each contribute whatever they can, the team fails. It's like putting together a jigsaw puzzle. Each person has a piece, and if even one piece is missing, the puzzle is impossible to complete.[18]

Support Norms of Reciprocity

In any effective long-term relationship, there must be a sense of reciprocity. If one partner always gives and the other always takes, the one who gives will feel taken advantage of, and the one who takes will feel superior. In such a climate, cooperation is virtually impossible. University of Michigan political scientist Robert Axelrod dramatically demonstrated the power of reciprocity in the well-known study of what's known as the Prisoner's Dilemma.[19] The dilemma is this: two parties (individuals or groups) are confronted with a series of situations in which they must decide whether or not to cooperate. They don't know in advance what the other party will do. There are two basic strategies—cooperate or compete—and four possible outcomes based on the choices players make: win-lose, lose-win, lose-lose, and win-win.

The maximum *individual* payoff comes when the first player selects an uncooperative strategy and the second player chooses to cooperate in good faith. In this "I win but you lose" approach, one party gains at the other's expense. If both parties choose not to cooperate and attempt to maximize individual payoffs, then both lose. If both parties choose to cooperate, both win, though the individual payoff for a cooperative move is less than for a competitive one (in the short run).

Bob invited scientists from around the world to submit their strategies for winning in a computer simulation of this test of win-win versus win-lose strategies. "Amazingly enough," says Bob, "the winner was the simplest of all strategies submitted: cooperate on the first move and then do whatever the other player did on the previous move. This strategy succeeded by eliciting cooperation from others, not by defeating them."[20] Simply put, people who reciprocate are more likely to be successful than those who try to maximize individual advantage.

The dilemmas that can be successfully solved by this strategy are by no means restricted to theoretical research. Similar predicaments arise every day: Should I try to maximize my own personal gain? What price might I pay for this action? Should I give up a little for the sake of others? Will others take advantage of me if I'm cooperative? Reciprocity turns out to be the most successful approach for such daily decisions, because it demonstrates both a willingness to be cooperative and an unwillingness to be taken advantage of. As a long-term strategy, reciprocity minimizes the risk of escalation: If people know that you'll respond in kind, why would they start trouble? And if people know that you'll reciprocate, they know that the best way to deal with you is to cooperate and become recipients of your cooperation.

Reciprocity leads to predictability and stability in relationships. It's less stressful to work with others when you understand how they will behave in response—especially to your own behavior in negotiations and disagreements.[21] Harvard professor of public policy

Robert Putnam explains, "The norm of generalized reciprocity is so fundamental to civilized life that all prominent moral codes contain some equivalent of the Golden Rule."[22] When you treat others as you'd like for them to treat you, it's likely that they'll repay you many times over.

This was precisely Florian Bennhold's reaction after interviewing with Wilson Rickerson, who ran his own consulting business on energy policy issues. "Wilson built our relationship on trust," says Florian. "He made clear that he was willing to take the first step. After a few hours, he invited me to work on a project with him, and he immediately started sharing his contacts with me mainly through direct introductions. I remember telling my wife how excited I was to work with him because I felt that he trusted my abilities." And the payoff was clear: "I knew that because of Wilson's trust, support, and the way he made me feel, I performed better than I ever expected." What's more, says Florian, "I felt compelled to reciprocate Wilson's trust."

Once you help others succeed, acknowledge their accomplishments, and help them shine, they'll never forget it. The "norm of reciprocity" comes into play, and they are more than willing to return the favor. Whether the rewards of cooperation are tangible or intangible, when people understand that they will be better off by cooperating, they're inclined to recognize the legitimacy of others' interests in an effort to promote their own welfare.

Structure Projects to Promote Joint Effort

People are more likely to cooperate if the payoffs for interdependent efforts are greater than those associated with working independently. Many people growing up in Westernized countries that emphasize individualistic or competitive achievement have the perception that they'll do better if everyone were each rewarded solely based on his or her individual accomplishments. They're wrong. In a world that's trying to do more with less, competitive strategies lose to strategies that promote collaboration.[23]

The motivation for working diligently on one's own job while keeping in mind the overall common objective is reinforced when it is the end result that gets rewarded and not simply individual efforts. Most profit-sharing plans, for example, are based on meeting the company's goals and not simply those of separate independent units or departments. Certainly each individual within the group has a distinct role, but on world-class teams, everyone knows that if he only does his individual part well, he is unlikely to achieve the group's goal. After all, if you could do it alone, why would you need a team? Soccer isn't a one-on-eleven sport; hockey isn't one-on-six; baseball isn't one-on-nine; basketball isn't one-on-five.[24] These sports require team effort—as do all organizational achievements.

Cooperative behavior requires individuals to understand that by working together they will be able to accomplish something that no one can accomplish on his or her own. Jim Vesterman considered himself a reasonably good team player, yet he learned an indelible lesson in the power of group effort when he joined the Marine Corps.[25] It started on his first day of boot camp at Parris Island as he and his fellow recruits learned to make their beds—when Jim learned that you can't survive without helping the guys next to you. His experience went something like this: the men are told that their objective is to have every bed in the platoon made; the drill instructor begins counting, and everyone has three minutes to make his bed ("hospital corners and the proverbial quarter bounce"); they step back in line when done. So, Jim explains, he made his bed, stepped back in line, and felt "pretty proud, because when three minutes were up, there weren't more than ten men who had finished." However, the drill instructor wasn't handing out any congratulations; rather, he was shouting out that they had all day to get this right, looking at all the beds that were unfinished.

Jim ripped off the sheets again . . . and again, and again. Finally the drill instructor looked him in the eye and pointed out, "Your bunkmate isn't done. What are you doing?" Apparently, Jim had been thinking that he was done while his bunkmate struggled. Finally, the light dawned on Jim, and working together with his bunkmate, they made both beds, and much faster than they had each done on his own. Still, not everyone in the platoon was finishing on time. The two of them looked at one another and realized that although they might be done, they had to help their buddies next to them, and then those next to them, and so on. Jim went from thinking that he'd do as good a job as he could on his assignment to "making beds for *anyone* who needed help" and appreciating that they were all in this together.[26]

You can also structure joint efforts by emphasizing long-term rather than short-term payoffs. That is, make certain that the long-term benefits of mutual cooperation are greater than the short-term benefits of working alone or competing with others. You need to get people to realize that by working together they can complete the project faster than by thinking about any short-term (or individual) victories resulting from doing their own thing or complaining or blaming or competing with others for scarce resources.

Support Face-to-Face Interactions

Group goals and roles, shared identity, reciprocity, and promoting joint effort are all essential for collaboration to occur, but positive face-to-face interaction is also vital. People can act as a cohesive team only when they can have some amount of face time with each other.

This is true not only locally but also in globally distributed relationships. Getting to know others firsthand is vital to cultivating trust and collaboration. And this need for face-to-face communication increases with the complexity of the issues,[27] as Wilson Chu, program manager at RingCentral, realized: "Until you see someone's face, they are not a real person to you."

This is why while managing an offshore development team, he asked people to turn on their webcams so that everyone could see one another. He felt that this made "everyone more comfortable with expressing their ideas because it made the interactions more personal—we each had more than just a name; we also had a face." It's the leader's job, as Wilson points out, to provide frequent and lasting opportunities for team members to associate and intermingle among disciplines, among departments, and across continents. Technology and social media can certainly enhance communications. Virtual connections abound, and in a global economy, no organization could function if people had to fly halfway around the world to exchange information, make decisions, or resolve disputes. That said, the stroke of a key, the click of a mouse, or the switch of a video doesn't get you the same results as an intimate in-person conversation. There are limits to virtual trust. Firsthand experience with another human being is just a more reliable way of creating identification, increasing adaptability, and reducing misunderstandings.[28]

Virtual trust, like virtual reality, is one step removed from the real thing. Human beings are social animals; it's in people's nature to want to interact, and bits and bytes make for a very weak social foundation.[29] It's certainly true that work relationships in today's global economy depend more and more on electronic connections, and many work "places" are virtual in nature. But you have to reconcile the reality of virtual organizations with the knowledge that building trust depends on getting to know one another deeply. In addition to relying on emails, instant messages, teleconferences, and videoconferences, you need to look to other technologies such as the bike, the car, the train, and the airplane.

People who expect durable, frequent face-to-face interactions in the future are more likely to cooperate in the present. Knowing that you'll have to deal again with someone tomorrow, next week, or next year ensures that you won't easily forget about how you've treated him and how he's treated you. This makes the impact of today's actions on tomorrow's dealings that much more pronounced. In addition, frequent interactions between people promote positive feelings on the part of each for the other. Encouraging people to transfer between team sites for a period of time ensures familiarity with the culture and practices of their peers. This notion of durable interactions may seem quaint and anachronistic in this global economic environment, in which speed is a competitive advantage and loyalty is no longer a strong virtue. But that doesn't make the reality disappear. Begin with the assumption that in the future you'll be interacting with this person again in some way and that this relationship will be important to your mutual success.

TAKE ACTION

Foster Collaboration

"You can't do it alone" is the mantra of exemplary leaders—and for good reason. You simply can't get extraordinary things done by yourself. Collaboration is the master skill that enables corporations, communities, and even classrooms to function effectively. Collaboration is sustained when you create a climate of trust and facilitate effective long-term relationships among your constituents. You have to promote a sense of mutual dependence—feeling part of a group in which everyone knows he or she needs the others to be successful. Without that sense of "we're all in this together," it's virtually impossible to keep effective teamwork going.

Trust is the lifeblood of collaborative teamwork. To create and sustain the conditions for long-lasting connections, you have to be able to trust others, they have to trust you, and they have to trust each other. Without trust you cannot lead, or get great things accomplished. Share information and knowledge freely with your constituents, show that you understand their needs and interests, open up to their influence, make wise use of their abilities and expertise, and—most of all—demonstrate that you trust them before you ask them to trust you.

The challenge in facilitating relationships is making sure people recognize how much they need one another to excel—how interdependent they really are. Cooperative goals and roles contribute to a sense of collective purpose, and the best incentive for people to work to achieve shared goals is the knowledge that you and others will reciprocate, helping them in return. Help begets help, just as trust begets trust. By supporting norms of reciprocity and structuring projects to reward joint efforts, you enable people to clearly understand that it's in their best interest to cooperate. Get people interacting and encourage face-to-face interactions as often as possible to reinforce the durability of relationships.

Exemplary leaders Foster Collaboration *by building trust and facilitating relationships*. This means you need to

- Explicitly say to your constituents, "I trust you." Saying it matters, and, obviously, you'd better mean it.
- Extend trust to others first, even if they haven't already extended it to you.
- Share information about yourself—your hopes, your strengths, your fears, your mistakes—the things that make you who you are.
- Spend time getting to know your constituents and find out what makes them tick.
- Show concern for the problems and aspirations others have.
- Listen, listen, and listen some more.
- Put the interests of the organization and of your constituents ahead of your own.
- Clearly articulate and frequently repeat the common goal that you are all striving to achieve, the shared values that are important, and the larger purpose of which everyone is a part.
- Do someone a favor. If he or she does one for you, reciprocate.
- Structure projects so that there is a common goal that requires cooperation.
- Make sure that people understand how they are interdependent with one another.
- Find ways to get people together face-to-face.

Use *The Leadership Challenge Mobile Tool* app to immediately integrate these activities into your life and make this practice an ongoing part of your behavioral repertoire.

CHAPTER 9

Strengthen Others

CASEY MORK AND HIS COLLEAGUES weren't quite sure what to make of their new manager. Initially they complained a lot because he didn't seem to be making decisions for them, and he didn't provide detailed instructions about how they should improve or change a document, as their previous manager had done. He also shared lots of "high-up information," which again, their previous manager had not bothered them with. He seemed a bit distant and didn't "get into the weeds" with his team members.

But as time went on, Casey realized that "this new fellow had really trusted us right from the start," and although initially his trust gave them the idea that they could get away with anything, they "learned that he knew enough about us that we weren't likely to sink the ship." As a consequence, a great deal more collaboration started to emerge between teams. They began talking with each other a lot more, and team members got to see each other in a whole new light. Because people started to gain a much better understanding of what they could deliver on and what they couldn't, fewer postsale complications arose, and productivity started to go up.

Unlike their previous manager, their new manager facilitated relationships and broke down barriers between functional groups. He offered them the chance to create their own boundaries, and they discovered that they needed relatively few to be effective. He shared information, involved people in discussions and deliberations, and allowed them discretion over their own decisions. As a result, Casey and his team began to realize that the team was accountable for their own success and failure. They became more self-determining. Casey observed that

> our team suddenly felt much more powerful as a result of this transfer of decision making. His praise began to look more like a conveyance of power. When he told us a project looked fantastic, and that he hadn't put much supervision into it, it made us feel like we created something, instead of executed on someone else's plan.
>
> He shared his power with us, which led to an increased ability and desire to execute. The previous manager kept the decision making to herself, didn't wholly trust us, and turned out to serve as not much more than a bottleneck. Given more opportunities to be self-directed and make real decisions, we began to gain this incredible new sense of competence and confidence—because we knew our success and failure was on us and us alone.

Looking back on this experience, Casey reflected about how "real latitude and not supervision allowed for the most efficient means of collaboration." Transferring power to group members, he noted, "also conveys trust, which will almost always lead to a better work product." Casey realized that the most effective leaders help people both feel and be more powerful and able to make things happen on their own.

Casey's experience illustrates how exemplary leaders make a commitment to *Strengthen Others*. They enable people to take ownership of and responsibility for their group's success by enhancing their competence and their confidence in their abilities, by listening to their ideas and acting on them, by involving them in important decisions, and by acknowledging and giving credit for their contributions.

Creating a climate in which people are fully engaged and feel in control of their own lives is at the heart of strengthening others. Exemplary leaders build an environment that develops both people's abilities to perform a task and their self-confidence. In a climate of competence and confidence, people don't hesitate to hold themselves personally accountable for results, and they feel profound ownership for their achievements.

To Strengthen Others, exemplary leaders engage in two essentials. They

- **ENHANCE SELF-DETERMINATION**
- **DEVELOP COMPETENCE AND CONFIDENCE**

Leaders significantly increase people's belief in their own ability to make a difference. They move from being *in control* to *giving over control* to others. becoming their coach. They help others learn new skills, develop existing talents, and provide the institutional supports required for ongoing growth and change. In the final analysis, leaders turn their constituents into leaders.

ENHANCE SELF-DETERMINATION

Leaders accept and act on the paradox of power: you become more powerful when you give your own power away. Long before empowerment was written into the popular vocabulary, exemplary leaders understood how important it was for their constituents to feel strong, capable, and efficacious. Constituents who feel weak, incompetent, and insignificant will consistently underperform; they want to flee the organization and are ripe for disenchantment, even revolution.

People who are not confident about their power, regardless of their organizational position or place, tend to hoard whatever shreds of influence they have. Powerless managers tend to adopt petty and dictatorial styles. Powerlessness also creates organizational systems in which political skills are essential, and "covering your backside" and "passing the buck" are the preferred modes of handling interdepartmental differences.[1]

To get a better sense of how it feels to be powerless as well as powerful, we've asked thousands of people over the past thirty years to tell us about their own experiences of being in these situations. Think of actions or situations that have made you feel powerless, weak, or insignificant, like a pawn in someone else's chess game. Are they similar to what others have reported?

Representative Actions and Conditions That People Report Make Them Feel *Powerless*

"No one was interested in, listened to, or paid attention to my opinion."

"People ignored or wouldn't answer my questions."

"I had no input into a hiring decision of someone who was to report directly to me."

"People picked me apart while I was making a presentation."

"My boss argued with me in front of my colleagues—even called me names."

"My decisions were not supported by my boss, even though he said he would back me up."

"Someone else took credit for my hard work and results."

"Information essential to my work was withheld, or I was out of the loop and the last to know key data that impacted my performance."

"My supervisor did not care for me as an individual."

"The manager belittled my skills, said she didn't feel that I would be able to be successful on this project, and made me feel insignificant."

"My supervisor pushed me to do things but wasn't willing to do them himself."

"I was given responsibility but no authority to hold others accountable."

"She made sly or negative remarks about my performance."

"My boss played favorites, and I wasn't one of them!"

Now think about what it's like when you feel powerful—strong, efficacious, like the creator of your own experience. Are your recollections similar to what others have experienced?

Representative Actions and Conditions That People Report Make Them Feel *Powerful*

"All the financial data were shared with me."

"I was asked to take on an important project that I had never done before."

"I was able to exercise my discretion about how we would handle a difficult, and delicate, situation."

"My manager (parent, teacher, coach, mentor) told me that I had great potential and that he/she believed in me."

"I was able to make decisions about key aspects of the project."

"The organization invested resources in helping me to learn how to do this job, or solve this problem, more effectively."

"My manager publicly expressed great confidence in my ability to handle the assignment."

"My supervisor told others about the great work I was doing."

"My boss showed appreciation and respect to me and my teammates."

"He took the time to let me know how I was doing and where I could be improving."

"She gave me the chance to both learn new skills and the opportunities to apply them."

As you examine what people say about powerless and powerful times, there is one clear and consistent message: *feeling powerful—literally feeling "able"—comes from a deep sense of being in control of your own life.* People everywhere share this fundamental need. When you feel able to determine your own destiny, when you believe you are able to mobilize the resources and support necessary to complete a task, then you will persist in your efforts to achieve. But when you feel controlled by others, when you believe that you lack support or resources, you show little commitment to excel. Even though you may comply, you still realize how much more you could contribute, if you wanted to.

Liz Wiseman, author and former Oracle vice president, makes similar points in her research about "Multipliers"—leaders who make everyone around them smarter—versus "Diminishers"—leaders who drain the energy and capability of those around them. Multipliers, she observes, invest in the success of others, and although they may jump in to teach and share their ideas, they always maintain the ownership and accountability that others have. Failing to do so creates dependency, and is the way of the Diminishers. They jump in, save the day, drive results through their personal involvement, and remind everyone how much smarter and more capable they are than everyone else is or even could be. In strengthening others, leaders adopt the assumptions of Multipliers, believing in essence that "people are smart and will figure it out" and that they "will get even smarter in the process."[2]

Any leadership practice that increases others' sense of self-determination, self-confidence, and personal effectiveness makes them more powerful and greatly enhances the possibility of their success.[3] Self-determination can be enhanced in a number of ways, based on three core principles which ensure that people are able to decide for themselves: choice, latitude, and personal accountability.

Provide Choices

Researchers use the term "organizational citizenship behavior" to describe those actions that employees take that are above and beyond their job descriptions or task requirements—that make the difference between ordinary and extraordinary individual and organizational performance.[4] These kinds of actions are illustrated in this story from Tim Haun, a personal trainer with the Decathlon Club, after he and his team experienced a change in senior management.[5]

One of the first changes the new leaders made was to set up a structure so that the trainers could earn health benefits, vacation time, and sick time. This change established a baseline level of trust, and showed the trainers that the new leadership cared about them and had their best interests and needs in mind. Monthly goals for the group were set around the number of hours worked, and this required trainers to set individual goals for themselves and to be responsible for recruiting clients to fill that number of hours. Their individual goals and the actual number of hours that each trainer worked were announced at monthly meetings. This newly required accountability and responsibility made all the trainers feel more in charge of their own destiny. They felt as though they were each running his or her own business within the larger business, which enhanced their own sense of control and power. In addition to this, the company hosted continuing education workshops, free of charge, at various points during the year. Trainers could choose to attend these events or not, but most of them did.

Trainers began suggesting ideas at their monthly team meetings, and many of them were implemented. For example, all the trainers had to wear uniforms, but there was a lag time before their new uniforms arrived, so one trainer suggested that they create shirts with different slogans on them each month, which they did for several months, with different people suggesting various slogans. Another trainer suggested that they start an "every trainer needs a trainer program," in which they trained each other. During the implementation of this program, they learned different training tips and tricks from each other and were able to observe each other at work, thus building their confidence in one another as a team.

The result, according to Tim, was an increase in their overall total number of billable hours (and thus salaries); giving the trainers choices built their commitment and productivity. As this story shows, leaders exercise guided autonomy: although they do set standards and hold everyone accountable for shared values and visions, they still give people the opportunity to make choices about how they will reach these objectives.

You want people to take initiative and be self-directed. You want them to think for themselves and not continually ask someone else, "What should I do?" This ability cannot be developed if you tell people what to do and how to do it. They really can't learn to act independently unless they get to exercise some degree of choice. If they have no freedom of choice and can act only in ways prescribed by the organization, then how can they respond when the customer or another employee behaves in ways that aren't in the script? If they have to ask the "boss" what to do—even if they think they know what needs to be done and feel they could do it—then they are going to be slowing down the entire organization. And if their boss doesn't know, then the boss will have to ask his or her manager. And up the ladder it goes. The only way to create an efficient and effective organization is to give people the chance to use their best judgment in applying their knowledge and skills. This implies, of course, that you've prepared them to make these choices and that you've educated them in the guiding principles of the organization.

Consider how Aruba Networks has done away completely with its vacation policy.[6] Like most every company, they used to spend a great deal of time and energy keeping track and reporting about vacations. Today they simply tell every employee to take his vacation when he needs it, for as long as he needs it, and the only proviso is that he has to make sure that the time off won't interfere with his work getting done. When you give people choices, they will find it harder to blame "the company" (or management) when things don't go their way or when they don't like the way things are going; because, after all, if they don't like the way something is being done, then they can do something about it—and taking initiative like this is one of the things leaders do. By providing choices, you are enabling others to lead themselves.

Structure Jobs to Offer Latitude

If you want higher levels of performance and greater initiative from your constituents, you must be proactive in designing work that allows them latitude, a close cousin of choice. To feel in control of their own work lives, people need to be able to take nonroutine action, exercise independent judgment, and make decisions that affect how they do their work, without having to check with someone else.[7] It means being creative and flexible—liberated from a standard set of rules, procedures, or schedules. Responsive service and extra employee efforts emerge when people have the necessary leeway to meet customer needs and sufficient authority to serve customer wants. David McCullough, a sales manager with a high-technology firm, told us about two personal experiences that illustrate how latitude in a job (or lack thereof) can either delight or frustrate a customer:

I wandered into the "Alpha" men's store at the local galleria. I needed some new slacks for work; so after trying several on, I selected a comfortable one that was on sale for about 60 percent off the regular price. Excited about my selection, I headed to the checkout counter. The cashier scanned the tag and informed me that the pants were actually not on sale. When I pointed out the fact that the tag had a sales amount written on it, he said there was nothing he could do because the computer was telling him differently. I insisted it was on the sales rack, that it wasn't my fault that someone didn't update the computer, and that I was entitled to the sales price on the tag. He finally picked up the phone and called his manager "upstairs." I don't know precisely who he talked to, but approximately fifteen minutes later, and with great embarrassment, he was finally given permission to give me the price that was indicated on the tag.

Not too long after this experience, I needed to buy a shirt and a new suit, so this time around I headed to "Beta" men's store. Again, I found myself gravitating toward the sales rack and found a nice dress shirt. It was also marked down, and when I went to checkout, the sales associate informed me that it had been placed on the wrong rack. Before I could say a word, he claimed this wasn't a problem and honored the discount advertised on the sales rack. I was ecstatic and as a result decided that I would just go ahead and look for the suit I needed right then and there; and I purchased one, not on sale, so the total transaction wasn't a trivial amount.

The fundamental difference between David's two experiences is that employees in one organization were trusted and given the latitude to use their judgment, whereas those at the other were viewed merely as cogs in some machine, neither trusted nor respected for their common sense. "There may be a certain amount of risk," David points out from his experience in sales, "in giving employees the latitude to make 'executive decisions.' However, along with this greater degree of trust comes a greater degree of accountability, resulting in a higher degree of customer satisfaction (and profitability)." These ideas don't just apply to frontline retail personnel. A study of the Fortune 200 revealed that in the most successful companies, divisional managers could spend ten times the amount that their counterparts could at the less successful organizations.[8]

Only adaptive individuals and organizations will thrive in today's dynamic global environment. This means you have to support more and greater individual discretion to meet the changing demands of customers, clients, suppliers, and other stakeholders. With increased discretion comes an increased ability to use and expand one's talents, training, and experience. The payoff is improved performance.

Foster Accountability

When people take personal responsibility and are held accountable for their actions, their colleagues are much more inclined to want to work with them and are more motivated to cooperate in general. Individual accountability is a critical element of every collaborative effort. Everyone has to do his or her part for a group to function effectively.

While leading a process improvement initiative for Citibank in the Philippines, Ana Aboitiz realized that she could not do everything herself and that she would have to get other people involved and responsible for the project's success. Although recently certified in Six Sigma methodology, she had little technical expertise around the bank's statement rendition process, and had never worked with these team members who were drawn from across various functional areas. Dividing tasks and assigning responsibilities, Ana said, "was very difficult for me. I had full responsibility for the project's success, and I did not know how to pass on this sense of accountability to team members that did not report to me directly. I was afraid that they would fail, and this would reflect on me." What did she do?

> I started the process of dividing tasks by acknowledging that I
> had little knowledge about the particulars of the statement
> rendition process and recognized that they had the technical
> expertise. As a result, I proposed that my role would be to
> provide guidance, Six Sigma training, as well as support for
> eliminating obstacles the team might encounter along the way.
> Just as I had proposed my own role, I decided to give each team

member a chance to identify responsibilities where they felt they could add the most value based on their expertise or interests. Given the opportunity to mold their role in the project, I noticed that they became more engaged in the project. Right away, they began to brainstorm out loud and interact with each other.

Ana shared her power (in this case, her knowledge) with the team and validated them by highlighting that they were the experts. She gave them choices and the latitude to take on responsibility because they were the stakeholders in this process. She made them powerful by following through on her promise that the ideas they came up with would be implemented on the operations floor. "I learned," said Ana, "that in order to foster accountability, you need to delegate authority and give others a chance to take responsibility. By trusting others with responsibility, you are letting them know you believe in them and that you have confidence that they can achieve it."

Ana understands something very fundamental about strengthening others. She knows that the power to choose rests on the willingness to be held accountable. She knows that the more freedom of choice people have, the more personal responsibility they must accept. There's also a bonus: the more that people believe that everyone else is taking responsibility for his or her part of the project—and has the competence to do it—the more trusting and the more cooperative they're going to be. People will be more confident in doing their part when they believe others will do theirs. This interconnectedness between choice and accountability takes on increasing importance in virtually linked global workplaces. In addition, as Ana notes, "when you allow others to take on responsibility, you open yourself up to being able to take on new responsibilities and learning opportunities." As others assume more responsibility, leaders can expend more energy in other areas, enhancing their own sphere of influence and bringing additional resources back to their units to be distributed once again among the group members.

Some believe that teams and other cooperative endeavors minimize individual accountability. They argue that if people are encouraged to work collectively, somehow they'll take less responsibility for their own actions than if they are encouraged to compete or to do things on their own. The evidence doesn't support this point of view.[9] It's true that some people become social loafers when working in groups, slacking off while others do their jobs for them. But this doesn't last for long, because their colleagues quickly tire of carrying the extra load. Either the slacker steps up to the responsibility, or the team wants that person out—provided the team has shared goals and shared accountability.

Enhancing self-determination means giving people control over their own lives. Therefore you have to give them something of substance to control and for which they are accountable. In Table 9.1, we offer a few suggestions on how you can foster individual accountability among your constituents.

Remember to provide the necessary resources—for example, materials, money, time, people, and information—for people to perform autonomously. There's nothing more disempowering than to have lots of responsibility for doing something but nothing to do it with. People's increased sphere of influence should be relevant to the pressing concerns and core technology of the business. Choosing the color of the paint may be a place to start, but you'd better give people influence over more substantive issues in time. For example, if quality is top priority, find ways to expand people's influence and discretion over issues of quality control.

> **TABLE 9.1** Ideas for Fostering Individual Accountability
>
> - Make certain that everyone in your organization, no matter the task, has a customer. The customer can be internal or external, but each person needs to know whom he or she is serving.
> - Substantially increase signature authority at all levels.
> - Remove or reduce unnecessary approval steps.
> - Eliminate as many rules as possible.
> - Decrease the amount of routine work.
> - Automate routine work wherever possible.
> - Assign nonroutine jobs.
> - Support the exercise of independent judgment.
> - Encourage creative solutions to problems.
> - Define jobs more broadly—as projects, not tasks.
> - Provide greater freedom of access, vertically and horizontally, inside and outside.

DEVELOP COMPETENCE AND CONFIDENCE

Choice, latitude, and accountability fuel people's sense of power and control over their lives. But as necessary as enhancing self-determination is, it's insufficient. Without the knowledge, skills, information, and resources to do a job expertly, and without feeling competent to skillfully execute the choices required, people feel overwhelmed and disabled. And even if they have the resources, there may be times when people don't have the confidence that they're allowed to use them or that they'll be backed up if things don't go as well as expected. And there may be times when they just lack the self-confidence to do what they know needs to be done.

Developing competence and building confidence are essential to delivering on the organization's promises and maintaining the credibility of leaders and team members alike. To make extraordinary things happen, you must invest in strengthening the capacity and the resolve of everyone in the organization. This is especially important during times of great uncertainty and significant challenge.

Think about a time when the challenge you faced was greater than the skills you had. How did you feel when the challenge was high but your skill was low? If you're like most people, you felt anxious, nervous, scared, and the like. Now think of a time when your level of skill was greater than the level of challenge in the job. How did you feel? Bored and apathetic, most likely. Do you do your best work when you're anxious or bored? Of course not; you do it when the challenge you face is just slightly greater than your current level of skill. That's when you feel stretched but not stressed out.

People often refer to being "in the flow" when they feel that they are performing effortlessly and expertly despite the difficulty of the experience. They are confident that their skills match the level of challenge of the experience, even though the challenge might be a bit of a stretch. Claremont Graduate University professor of psychology Mihaly Csikszentmihalyi has spent his entire academic career studying the relationship of challenge and skill to optimal performance, and he finds that "when high challenges are matched with high skills, then the deep involvement that sets flow apart from ordinary life is likely to occur."[10] This relationship is illustrated graphically in Figure 9.1.

Although flow is not possible with every single task in every single situation, it's something that is characteristic of peak perfor-

FIGURE 9.1 Optimal Performance, Challenge, and Skill

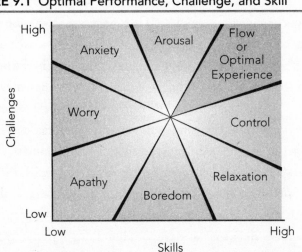

Source: M. Csikszentmihalyi, *Finding Flow: The Psychology of Engagement with Everyday Life* (New York: Basic Books, 1997), 31. Copyright © 1998 Mihaly Csikszentmihalyi. Reprinted with permission of Basic Books, a member of the Perseus Book Group.

mances. Exemplary leaders strive to create the conditions that make flow possible. That means they need to continuously assess their constituents' capacity to perform in the context of the challenges they face. Such assessment requires attention to the skills and the willpower of each person they lead.

Rakesh Soundaranathan put these principles into action when he was a senior member of Oracle's direct sales force. He realized that when new sales reps came on board, they were being inundated with so much information that they felt as though they were "drinking from a fire hose." Rakesh introduced a mentor program to help guide new hires in acquiring the requisite skills and creating the conditions for them to meet the challenges they faced. Whenever a new sales rep—someone at the company for less than three months— had a question, Rakesh said that "I would step away from my desk, walk over to them, and answer their question as best I could." Sometimes that meant going into a conference room, armed with product collateral and finance textbooks. He would sketch out diagrams, processes, or technology infrastructures to help the fledgling rep understand the products and marketplace. Sometimes their questions were around internal processes within Oracle—such questions as "How should we communicate with cross-functional teams?" or "What is the best way to write an executive summary?" Other senior sales reps took on mentees; indeed, after a while, these reps started meeting themselves to discuss how mentorship of the new sales reps was coming along. Their coaching, Rakesh noted, "made a tremendous difference in retention, but more importantly it built everyone's sense of competence and created strong collaborative efforts."

Educate and Share Information

People can't do what they don't know how to do. So when you increase the latitude and discretion of your constituents, you also have to increase expenditures on training and development. When people aren't sure about how to perform the critical tasks or are fearful of making mistakes, they may be reluctant to exercise their judgment. "Ensuring that employees are given the training they need and involving them in decisions that impact their work creates both competence and commitment," observe Michael Burchell and Jennifer Robin, authors of *The Great Workplace*. In their research, they find that "Great Place to Work" companies view training and development as a way of supporting employees and showing respect for them and their customers: "They understand that as the business continues to grow, they will need employees who can readily step into tomorrow's jobs rather than having them develop necessary skills on the fly, hiring from the outside, or simply losing market opportunity."[11]

Strengthening others requires up-front investments in initiatives that develop people's competencies and foster their confidence. These investments produce profits: companies that spend more than the average amount on training have a higher return on investment than companies that are below-average spenders.[12] Organizations that have invested more than the average amount of money on training enjoy higher levels of employee involvement and commitment and better levels of customer service, along with greater understanding of and alignment with company visions and values.

Here's what Erika Long did when she was faced with a lack of skills in some of her team members at Macys.com:

> I knew that they needed certain training, not only to grow as individuals but to complete the tasks assigned to them. To remedy this, I worked with each team member, teaching them certain buyer responsibilities and explaining critical situations. An issue came through from one of our vendors, and instead of solving it on my own I called the assistant buyer over and walked her through how I would think about fixing the problem. It was clear that she understood, and the next time was able to do it herself.
>
> We also created smaller teams, partnerships, where each person got to know one another better and helped develop each other's skills and confidence. With that confidence came better understanding and trust in one another. By educating, training, and coaching the other team members, they built self-confidence, and our team became even stronger.

Sharing information with constituents—which showed up prominently on the list of what made people feel powerful, and the lack of which was frequently cited as making people feel powerless—is another significant educational tactic. Strategist Nilofer Merchant echoes this observation: "Everyone is better off when they know why decisions are made with as much accuracy as possible. It gives them an understanding of what matters and provides information on which to base the trade-offs constantly being made at every level. When reasons behind decisions are not shared, the decisions seem arbitrary and possibly self-serving."[13] This is what Erika found when she brought her team together and explained to them their challenges and opportunities. She outlined the tasks that needed to be completed and the projects she wanted the team to take on. She shared with them what upper management expected. Erika went on to say,

> Managers often think that withholding information will help the team be more focused; or perhaps it has to do with wanting the power for themselves. However, I found that sharing information fosters collaboration and communication among the team. Getting everyone on "the same page" not only helped them feel like they were an important and valued member of the team, but it also actually helped the work process. The more information they had, the more they understood why they were doing what they were doing, and the more "bought-in" to the team's overall goal they were.

For leaders, developing the competence and confidence of their constituents so that they are more qualified, more capable, and more effective and are leaders in their own right reflects their appreciation of the truth that they can't get anything extraordinary accomplished all by themselves. Making people smarter is the job of every leader. In today's world, if your constituents aren't growing and learning in their jobs, they're highly likely to leave and find better ones.

Organize Work to Build Competence and Ownership

People confronted critical organizational issues in their personal-best leadership case studies. Although it may seem obvious that people do their best when the work is critical to success, this principle is often lost in the day-to-day design of work. Organize assignments so that people feel that their work is relevant to the pressing concerns of the business. Enrich their responsibilities so that they experience variety in their tasks and have opportunities to make meaningful decisions about how their work gets accomplished. Make sure that your constituents are well represented on the task forces, committees, teams, and problem-solving groups dealing with the critical tasks and issues in your organization. Involve them in programs, meetings, and decisions that have a direct impact on their job performance.

Your constituents can't act like owners and provide leadership if they lack a fundamental understanding of how the organization operates. To fully comprehend critical organizational issues and tasks, they need to be able to answer such questions as "Who are our most important customers, clients, suppliers, and stakeholders? How do they perceive us?" "How do we measure success?" "What has our track record been over the past five years?" "What new products or services will we initiate in the next six months?" If your constituents can't answer critical questions like these, how can they work together to transform shared values and common purposes into reality? How can they know how their performance affects other teams, units, divisions, and ultimately the success of the entire enterprise or endeavor? How can they feel very strong or capable if they don't know the answers to the same questions every "owner" or CEO would know?[14]

When Raj Limaye joined Datapro (India) as deputy manager, his group wasn't feeling very competent or successful. To deal with these sentiments, he immediately implemented regular meetings, with new themes and new chairs each week, and made a concerted effort to get everyone present to share his or her ideas. He met with group members individually and asked them what they wanted to do in their jobs. Although their answers were not all the same, Raj made certain that he found challenging extensions to the tasks they were performing, and added variety to each job: "I tried removing unnecessary routine tasks wherever possible; and, if not, then these were rotated. In six months we had reduced the routine tasks to a minimum, as everyone shared ideas about how to improve these tasks or find alternatives. We helped everyone become more competent by creating a learning climate where people needed to look beyond their own job descriptions and organizational boundaries. People were assigned important tasks, and I made them accountable at the same time."

Like Raj and Erika, exemplary leaders carefully look at what constituents are doing in their jobs and figure out where and how their tasks and positions could be enriched. They provide sufficient information so that constituents feel that they have the perspective of owners in making decisions, which consequently fosters greater competence and enhances their self-confidence.

Foster Self-Confidence

Even if people know how to do what needs to be done, a lack of confidence may stop them from doing it. Strengthening others is a key step in a psychological process that affects individuals' intrinsic needs for self-determination. People have an internal need to influence other people and life's events so as to experience some sense of order and stability in their lives. Feeling confident that they can adequately cope with events, situations, and people puts them in a position to exercise leadership. Without sufficient self-confidence, people lack the conviction for taking on tough challenges. The lack of self-confidence manifests itself in feelings of helplessness, powerlessness, and crippling self-doubt. By building constituents' self-confidence, you are building their inner strength to plunge ahead in uncharted terrain, to make tough choices, to face opposition and the like because they believe in their skills and decision-making abilities.[15]

Empirical studies document how self-confidence affects people's performance. Managers were told, in one study, that decision making was a skill developed through practice: the more one worked at it, the more capable one became. Another group of managers was told that decision making reflected their basic intellectual aptitude: the greater one's underlying cognitive capacities, the better his or her decision-making ability. Working with a simulated organization, both groups of managers dealt with a series of production orders requiring various staffing decisions and the establishment of different performance targets. When faced with difficult performance standards, those managers who believed that decision making was an acquirable skill continued to set challenging goals for themselves, used good problem-solving strategies, and fostered organizational productivity. Their counterparts, who believed that decision-making ability was latent (that is, you either have it or you don't), lost confidence in themselves over time as they encountered difficulties. They lowered their aspirations for the organization, their problem-solving deteriorated, and organizational productivity declined.[16]

In a related set of studies, one group of managers was told that organizations and people are easily changeable. Another group was told, "Work habits of employees are not that easily changeable, even by good guidance. Small changes do not necessarily improve overall outcomes." Those managers with the confidence that they could influence organizational outcomes through their actions maintained a higher level of performance than those who felt that they could do little to change things.[17] A study of entry-level accountants revealed that those with the highest self-confidence were rated ten months later by their supervisors as having the best job performance. Their level of self-confidence was a stronger predictor of job performance than the actual level of skill or training they had received before being hired.[18]

These studies document what experience underscores: having confidence and believing in your ability to handle the job, no matter how difficult, are essential in promoting and sustaining consistent effort. By communicating to constituents that you believe that they can be successful, you help them extend themselves and persevere.[19]

Coach

Although it's true that exemplary leaders communicate their confidence in others, you can't just tell people they can do something if they really can't. There's a direct connection between self-confidence and competence. You need to coach constituents, because no one ever got to be the best at anything without the constructive feedback, probing questions, and active teaching of respected coaches.[20] Among sales managers, for example, developing others has been shown to be the competency most frequently found among those at the top of their field.[21] In a three-year study of the impact of training, it was found that the high-improvement learners were four times more likely to have had one-on-one conversations with their managers than individuals who showed little or no improvement.[22] In other words, it wasn't the training that had the most effect on improvement; it was the coaching that followed it. You have to make yourself available to offer advice and counsel as people apply what they have learned in real-time situations.

Abhijit Chitnis provides testament to how coaching made a difference in his development. He was just starting out in the corporate world, and he was facing his first "really tough" consulting assignment:

> I had to deliver a critical solution proposal for my client, and I was chosen to be the one who would make the presentation. However, since this was my first client presentation, in front of a sizeable and senior audience, I was tense and a bit underconfident. My boss, however, showed full confidence in me and coached me to take advantage of this opportunity. He said that the team had worked hard to deliver the solution, and he had absolute confidence in our proposal. During the presentation, I made a minor mistake in my delivery, and at the break he stood by me, said it was going great, not to worry and that the client absolutely loved the proposal. This really boosted my confidence, and I went on to finish the presentation with great applause.

Looking back on this experience, Abhijit appreciated how "leaders have to coach their teams and keep the motivation and energy flowing so that people can reach their full potential."

When at their best, leaders never take control away from others. They leave it to their constituents to make decisions and take responsibility for them. When leaders coach, educate, enhance self-determination, and otherwise share power, they're demonstrating profound trust in and respect for others' abilities. When leaders help others grow and develop, that help is reciprocated. People who feel capable of influencing their leaders are more strongly attached to those leaders and more committed to effectively carrying out their responsibilities.[23] They own their jobs.

Strengthening others involves paying attention and believing that people are smart enough to figure things out for themselves, if given the opportunity and provided with support and coaching. Coaching stretches people to grow and develop their capabilities, and it provides them with opportunities to both hone and enhance their skills in challenging assignments.

Good coaches also ask good questions. Frances Hesselbein, former CEO of the Girls Scouts of the U.S.A. and founding president of the Leader to Leader Institute, says her personal motto is "Ask, don't tell." She learned it from Peter Drucker, who said, "The leader of the future asks; the leader of the past tells."[24] The benefits of asking questions are numerous. For one, it gives other people the room to think and to frame issues from their own perspective. Second, asking questions indicates an underlying trust in people's abilities by shifting accountability, and it has the benefit of creating almost immediate buy-in for the solution. (After all, it's their idea.) Asking questions also puts leaders in a coaching position, more of a guiding role, which frees them up to think more freely and strategically.

Neera Patel, finance manager with Applied Materials, richly describes her own experiences of coaching one of her direct reports through asking questions:

The objective of the meeting was to teach her how I dealt with a mapping issue in the financial systems. I thought about how I could approach this entire meeting without speaking in statements. I was able to get through 80 percent of the meeting with questions only. Thinking back to how the meeting went, I am shocked at what I learned about how to lead others. I was able to pull information out of her, thereby guiding her to learn what the issue was and how to approach it without having to work as hard. It was amazing! I also learned that she knew more than I gave her credit for, which is something I would not have known had I approached this another way.

I first showed her the reports out of the two financial systems and asked, "What do you see wrong here?" Then I asked her, "What seems to be off between the systems? What is the specific trigger that is causing these mapping issues? How can we approach the fix? Is this a temporary fix? How can we fix this permanently? Who are the players that need to be involved in the permanent fix? What are all the steps needed?" I found that I was able to do less explaining and essentially shifted the burden of thinking and accountability to her. I made her feel much better about herself and confident as well.

The success of every organization is a shared responsibility. As we said in Chapter Eight, you can't do it alone. You need a competent and confident team, and the team needs a competent and confident leader. Coaching is an essential part of exemplary leadership. And while you're at it, think about getting a coach yourself. There's no better way to model the behavior you expect from others than by doing it yourself.

TAKE ACTION

Strengthen Others

Strengthening others is essentially the process of turning constituents into leaders—making people capable of acting on their own initiative. A virtuous cycle is created as power and responsibility are extended to others and as they respond successfully. Leaders strengthen others when they make it possible to exercise choice and discretion, when they design options and alternatives to the ways that work and services are produced, and when they foster accountability and responsibility that compel action.

Leaders develop in others the competence, as well as the confidence, to act and to excel. They make certain that constituents have the necessary data and information to understand how the organization operates, gets results, makes money, and does good work. They invest in people's continuing competence, and they coach people on how to put what they know into practice, stretching and supporting them to do more than they might have imagined possible. Exemplary leaders use questions to help people think on their own, and coach people on how to be at their best.

To Enable Others to Act, you must *strengthen others by increasing their self-determination and developing competence.* This means you need to

- Take actions that make people feel powerful and in control of their circumstances.
- Let people make choices about how they do their work and serve their customers.

- Structure jobs so that people have opportunities to use their judgment.
- Provide the necessary resources (especially information) to perform effectively.
- Do away with routine assignments as quickly as possible.
- Find a balance between people's skills and the challenges associated with their work.
- Educate, educate, and educate yourself and your constituents.
- Promote an ownership perspective by making sure that people understand the big picture of how the enterprise operates.
- Demonstrate your confidence in the capabilities of constituents and colleagues.
- Set aside the time necessary to coach.
- Ask questions; stop giving answers.

Use *The Leadership Challenge Mobile Tool* app to immediately integrate these activities into your life and make this practice an ongoing part of your behavioral repertoire.

ENCOURAGE
THE HEART

Getting extraordinary things done in organizations is hard work. The climb to the summit is arduous and steep. Leaders encourage others to continue the quest. They inspire others with courage and hope.

Leaders give heart by visibly recognizing people's contributions to the common vision. With a thank-you note, a smile, and public praise, the leader lets others know how much they mean to the organization.

Leaders express pride in the accomplishments of their teams. They make a point of telling the rest of the organization about what the teams have achieved. They make people feel like heroes.

Hard work can also be fun work. Hoopla is important to a winning team. Everybody loves a parade. Leaders find creative ways to celebrate accomplishments. They take time out to rejoice in reaching a milestone.

And what sustains the leader? From what source comes the leader's courage? The answer is love. Leaders are in love— in love with the people who do the work, with what their organizations produce, and with their customers.

In the next two chapters, we will see how you must

- **Recognize Contributions by showing appreciation for individual excellence.**
- **Celebrate the Values and Victories by creating a spirit of community.**

CHAPTER 10

Recognize Contributions

FROM HER VERY FIRST DAY at Ambition Group—a leading provider of recruitment and career services, with operations in Australia, the United Kingdom, and Asia—Jade Lui experienced "a strong sense of community and an encouraging culture." Her first meeting was with Guy Day, the managing director. "Guy personally greeted me, spent an hour introducing me to the firm's corporate vision and values, then introduced me to each and every person in the office," Jade told us. "I was pleasantly surprised that the most senior executive actually devoted such time and effort to bringing on board the most junior new recruit. He showed that he cared."

One of the regular practices at Ambition was for each consultant to write his or her successful new placements onto one of the several whiteboards throughout the office. These postings detailed the candidate, the client employer, and the billing amount. Jade said,

> Every time a consultant got up to write on the whiteboard, the entire office would cheer. And every morning when he arrived

at the office, Guy would walk around the floor and chat with individual consultants regarding their new placements. He was concerned not only about the billing amount; he would also inquire about the process, the challenges, how the consultants surmounted those hurdles, and what people learned from the experience. Guy also volunteered to attend client meetings with the consultants. This solidified his presence in the firm-client interface and also demonstrated his genuine interest in our work.

Guy's personal involvement and interest were evident in the quarterly coffees he would host with each individual consultant to provide performance feedback and to discuss development areas and career growth opportunities. During monthly meetings, Guy would ask every consultant to share a success story, giving him or her an opportunity to showcase a job well done in front of fellow colleagues. Guy also offered his personal commendation to select consultants each month, not for their revenue generation, but for their contribution to shared values like teamwork, creativity, and quality service. "These gestures," Jade explained, "were especially encouraging because they conveyed the notion that profitability was not the only performance metric we were measured against. He cared a lot about our contribution to company culture and long-term firm values as well."

To foster a sense of spirit and community, regular celebrations were held for everyone in the firm—including the management team, front-office consultants, and back-office support staff. Month ly birthday parties, quarterly bashes, annual Christmas parties, and community service days offered opportunities for cross-department rapport building and, more important, for everyone in the firm to get to know one another on a more personal level.

Guy won over the hearts of his constituents, and the result, Jade said, "was that the firm came easily together to work toward common goals, and staff in general had a greater sense of satisfaction at work, and we made lots of money!" Throughout her tenure at Ambition, Jade said, "there was never a day that went by that I did not feel motivated or enthusiastic about going to work. I felt that my work mattered, because it was recognized."

Just as Guy did with Jade, all exemplary leaders make the commitment to *Recognize Contributions*. They do it because people need encouragement to function at their best and to persist for months when the hours are long, the work is hard, and the task is challenging. Getting to the finish line of any demanding journey demands energy and commitment. People need emotional fuel to replenish their spirits. They need the will to continue and the courage to do something they have never done before. No one is likely to persist for very long when he or she feels ignored or taken for granted. It's your job to make sure that your constituents feel that their work matters and that they make a difference. It's your job to recognize their contributions to success by showing your appreciation for individual excellence.

To Recognize Contributions, you need to utilize these two essentials:

- **EXPECT THE BEST**
- **PERSONALIZE RECOGNITION**

By putting these essentials into practice, you uplift people's spirits and arouse the internal drive to strive. You stimulate their efforts to reach for higher levels of performance and to aspire to be true to the visions and values of the organization. You help people find the courage to do things that they have never done before.

EXPECT THE BEST

Belief in others' abilities is essential to making extraordinary things happen. Exemplary leaders elicit high performance because they strongly *believe in* the abilities of their constituents to achieve even the most challenging goals. That's because positive expectations profoundly influence not only your constituents' aspirations but also, often unconsciously, how you behave toward them. Your beliefs about people are broadcast in ways you may not even be aware of. You give off cues that say to people either "I know you can do it" or "There's no way you'll ever be able to do that." You can't realize the highest level of performance unless you let people know in word and deed that you are confident that they can attain it.

Social psychologists have referred to this as the "Pygmalion effect," from the Greek myth about Pygmalion, a sculptor who carved a statue of a beautiful woman, fell in love with the statue, and appealed to the goddess Aphrodite to bring her to life. His prayers were granted. Leaders play Pygmalion-like roles in developing their constituents. Ask people to describe the best leaders they've ever had, and they consistently talk about individuals who brought out the best in them. They say things like, "She believed in me more than I believed in myself" or "He saw something in me even I didn't see."

Exemplary leaders bring others to life, figuratively speaking. These leaders dramatically improve others' performance because they care deeply for them and have an abiding faith in their capacities. Constituents are able to respond positively to these expectations not only because they have the abilities but also because leaders are more nurturing, supportive, and encouraging toward people in whom they believe. Research on the phenomenon of self-fulfilling prophecies provides ample evidence that people act in ways that are consistent with others' expectations of them.[1]

When you expect people to fail, they probably will. If you expect them to succeed, they probably will. James Stout, an energy resource analyst at Public Finance Solutions and Engineering, thinks back on one of his early internships, and attributes his positive experience in that company in large part to the way he was made to feel like a valuable contributor:

> When I arrived on the job, I knew that there were high
> expectations for my performance. Along with the standard
> pleasantries, I was greeted with a work plan for my projects
> spelled out in calendar format. What could have been
> intimidating was not, for my manager made it clear that she
> had hired me because she felt confident in my skills and
> internal drive. I felt empowered to do my job and to do it with
> independence and pride. I was given the freedom to review the
> work plan and to discuss the projects with my manager if I felt
> they were somehow not right for me.

The best leaders bring out the best in their constituents. If the potential exists within someone, exemplary leaders always find a way to release it. The emerging field of positive organizational psychology provides solid evidence that leaders who create an affirmative orientation in organizations, foster virtuousness among people, and focus on achieving outcomes beyond the norm are significantly more successful.[2] There's increasing proof that it pays to be positive.

Show Them You Believe

As social scientists have documented, leaders' positive expectations aren't just fluff.[3] They're not just about keeping a positive outlook or getting others psyched up. The expectations you hold as a leader provide the framework into which people fit their own realities. They shape how you behave toward others and how they behave on the task. Maybe you can't turn a marble statue into a real person, but you can draw out the highest potential of your constituents. Here's how Patti Kozlovsky, senior consultant at PKM Consulting, did it:

I let team members know that I really thought they could do the job, and I trusted their judgment to find the information and extract what was needed in a timely manner. In our group meetings, as we reviewed the information team members were contributing, I made a conscious effort to thank members for what they had contributed rather than commenting on what had not been done. What impact did this have? First of all, there was less tension in the group, and team members felt as though everyone was participating to their fullest capacity. Instead of sniping at each other over what was not done, people were generally supporting one other, sharing resources and letting their colleagues know what they had found, and sharing ideas about where others might find critical data.

It was also interesting that team members were genuinely interested in what others had discovered and how that connected with information they had gathered. Because the team had confidence in each other's abilities, this strengthened our respect for one another and made it easy to incorporate multiple perspectives into our final product. This experience taught me that people live up to our expectations. If you express confidence in their abilities, they will put their heart into whatever project is on the table.

Patti acknowledged that she wasn't always comfortable giving over control to her teammates, but she had clearly learned that her holding positive expectations of high performance and motivation in others, along with recognizing them for their contributions, easily beat the alternative of command-and-control management. For your constituents to be successful on a job, you have to make certain that they feel that they belong, are accepted and valued, and have the skills and inner resources needed to be successful.

Believing in others is an extraordinarily powerful force in propelling performance.[4] If you want your constituents to have a winning attitude, you have to do two things. First, you have to believe that your constituents are already winners. It's not that they will be winners someday; they are winners right now! If you believe that people are winners, you will treat them that way. Second, if you want people to be winners, you have to behave in ways that communicate to them that they are winners—not just through your words but also through tone of voice, posture, gestures, and facial expressions. No yelling, frowning, cajoling, making fun of them, or putting them down in front of others. Instead, it's about being friendly, positive, supportive, and encouraging. Offer positive reinforcement, share lots of information, listen deeply to people's input, provide them with sufficient resources to do their jobs, give them increasingly challenging assignments, and lend them your support and assistance.[5]

It's a virtuous circle: you believe in your constituents' abilities; your favorable expectations cause you to be more positive in your actions; and those encouraging behaviors produce better results, reinforcing your belief that people can do it. And what's really powerful about this virtuous circle is that as people see that they are capable of extraordinary performance, they develop that expectation of themselves. Another virtuous circle begins.

Be Clear About the Goals and the Rules

Positive expectations are necessary to generate high performance, but that level of performance isn't sustainable unless people are clear about ground rules and outcomes. When you were a kid you might have read Lewis Carroll's *Alice's Adventures in Wonderland*. Remember the croquet match? The flamingos were the mallets, the playing-card soldiers were the wickets, and the hedgehogs were the balls. Everyone kept moving, and the rules kept changing all the time. There was no way of knowing how to play the game or what it took to win. You don't have to fall down the rabbit hole to know how Alice felt.

Sachin Gad, project director with a high-technology company, recalled a time when he learned how essential it is to be clear about what you're trying to accomplish and how to accomplish it, especially when the going gets tough.[6] Faced with a situation where timelines were not only challenging but ever changing—where documentation was unclear and the customer's requirements were considered "unrealistic"—Sachin found, not surprisingly, that morale and motivation on the project team were low. He spent considerable time listening to everyone involved, held sales responsible for realistically managing customer expectations, and worked together with others to set clear guidelines that addressed conflicting resource requirements. At the same time, he systematically tracked achievement and identified and recognized high performers. Over the course of a single year, the situation improved significantly: employee attrition within the program fell 55 percent, and employee satisfaction improved by more than 34 percent.

Just believing that people can succeed is only part of the equation. If you want people to give their all, to put their hearts and minds into their work, you must also make certain that people know what they are supposed to be doing. You need to clarify what the expected outcomes look like and make sure that there are some consistent norms governing how the game is played.

Both goals and values provide people with a set of standards that concentrates their efforts. Goals are shorter term, and values (or principles) are more enduring. Values and principles serve as the basis for goals. They're your standards of excellence, your highest aspirations, and they define the arena in which goals and metrics must be set. Values mediate the path of action. Goals release the energy.

The ideal state—on the job, in sports, and in life generally—is often called "flow." "Flow experiences," as described in Chapter Nine, are those times when you feel pure enjoyment and effortlessness in what you do.[7] To experience flow, it's necessary to have clear goals, because they help you concentrate and avoid distractions. By having an intention to do something that is meaningful to you, by setting a goal, you take purposeful action. Action without goals, at least in an organizational context, is just busywork. It's a waste of precious time and energy.

But what do goals have to do with recognition? They give recognition context. People should be recognized for achieving something, for doing something extraordinary—coming in first, breaking a record, setting a new standard of excellence. Leaders should absolutely make sure they affirm the worth of every one of their constituents. But for recognition to be meaningful and for it to reward appropriate behaviors, you have to have an end in mind. Goals help people keep their eyes on the vision. Goals and intentions keep them on track. They help people put the phone in do-not-disturb mode, shut out the noise, and schedule their time. Goal setting affirms the person, and, whether you realize it or not, contributes to what people think about themselves.

THE LEADERSHIP CHALLENGE

Give Regular Feedback

People need to know if they're making progress toward the goal or simply marking time. Their motivation to perform a task increases only when they have a challenging goal *and* receive feedback on their progress.[8] Goals without feedback, or feedback without goals, has little effect on people's willingness to put extra effort (or motivation) into the task, as the research findings in Figure 10.1 illustrate.

Just announcing that the idea is to reach the summit is not enough to get people to put forth more effort. They need information on whether they're still climbing in the right direction, making progress toward the top, or sliding downhill. With clear goals and detailed feedback, people can become self-correcting and can more

FIGURE 10.1 The Impact of Goals and Feedback on Motivation

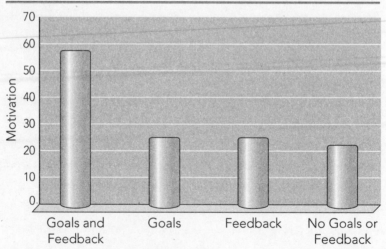

Source: A. Bandura and D. Cervone, "Self-Evaluative and Self-Efficacy Mechanism Governing the Motivational Effects of Goal Systems," *Journal of Personality and Social Psychology* 45 (1983): 1017–1028.

easily understand their place in the big picture. With feedback they can also determine what help they need from others and who might be able to benefit from their assistance. Under these conditions, they will be willing to put forth more productive effort. When there is no feedback, production will be less efficient and will exact a significant toll in the form of increased levels of stress and anxiety.

That is exactly why Harun Özkara, project manager in the R&D department at an Istanbul-based HVAC manufacturing company, initiated "the Friday Meetings."[9] For a time, the department was without a senior manager and experienced high turnover and low morale. One Friday afternoon just before the workweek ended, Harun called a meeting. Everybody was curious about this unexpected meeting, fearing that more organizational changes and layoffs would be announced. The meeting began with Harun sharing the results of his conversations with all the other department managers regarding their thoughts about R&D and what could be done better. The feedback was sobering, but Harun wanted to set a clear direction together for the division so that they didn't lose their way in these times of uncertainty. This first meeting began what became a weekly ritual for the R&D department.

In these meetings, all the department members gathered together in a big conference room in the factory. The meeting usually started with an update on the current condition of the department. Members discussed any problems they had or difficulties they were experiencing in getting tasks done. They aired common issues and explored solutions. Although these meetings were about solving problems and improving performance, it was the feedback that was the spark for these discussions and for the department's continued productivity.

Feedback is at the center of any learning process. For example, consider what happens to your self-confidence without feedback.

In a study, people were told that their efforts would be compared with how well hundreds of others had done on the same task. They received praise, criticism, or no feedback on their performance. Those who heard nothing about how well they did suffered as great a blow to their self-confidence as those who were criticized. Only those who received positive feedback improved.[10] Saying nothing about a person's performance doesn't help anyone—not the performer, not the leader, and not the organization. People hunger for positive feedback. They really do prefer to know how they are doing, and no news generally has the same negative impact as bad news. In fact, people actually would prefer to hear bad news rather than no news at all.

Without feedback there is no learning—it's the only way for you to know whether or not you're getting close to your goal and whether or not you're executing properly. Feedback can be embarrassing, even painful. While most people realize intellectually that feedback is a necessary component of self-reflection and growth, they are often reluctant to make themselves open to it. They want to look good more than they want to get good! Researchers consistently point out that the development of expertise or mastery requires one to receive constructive, even critical, feedback.[11]

Moreover, setting the right climate for feedback is critical. Reviewing past behavior can't be a search for culprits or an opportunity to fix the blame. Make sure you "test for understanding" when you give feedback. See if the recipient of your feedback can put into his own words what he believes you have said—to your satisfaction—and in this way ensure that you are both on the same page. Test out some hypotheses about possible future actions to see if these would address the issues being raised.

When leaders provide a clear sense of direction and feedback along the way, they encourage people to reach inside and do their best. Information about goals and about progress toward those goals strongly influences people's abilities to learn and to achieve.[12] Because encouragement is more personal and positive than other forms of feedback, it's more likely to accomplish something that other forms cannot: strengthening trust between leaders and constituents. Encouragement, in this sense, is the highest form of feedback.

PERSONALIZE RECOGNITION

One of the more common complaints about recognition is that far too often it's highly predictable, routine, and impersonal. A one-size-fits-all approach to recognition feels insincere, forced, and thoughtless. Over time it can even increase cynicism and actually damage credibility. Maurice Chan provided personal testimony to the weaknesses of this strategy when he told us about his experience working as an engineer in a multinational telecommunications company. The Hong Kong branch adapted an incentive scheme from headquarters to reward staff achievements:

> I got such a reward almost every year. The intention of this incentive scheme was great. However, the prize was nothing much, maybe a few thousand dollars and an email telling you that the money was already banked in your account. No one would come to your cube and talk to you about what you had achieved. It made the incentive scheme just like a "bureaucratic procedure." It didn't make me or anyone else very excited about getting the reward.

Recognition should be personalized; otherwise it will quickly be forgotten and discounted. It should be made and expressed from your heart. Try to step into the shoes of other people and ask yourself, "What do I wish other people would do to celebrate and recognize my contribution?" Let your answer to this question guide your own behavior with others.

Alexey Astafev echoes Maurice's observations. Alexey was involved with international business development for the Russian railways administration, and he still remembers the day when his department head called him into the office and silently handed him a merit citation from the CEO, along with a bonus certificate. The peculiar thing, said Alexey,

> was that the bonus amount was determined by the CEO
> himself—marked with his pen over the standard sum that
> usually was given out with that type of award. But I don't even
> remember now how much it was! Probably because the way I
> was rewarded was neither "personalized" nor "visible." He told
> me that he was doing this privately because he didn't want
> others to envy me. I tried to understand it back then, but failed
> to. And it surely had no big impact on my performance.

What Alexey learned from this experience, and many others like it, was, in his words,

> that in order to encourage people to do their best, you should
> be able to recognize their achievements and make them feel
> trusted and valued. It has to be personal, precise, and visible.
> Even if it is a great reward, if you don't give it out right—or get
> it right—it will be forgotten soon without achieving the
> purpose of bringing out the best in people. On the other hand,
> even a small appraisal such as a "thank you" which is tailored

and meant specifically to you, can inspire people to great performance.

When we've asked people to tell us about their "most meaningful recognition," they, like Maurice and Alexey, consistently report that it's "personal." They say that it feels special. That's why it's so important for leaders to pay attention to the likes and dislikes of each and every individual. You get a lot more emotional bang for your buck when you make recognition and rewards personal. "A sincere word of thanks from the right person at the right time can mean more to an employee than a raise, a formal award, or a whole wall of certificates and plaques," writes Bob Nelson in *1001 Ways to Reward Employees.*[13] As he points out, "Part of the power of such rewards comes from the knowledge that someone took the time to notice the achievement, seek out the employee responsible, and personally deliver praise in a timely manner." When it comes to encouraging the heart, personalizing recognition pays off.

Get Close to People

"'*Shukriya* ["thank you" in Hindi]. You have done an awesome job' was the first thing I read in the morning," says Meghana Mehta. This was an email sent to her by Beth, her indirect manager and also her internal customer from Citibank. "I was highly elated reading this email," Meghana told us. It was evidence, she said, that

Beth had gone an extra mile to learn Hindi and to appreciate my work. It was a small gesture, but so dearly valued that I still remember it after ten years. Though she was not my reporting manager and also not even in my same location, she had made a personal connection with me. For example, she knew I am a chocolate lover and used to bring my favorite chocolates especially for me. At the end of the project, she gave all of us an engraved star that read "The Star Team of Citidirect," which I still have displayed on my cubicle today. Such appreciation had never been done in India, and this was a tremendous morale-boosting event for us.

As Meghana's story illustrates, to make recognition personally meaningful, you first have to get to know your constituents. If you're going to personalize recognition and make it feel genuinely special, you'll have to look past the organizational diagrams and roles people play and see the person inside. You need to get to know who your constituents are, how they feel and what they think. For Beth, this meant learning at least a few words in another language, and learning about what sort of treat would be special for Meghana. This means that as a leader, you need to be regularly walking the halls and plant floors, meeting often with small groups, and hitting the road for frequent visits with associates, key suppliers, and customers. Paying attention, personalizing recognition, and creatively and actively appreciating others increase their trust in you. This kind of relationship is even more critical as workforces are becoming increasingly global and diverse. If others know that you genuinely care about them, they're more likely to care about you. This is one important way that you bridge cultural divides.

Because proximity is the single best predictor of whether two people will talk to one another, you have to get close enough to people if you're going to find out what motivates them, what they like and don't like, and what kinds of recognition they most appreciate. Yet managerial myth says that leaders shouldn't get too close to their constituents, that they can't be friends with people at work.[14] Well, set this myth aside. Over a five-year period, researchers observed groups of friends and groups of acquaintances (people who knew each other only vaguely) performing motor-skill and decision-making tasks. The results were unequivocal. The groups composed of friends completed, on average, more than three times as many projects as the groups composed merely of acquaintances. In terms of decision-making assignments, groups of friends were over 20 percent more effective than groups of acquaintances.[15] Other studies have shown that employees who have a friendly relationship with their manager are two-and-a-half times more satisfied with their jobs.[16]

Darren Gest, human capital senior consultant at Deloitte[17] in Chicago, recalled an early experience where he was the "low man on the totem pole" on a financial services project that featured a Fortune 500 client and the top human capital leadership in Deloitte:

> I expected a high-pressure work environment: Darren do this, Darren do that. Pay your dues. Earn your place here. Prove your worth. Go run the numbers and come back with a latte. Instead, Marc Kaplan, my senior manager, took me out to dinner that evening to introduce me to the city and laid out my role and expectations in the clearest and most concise way possible. "You are like the point guard on this team," he said. "We need you to assist us with reports, meetings, scheduling, and presentations. Your role is really important; it's the nerve center of the team." He gave me my dignity back. He humanized the experience and opened up the channels of communication. He showed that he cared about me, and in turn, I wanted to show him how much I cared.

Although it was many years ago, Darren remembers opening up an email from Alice Kwan, a Deloitte principal who thanked him for his efforts on a project:

> "We are getting close to our goal and could not have done it without your analysis. I just wanted to thank you." I was amazed that Alice took the time to recognize my efforts. She continued, "I remember at dinner you mentioned that you have never tried lobsters. Let me take you out for lunch on Wednesday and we can talk about your career aspirations." Hands down, that lunch provided a backdrop for the most meaningful conversation I have had at Deloitte. I am now on an assignment with our team in Hyderbad (India)—if she called me right now, no matter where I was in the world, I would drop what I was doing to readily assist her with a project need.

That's exactly what happens when you get close to people, especially through personalizing recognition and appreciation. The payoff from connecting with team members on a meaningful level, according to Darren, is that this will be "reciprocated with loyalty." He explained: "I suspect that Alice knew that our one-hour lunch would translate into a lifetime of high performance for me—because I had been incentivized by her recognition and was grateful for her appreciation. As a leader, I now know that sincere recognition and personalized appreciation can translate into endless productivity and loyalty. The heart is a powerful tool, and when tapped into, it will do amazing things for the people by whom it is encouraged."

People are just more willing to follow someone with whom they have a relationship, as Darren's experiences attest. Relationships are built on trust. An open door is a physical demonstration of a willingness to let others in. So is an open heart. To become fully trusted, you must be open to and with others. This means disclosing things about yourself in order to build the basis for a relationship. This means telling others the same things you'd like to know about them—talking about your hopes and dreams, your family and friends, your interests and your pursuits.

Certainly, disclosing information about yourself can be risky. You can't be sure that other people will like you, appreciate your candor, agree with your aspirations, buy into your plans, or interpret your words and actions in the way you intend. But by demonstrating the willingness to take such risks, you encourage others to take a similar risk—and thereby take the first steps necessary to build *mutual* trust, the foundation for any relationship.

Be Creative About Incentives

Donna Wilson, the VP and general manager of station KJRH, the NBC affiliate in Tulsa, Oklahoma, got creative in her efforts to personalize recognition. She figured that if she took $300 of her own money and spent it on recognition efforts, it probably would not touch that many people. So she split that money among fifteen people and asked *them* to spend it over the course of a month to encourage the hearts of others.[18]

Donna thought this would be really fun to do—and it sure was. Some gave gas cards to photographers (to ease the burden of rising prices at the pump) or iTunes cards to IT folks (so that the song fit the person rather than being something "generic"), and some gave mementoes to people outside their department (which, Donna said, was quite unusual). Someone created "the Big Fish" award so that recognition could go on and on long after the month had passed. A giant plastic fish was hung over the cubicle of the "star performer" from sales each month; there was plenty of friendly competition to become the Big Fish. Some bought lunch for folks; several had some buttons made up that said "I encourage," and handed them out to people they saw doing good work around the station.

As Donna's experience underscores, leaders don't need to rely exclusively on the organization's formal reward system, which offers only a limited range of options. After all, promotions and raises are scarce resources. And don't make the mistake of assuming that individuals respond only to money. Although salary increases and bonuses are certainly valued, individual needs for appreciation and rewards extend much further than cash.

Jane Binger, executive director of leadership development and education for Lucile Packard Children's Hospital at Stanford, for years has asked people during job interviews and meet-and-greet appointments how they would like to be recognized. She has found that most just want a simple gesture acknowledging that their work was appreciated and valued—usually taking the form of a personal note or email, a comment during a meeting or in the hall, or just a stop by their office. "They want to know that I value them. That I think they are doing a great job. And that I am not taking them or their contribution for granted. This doesn't require any over-the-top grand actions," says Jane.

Spontaneous, unexpected rewards are often more meaningful than expected, formal ones. "The form of recognition that has the most positive influence on us and that should be used most often is on-the-spot recognition," says Sonia Clark, vice president of human resources for several high-technology firms. "When something really terrific happens, I comment on it right away and to anyone who might be close enough to hear." Rewards are the most effective when they're highly specific and given in close proximity to the appropriate behavior. One of the most important results of being out and about as a leader is that you can personally observe people doing things right and then reward them either on the spot or at the next public gathering.

Your options are quite limited if you rely exclusively on the organization's formal reward system. There is usually too much of a time lag between performance and rewards. Our research found that the time lapse between performance and promotion is often more than six months.[19] It's tough to remember exactly what you did to earn the promotion when the feedback follows a half-year later. And although it's true that money may get people to do the job, it doesn't get them to do a particularly outstanding job.[20]

People respond to all kinds of informal recognition and rewards.[21] That's the beauty of being creative and personalizing them. You have lots and lots of options. We've seen people give out stuffed giraffes, rainbow-striped zebra posters, T-shirts, mugs with team photos, crystal apples, rides in a classic car, clocks, pens, plaques, and hundreds of other creative expressions of appreciation. We've seen it done verbally and nonverbally, elaborately and simply. There are no limits to kindness and consideration.

It's important to understand that genuine recognition does not have to include anything tangible. Exemplary leaders make tremendous use of intrinsic rewards—rewards that are built into the work itself, including such factors as a sense of accomplishment, a chance to be creative, and the challenge of the work—all directly tied to an individual's effort. These rewards are far more important than salary and fringe benefits in improving job satisfaction, commitment, retention, and performance.[22] Praise and coaching are significant forms of recognition as well. Often it's the simple, personal gestures that are the most powerful rewards, which is exactly what Jacqueline Wong experienced. Jacqueline recalls how she felt when her CEO, stationed in Singapore, flew to the Hong Kong branch to thank her:

> The sincere and timely appreciation and the simple "thank you" encouraged my heart. It created a sense of well-being and a sense of belonging to the team. While I used to think I was only motivated by monetary rewards, the recognition by someone important greatly contributed to my sustained and accelerated drive to further uphold the responsibility bestowed upon me by my CEO. It was an important lesson for me. It is the power, the refreshing energy, which touches the heart that makes me challenge myself to improve.

It's all about being considerate. The techniques that you use are less important than your genuine expression of caring. People appreciate knowing that you care about them, and they are more caring about what they are doing as a result. When you genuinely care, even the smallest of gestures reap huge rewards.

Just Say Thank You

Not enough people make enough use of the most powerful but inexpensive two-word rewards—"thank you." In fact, that's exactly what they found at Sullivan and Cromwell, one of the oldest and most respected law firms in the United States. For years, they noticed that they were routinely losing high-value first-year associates recruited from the top law schools, and they conducted a survey to find out why. What they found was a shock: it wasn't because of the money, the hours, or the work. It was because the young lawyers didn't feel appreciated by the partners. So the firm instituted a very simple policy: every partner was required to say "Please" and "Thank you" whenever he or she made a request. In one year, attrition was reversed, and Sullivan and Cromwell was voted the best law firm to work for by *American Lawyer* magazine.[23]

Ian Foo, IT strategy and transformation consultant with Accenture in Singapore, would be the first to admit that it took him a while to appreciate how important recognizing contributions is to achieving excellent results. He's results-oriented, and hadn't focused on the personal side of business. But as he began to reflect about this he concluded, "I think the key lesson is that everyone needs to be told what they are doing well and how to improve, despite often feeling that it is obvious. This is because thanking someone is one of the first manners we teach to our children, yet people in the workforce often feel underappreciated because 'we are just doing our jobs.'"

Ian's insight is important. Personal congratulations rank at the top of the most powerful nonfinancial motivators identified by employees.[24] There are few if any more basic needs than to be noticed, recognized, and appreciated for one's efforts. It's true for everyone—volunteers, teachers, doctors, priests, politicians, salespeople, customer service representatives, maintenance staff, and executives. Little wonder, then, that a greater volume of thanks is reported in highly innovative companies than in low-innovation firms.[25] Extraordinary achievements bloom more easily in climates in which performance is nurtured with a higher volume of appreciative comments.[26] Studies show that work teams in which the ratio of positive to negative interactions is greater than three to one are *significantly* more productive than those teams that haven't achieved this ratio.[27]

It is always worth the few extra moments to recognize someone's hard work and contributions. All too often, people forget to extend a hand, a smile, or a simple thank you. People naturally feel a little frustrated and unappreciated when their manager or a colleague takes them for granted. Sometimes this can be overlooked because people are under the pressure of deadlines, and the mandate to deliver on time overtakes expressing gratitude. But it's really important that you stick around for that extra minute to say thanks.

Olivia Lai recalls that when she took the lead in managing the customer service support team at Kimberly-Clark, she always made sure that she said "Thank you" or "I really appreciate your help" before she ended meetings or walked away from people's desks. "You should see the smile that it generates," she beams. "It gives them a warm feeling knowing that their work was welcomed and recognized by others." Olivia remembers one occasion when she had just returned from a three-day vacation:

The first thing I did was to stop at my team's cubicles. I didn't even check email; I didn't want to read about what happened while I was gone. I wanted to hear it from my team. I stopped by each person individually and thanked him or her for holding down the fort. They spent fifteen minutes giving me a full update, but no one looked stressed. They were glad to have me back so they could get approvals on paperwork and process changes, but it was as if I had never left. And the best part? As I got up to leave, I received a hug from each one of them. It was such a nice feeling to be back and have my team again.

What I realized as I was walking back to my office was that recognition goes both ways. They appreciated the extra time I spent with them. They appreciated that I didn't read all my emails first before hearing their version of what happened the last few days. I trusted them to do their job and do it well. At the same time, I felt appreciated knowing I had a great team that not only could work together competently, but also enjoyed working with me. It gives me the extra boost of confidence to do an even better job as their manager.

A few moments spent together empowered Olivia's team to work even harder. They wanted not only to live up to her expectations but also to go above and beyond. When you take the time to set the bar high and make it known that you believe people can excel, you will notice extraordinary results. And you will foster strong team collaboration and unity. "If I can empower my team to work together and be excited about coming to work every day, then that's all I can ask for," Olivia said. For a leader, it's not about just achieving financial results and delivering on annual objectives. It's also about creating a winning team through trust and through a personal connection. This includes extending a simple pat on the back, a handshake, a smile, and a 'Thank you for your hard work.'"

Making a point of regularly saying thank you goes a long way in sustaining high performance. Personalized recognition comes down to being thoughtful. It means knowing enough about another person to answer the question, "What could I do to make this a memorable experience so that this person will always remember how important his or her contributions are?"

TAKE ACTION

Recognize Contributions

Exemplary leaders have positive expectations of themselves and of their constituents. They expect the best of people and create self-fulfilling prophecies about how ordinary people can produce extraordinary actions and results. Exemplary leaders' goals and standards are unambiguous, helping people focus on what needs to be done. They provide clear feedback and reinforcement. By maintaining a positive outlook and providing motivating feedback, they stimulate, rekindle, and focus people's energies and drive.

Exemplary leaders recognize and reward what individuals do to contribute to the vision and values. They express their appreciation far beyond the limits of the organization's formal systems. They enjoy being spontaneous and creative in saying thank you. Personalizing recognition requires knowing what's appropriate individually and culturally. Although recognizing someone's efforts may be uncomfortable or embarrassing at first, it really isn't difficult to do. And it's well worth the effort to make a connection with each person. Learn from many small and often casual acts of appreciation what works for each of your constituents and how best to personalize recognition.

To Encourage the Heart, you must *recognize contributions by showing appreciation for individual excellence.* This means you have to

- Make sure people know what is expected of them.
- Maintain high expectations about what individuals and teams can accomplish.
- Communicate your positive expectations clearly and regularly.
- Let people know that you believe in them, not just in words, but also through actions.
- Create an environment that makes it comfortable to receive and give feedback—including to you.
- Link recognition and rewards with performance outcomes so that only those who meet or exceed the standards receive them.

- Find out the types of encouragement that make the most difference to others. Don't assume you know. Ask. Take the time to inquire and observe.
- Connect with people in person. Stop by and visit them in their workspaces.
- Be creative when it comes to recognition. Be spontaneous. Have fun.
- Make saying thank you a natural part of your everyday behavior.
- Don't take anyone for granted.

Use *The Leadership Challenge Mobile Tool* app to immediately integrate these activities into your life and make this practice an ongoing part of your behavioral repertoire.

RECOGNIZE CONTRIBUTIONS

CHAPTER 11

Celebrate the Values and Victories

ALL OVER THE WORLD, people celebrate. They take time off work to gather to mark an important occasion. They march in elaborate parades down the city's main street to shower a championship team with cheers of appreciation. They set off fireworks to commemorate great historic victories or the beginning of a new year. They convene impromptu ceremonies in the company conference room to toast the award of a new contract. They attend banquets to show their respect for individuals and groups who've accomplished an extraordinary feat. They get all dressed up in tuxedos and gowns— and sometimes in very silly costumes—to rejoice at the passing of another season. They sit down at elaborate feasts to give thanks for the bountiful harvest. They get together with colleagues at the end of a grueling work session and give each other high-fives for a job well done. And in tragic times, people gather together in eulogy and song to honor those who showed courage, conviction, and sacrifice.

Why do people take time away from their jobs to come together, tell stories, and raise their spirits? Because celebrations are among the most significant ways people all over the world proclaim respect and gratitude, renew a sense of community, and remember shared values and traditions. They are as important to an organization's long-term health as is the daily performance of tasks.

Leaders at DeVry, a global provider of educational services and one of the largest publicly held educational organizations in the world, understand this very well. They know that it takes the highest levels of integrity, dedication, and excellence to serve their students and colleagues well. And they know that to sustain this kind of exemplary performance, they need to take time out to strengthen relationships, celebrate successes, and reaffirm commitment. At DeVry, the TEACH Summit and PRIDE event is one of the most important ways they accomplish this. Each annual celebration is unique, but they all share a common purpose. It is, explained Daniel Hamburger, president and CEO, "a rare opportunity for us to gather our leaders and highest performers together to recognize excellence in the things that matter most to us."

On the first night of one TEACH Summit we observed, more than 250 DeVry leaders gathered for the inaugural dinner, where senior leaders recognized several individuals who had been exemplary at living DeVry's TEACH values. (TEACH is an acronym for Teamwork and Communication, Employee Focus, Accountability + Integrity = Ownership, Continuous Improvement, and Help Our Students Achieve Their Goals.) They presented the Talent Developer Award for modeling employee focus, the Change Leadership Award for continuous improvement, and the Leadership Excellence Award for truly demonstrating and living the DeVry purpose, vision, and values as a whole. The spirit of appreciation on that first night set the tone for three days of educational sessions, team-building activities, and recognition ceremonies.

The next day, DeVry leaders welcomed 375 very special employees—the year's PRIDE (Professional Recognition of Integrity and Dedication to Excellence) honorees. They had been invited so that senior leaders could thank them for exemplifying TEACH values and for going above and beyond in service of DeVry's students. And, at this particular event, organization leaders also went above and beyond to show their gratitude to the honorees. They put on red DeVry T-shirts and congratulated PRIDE members arriving at the airport, rode with them on the bus to the hotel, greeted them when they got to the lobby, and guided them to the registration area. At dinner that evening, leaders held the doors open for the PRIDE honorees and cheered loudly as they ceremoniously received their individual awards. It was an extraordinary evening, and something that all recipients remember for the rest of their lives. Lori Mendicino, program manager at DeVry University and a winner in a prior year of a PRIDE award, told us that receiving this recognition was "more exciting than I can even begin to tell you. It's an honor, and to see that the leaders understand what you do and value what you do is just phenomenal."

The awards ceremony was followed by another day of learning and community building. Together leaders and honorees explored, through presentations, videos, and interactive activities, the meaning and importance of TEACH values. They took part in a TEACH quiz show, renewed their commitment by making short "I TEACH" videos, and focused attention on creating a culture of service. To cap the event off, DeVry employees had great fun building bicycles and then donating them to local kids—an intense learning experience about the "T" value of Teamwork and Communication, as well as a reaffirmation of DeVry's philosophy of "Doing Well by Doing Good."

Bill Hughson, president of DeVry's Healthcare Group, says that although it's important to take time to celebrate outstanding achievement for its own sake, he reaffirms that celebrations are important ways that leaders and their organizations also communicate what is important to them:

It has been said that an organization produces most what it honors most. We believe that publicly recognizing and celebrating those who exemplify our purpose, vision, and values is the best possible way to encourage others to behave consistently with them as well. How the accomplishments are celebrated is just as important as what is celebrated. If executed publicly and with thoughtfulness and intentionality, celebrations make clear what activities, behaviors, and outcomes the organization values, and therefore what it takes for employees to be successful in the organization, in a very powerful way.

The experience of DeVry's leaders is confirmed in our research. Performance improves when leaders publicly honor those who have excelled and who have been an example to others. That is why exemplary leaders make a commitment to *Celebrate the Values and Victories* by mastering these essentials:

- **CREATE A SPIRIT OF COMMUNITY**
- **BE PERSONALLY INVOLVED**

When leaders bring people together, rejoice in collective successes, and directly display their gratitude, they reinforce the essence of community. Being personally involved makes it clear that everyone is committed to making extraordinary things happen.

CREATE A SPIRIT OF COMMUNITY

Human beings are social animals—hardwired to connect with others.[1] Otherwise everyone would live like hermits, working alone, eating alone, shopping alone, sleeping alone, and avoiding contact with others. It's an absurd notion, but many organizations operate as if social gatherings were a nuisance. They aren't. People are meant to do things together, to form communities, and in this way demonstrate a common bond.

When social connections are strong and numerous, there's more trust, reciprocity, information flow, collective action, and happiness—and, by the way, greater wealth.[2] Some of the fastest-growing and most successful businesses these days are evidence of the need for social connection. Facebook, Foursquare, Friendster, Google+, LinkedIn, StumbleUpon, Twitter, and Pinterest are only a few of the more than two hundred (and growing) social networking sites with over one hundred million users.[3] Research indicates that "social networking site users have more friends and more close friends" than nonusers[4] and may be reversing what had been a three-decade-long downward trend toward people's being less involved in communities. Social capital has been added to physical and intellectual capital as a major source of success and happiness.

Corporate celebrations are among the best ways to capitalize on the need to connect, to socialize, and to form community. Research on corporate celebrations has found that "Celebrations infuse life with passion and purpose. . . . They bond people together and connect us to shared values and myths. Ceremonies and rituals create community, fusing individual souls with the corporate spirit. When everything is going well, these occasions allow us to revel in our glory. When times are tough, ceremonies draw us together, kindling hope and faith that better times lie ahead."[5] In acknowledging community, leaders create a sense of team spirit, building and maintaining the social support necessary to thrive, especially in stressful and uncertain times.

Sometimes celebrations can be elaborate, but more often they are about connecting everyday actions and events to the values of the organization and the accomplishments of the team. Exemplary leaders seldom let an opportunity pass to make sure that constituents know why they're there and how they should act in service of that purpose. For example, Kurt Richarz, executive vice president of sales at Seagate Technology, uses regular monthly conference calls with the entire sales organization to shine the spotlight on people who have recently been given "Standing Ovations."[6] This program is very simple: peers nominate colleagues by filling out a brief form highlighting their contributions or achievements. The form is forwarded on not only to the recipient but to the recipient's manager as well. Even more important, the recipient's photo and summary of accomplishments are featured on the monthly sales call, and Kurt reserves time to highlight and congratulate the "heroic efforts" of people in supporting the sales organization. He tells everyone it's "one of my favorite parts of the call." Afterwards, Kurt goes on to thank the nominators. After all, he says, "you guys are all very busy, and I appreciate you taking the time to do this." This public, enthusiastic, and heartfelt recognition goes a long way in making both the recipients and bystanders feel that they are valued, and toward building a positive, empowering community.

Whether they're to honor an individual, group, or organizational achievement or to encourage team learning and relationship building, celebrations, ceremonies, and similar events offer leaders the perfect opportunity to explicitly communicate and reinforce the actions and behaviors that are important in realizing shared values and shared goals. Exemplary leaders know that promoting a culture of celebration fuels the sense of unity essential for retaining and motivating today's workforce. Besides, who really wants to work in a boring place that neither remembers nor celebrates anything? David Campbell, former senior fellow with the Center for Creative Leadership, says it well: "A leader who ignores or impedes organizational ceremonies and considers them as frivolous or 'not cost-effective,' is ignoring the rhythms of history and our collective conditioning. [Celebrations] are the punctuation marks that make sense of the passage of time; without them, there are no beginnings and endings. Life becomes an endless series of Wednesdays."[7]

Celebrate Accomplishments in Public

As we noted in the previous chapter, individual recognition increases the recipient's sense of worth and improves performance. Public celebrations have this effect as well, and they add other lasting contributions to the welfare of individuals and organizations that private individual recognition can't accomplish.[8] It's these added benefits that make celebrating together so powerful.

For one thing, public events are an opportunity to showcase real examples of what it means to "do what we say we will do." When the spotlight shines on certain people, and stories are told about their actions, they become role models. They represent how the organization would like everyone to behave, and demonstrate concretely that it is possible to do so. Public celebrations of accomplishment also build commitment, both among the individuals being recognized ("Keep up the good work; it's appreciated") and among those in the audience ("Here are people just like you who are examples of what we stand for and believe in. You too can do this. You too make a significant contribution to our success").

This was precisely the reflection that MT Vu, program analyst at Lockheed Martin, shared with us: "I received an Operational Excellence Award for my contribution to a new business proposal. The award was presented in front of all my peers and management. I felt a great sense of pride and fulfillment. This encouraged me to continue to perform well to show my peers and management that the award represented my values." She said that this public acknowledgment not only energized her but also "revalidated to others that great performance will be recognized."

Public ceremonies also serve as a collective reminder of why people are there, of the values and visions they share. By making celebrations a public part of organizational life, leaders create a sense of community. The process of creating community helps ensure that people feel that they belong to something greater than themselves and that they are working together toward a common cause. Celebrations serve to strengthen the bond of teamwork and trust.

Jan Pacas, general manager of Hilti Australia, which provides leading edge technology to the global construction industry, understood this when he instituted the "Champions League."[9] Because teamwork is one of the four nonnegotiable values at Hilti Australia—the other three are integrity, courage, and commitment—Jan wanted to make sure that people knew that it wasn't just the sales force who was responsible for top-level results. There were also many people in support functions who contributed to the company's success.

To ensure that these behind-the-scenes folks did not go unnoticed, Jan introduced peer-nominated awards for people in nonmanagerial roles who had demonstrated outstanding customer focus. Anyone in the company could submit a nomination along with a story to support their nomination, which the executive management team reviewed to make sure that the candidates consistently lived the company's values. The process took nine months, and the final winners were not selected until the last week. The first of the Champions League awards were given out at the gala dinner to celebrate Hilti's fifty years in Australia, and there was an air of excitement as Jan read the list of recipients. No one knew until that moment who would be walking up on stage, and it was inspiring to see 250 people give a standing ovation to those who exemplified the shared values of Hilti. "The announcement of the Champions League winners was the pièce de résistance to an overall great two-day event," Jan said. "It was not about the prize, although the prize was very exciting; it was the feeling that you had been selected by your peers for something very, very special that *you* had achieved. . . . It made everybody proud being a winner of this, and at the same time it cemented the 'high expectations–high rewards' culture with all staff."

Some people are reluctant to recognize people in public, fearing that it might cause jealousy or resentment. Allay these fears. All winning teams have Most Valuable Players, and usually it's the team that selects them. Public celebrations, like the Champions League awards, are important opportunities to reinforce shared values and to recognize individuals for their contributions. They give you the chance both to say thanks to specific individuals for their outstanding performance and to remind people of exactly what it is that the organization stands for.

Private rewards may work fine to motivate individuals, but they don't have the same impact on the team. To generate community-wide energy and commitment for the common cause, you need to celebrate successes in public.

Provide Social Support

Supportive relationships at work—relationships characterized by a genuine belief in and advocacy for the interests of others—are critically important in maintaining personal and organizational vitality.[10]

Ceremonies and celebrations are opportunities to build healthier groups, to enable members of the organization to know and care about each other.

One of the significant lessons learned from an extensive ten-year study of service quality is that social support networks are essential for sustaining the motivation to serve. Shortfalls in service performance are highly correlated with the absence of social support and teamwork.[11] Indeed, an antidote to service burnout is ensuring that coworkers support one another and feel a sense of achieving together. People who don't like the folks they're working with don't stay around very long. Working with others on your team should be energizing, rejuvenating, even inspirational and fun.

This is just what Ferhat Zor experienced when he was working on a warehouse performance management project with Borusan Logistics (Turkey). The Tuzla warehouse manager reviewed the performance of the various operational units at his monthly meetings and made the point that they needed to support and help one another. These meetings always ended, according to Ferhat, with celebrating their accomplishments as an entire group. Sometimes the celebrations were quite lavish—everyone would be taken out for dinner—other times, more simply, dessert was served in the warehouse after lunch or dinner, and group members enjoyed one another's company. After the group successfully completed one very challenging project, a "spontaneous" surprise party was held, and each and every employee was personally congratulated. Ferhat explained that "their happiness and pride were evident." Lots of photographs were taken, and later these pictures were shared on the Web with other divisions. A few months later, their accomplishment was highlighted in the company's newsletter, "in order," said Ferhat, "to show that each person makes an important contribution and each doing their best makes the company a success."

Research across a wide variety of disciplines consistently demonstrates that this kind of social support enhances productivity, psychological well-being, and even physical health. Researcher and former Harvard teaching fellow Shawn Achor, for example, has found that among undergraduate students "social support was a far greater predictor of happiness than any other factor, more than GPA, family income, SAT scores, age, gender, or race."[12] Other studies have found that social support not only enhances wellness but also buffers against disease, particularly during times of high stress. This latter finding is true irrespective of an individual's age, gender, or ethnic group. Even after adjusting for such factors as smoking and histories of major illness, people with few close contacts were two to three times more likely to die during the study period than those who regularly had friends to turn to.[13] In fact, George Vaillant, Harvard professor of psychiatry, who directed the world's longest continuous study of physical and mental health, when asked what he had learned from his forty years of research, said that "the only thing that really matters in life are your relationships to other people."[14]

Social support is not just good for your physical and mental health. It's also vital to outstanding performance. Consider what researchers found when analyzing the speeches of baseball players when they were inducted into the National Baseball Hall of Fame. As elite athletes, they had achieved the highest recognition in a field demanding top physical skills. Yet for almost two-thirds of them, their words of appreciation were less about technical or practical assistance than about such factors as emotional support and friendship. Social support was mentioned even more prominently for those elected in their very first year of eligibility.[15]

What's true at home, in the community, and on the playing field is just as true at work. Research indicates, for instance, that "if you have a best friend at work you are significantly more likely to engage customers, get more done in less time, have more fun on the job, have a safe workplace with fewer accidents, innovate and share ideas, feel informed and know that your opinion counts, and have the opportunity to focus on your strengths each day."[16] Friends are not only good for your health but good for business. There is plenty of opportunity for strengthening these relationships because, unfortunately, only 18 percent of people report that their organizations offer opportunities to develop friendships at work.[17]

Our files are full of personal-best leadership cases in which strong human connections produced spectacular results. Extraordinary accomplishments are achieved when everyone gets personally involved with the task and with other people. When people feel a strong sense of affiliation and attachment to their colleagues, they're much more likely to have a higher sense of personal well-being, to feel more committed to the organization, and to perform at higher levels. When people feel distant and detached, they're unlikely to get much of anything done.[18]

Leaders understand that what makes people most miserable is being alone. Celebrations provide concrete evidence that individuals aren't alone in their efforts, that other people care about them, and that they can count on others. People are reminded that they need each other, that their work gets done because they're connected and caught up in each other's lives. Celebrations reinforce the fact that it takes a group of people working together with a common purpose, in an atmosphere of trust and collaboration, to get extraordinary things done. By making achievements public, leaders build a culture in which people know that what they do is not taken for granted, and clearly feel that their efforts are appreciated and applauded.

Invest in Fun

Fun isn't a luxury, even at work. Every personal-best leadership experience was a combination of hard work *and* fun. In fact, most people agreed that without the enjoyment and the pleasure they experienced with others on the team, they wouldn't have been able to sustain the level of intensity and hard work required to do their personal best. People simply feel better about the work they're doing when they enjoy the people they're working with.[19] Every day might not be all laughs, but if it's all drudgery, then it's hardly worth the effort to get out of bed and come to work.

Joie de Vivre Hospitality—the country's second-largest boutique hotelier—was celebrating their twentieth anniversary, and founder-CEO Chip Conley decided to throw a "Joy party" in celebration of the company's name (French for "joy of life") and the company's mantra ("Create joy"). For years, the company's three thousand employees had often worn blue wrist bands with this mantra imprinted on it, and one of the core values of the organization was to create opportunities to celebrate joy with employees, customers, and even innocent bystanders.

The company invited ten thousand women from around California—all with the name Joy—to a party at their new, luxury Hotel Vitale on San Francisco's waterfront. The first twenty-five who gave them an affirmative RSVP were given a free hotel room for the night of the event so that they could have a Joy slumber party. Chip said,

> That night, I showed up and saw smiles everywhere. We ended up with a roomful of joy (and Joys), 125 women sharing the same name, along with their husbands, significant others, friends, and children. What was miraculous was how those

strangers bonded so quickly through their stories of "being Joy," as if they were long-lost friends. There were lots of Joy-full tears. It was one big love bubble, not just for the Joys and their families but also for our employees, who realized the significance of our company name and our mission of creating joy in the world. To this day, many Joie de Vivre employees say this is one of their fondest memories in the company.

It's easy to imagine the fun people had in thinking about, planning, and eventually en-Joy-ing this event. And, although the intent of the event wasn't necessarily to drive business, that hotel received a large new piece of business, a corporate retreat that more than paid for the party, thanks to the word of mouth from the event.

Having fun sustains productivity, creating what researchers refer to as "subjective well-being." And it's not all about parties, games, festivities, and laughter. Wayne Tam describes his manager Stephen Barkhuff, director of planning tools, at Bank of America, as a quantitative guy who really enjoyed problem solving and logic problems:

He really had fun dissecting complex computer code or translating business processes to functional specifications. While these tasks could be quite difficult, he was always positive and built up our skills so that we could meet these challenges with the same attitude he had. He encouraged the heart by showing us how to have fun with this work. Many of us reporting to him often worked together on complex problems and encouraged each other as well. Since we often had fun completing these challenges, we also shared the passion that Steve had with his work.

Wayne went on to say that "I learned that though you get paid to do a job, it's better to be able to enjoy what you do and have fun."

When you appreciate Chip's Joy party and how Steve was able to make solving challenging problems fun, you can also understand that these leaders—and hundreds of others we studied—are passionate about their purpose, what they believe in, and how they pass this on to others. They know that work in today's organizations is difficult and demanding, and in this climate people need to have a sense of personal well-being in order to sustain their commitment. And leaders set the tone. When leaders openly demonstrate the joy and passion they have for their organizations, team members, clients, and challenges, they send a very loud message to others that it's perfectly acceptable for people to make public displays of playfulness; it is more than okay to show enthusiasm both at work and for the work you do.

GET PERSONALLY INVOLVED

Remember what we said at the beginning of this book: leadership is a relationship. People are much more likely to enlist in initiatives led by those with whom they feel a personal attachment. We started our discussion of personal-best leadership with Model the Way, and we've come full circle. If you want others to believe in something and behave according to those beliefs, you have to set the example by being personally involved. You have to practice what you preach. If you want to build and maintain a culture of excellence and distinction, then you have to recognize, reward, reinforce, and celebrate exceptional efforts and successes. You have to get personally involved in celebrating the actions that contribute to and sustain the culture. And if you want people to have the courage to continue the quest in the face of great adversity, you have to encourage them yourself.

What you preach and what you celebrate must be one and the same. If they aren't, the event will come off as insincere and phony—and your credibility will suffer. The celebration must be an honest expression of commitment to key values and to the hard work and dedication of the people who have lived the values. Elaborate productions that lack sincerity are more entertainment than encouragement. It's authenticity that makes conscious celebrations work.

When it comes to sending a message throughout the organization, nothing communicates more clearly than what the leaders do. By directly and visibly showing others that you're there to cheer them along, you're sending a positive signal. When you set the example that communicates the message, "Around here we say thanks, show appreciation, and have fun," others will follow your lead. The organization will develop a culture of celebration and recognition. Everyone becomes a leader, everyone sets the example, and everyone takes the time to celebrate the values and victories. When leaders are encouraging, others follow their example, and organizations develop a reputation for being great places to work. They're magnetic, attracting and retaining employees and customers far better than their competitors can. People form a strong bond with these institutions. They're proud to be affiliated. Employees want to excel, business partners want to delight, and customers want to stay loyal for a lifetime.

Wherever you find a strong culture built around strong values, you'll also find endless examples of leaders who personally live the values. You have to set the example of what's expected and what will be rewarded by being personally involved, which is precisely what Beth Taute described to us about a manager (Jo) she worked with at Citibank, who headed up a small team of analysts responsible for the mammoth task of upgrading the human resources system, which involved over 150,000 employees dotted across more than fifty-two countries: "Jo had taken on the task because she felt her team could do it. She shared her belief in the team's ability to do it with them in their weekly team meeting. She then sat with each of them individually in one-to-one meetings to allow them to express their fears or reservations. She wanted each person in her team to feel as though his or her opinions were important enough to be considered individually."

Jo got the ball rolling, and within a few days the team members were up to their necks in various systems and issues. They were rarely out of the office before midnight due to the tight time constraints placed on them, and Jo was right alongside them at all times. She even moved out of her office onto the floor to be closer to them, and they converted her office to a meeting room for the various conference calls they were making. She often had to leave the office early to pick her daughter up and take her home, but would always return with pizza, late-night snacks, or coffee to keep the team fed and content.

Jo showed her appreciation in various ways that other managers did not—even if it cost her time and personal funds. She would do small things, such as taking the team out for a surprise lunch. She let team members leave early if she knew they had something special happening in the evening. She let team members with children come in late or leave early on special occasions like birthdays so that they could spend the morning or afternoon with them. She knew they were putting in more hours per week than was required and wanted them to know that the hours were appreciated. Small and silly gifts with hidden jokes or meaning were scattered on everyone's desks. The result, according to Beth, was that "her team was completely dedicated to her. She was an inspiration to them, and that meant they would work until all hours to ensure this project was completed."

Jo knew that the project was an enormous undertaking, and so did her team. Because of her hands-on personal involvement, her team wanted to show her, by meeting and trying to exceed her expectations, that her confidence and trust in them were correctly placed. She was their chief cheerleader and supporter. She was also their first line of help when they needed it, as well as the biggest believer in their ability to succeed. She mounted a huge poster in what had been her office documenting country by country where they were making inroads and where they had to do more work. Her enthusiasm for the project and their ability to complete it spilled over to the team. Every time they reached a milestone, they would go out for a celebratory drink. Said Beth,

> Jo had such close relationships with a varied group of individuals and knew which buttons to push to get each individual to perform beyond their comfort zone and to remain dedicated to the cause. She made coming to work and being there late seem fun and not like a hard slog. I learned that leaders have to be involved and connected with what's going on and that the best recognition is ongoing, without being expected or predictable. To have done great work and be recognized by Jo was more than any other recognition team members wanted.

It's this kind of personal dedication and involvement that earns leaders the respect and trust of their teams. It's what builds credibility and loyalty. It's also what develops an engaged and productive workforce.

Show You Care

Leaders make sure that people know they are being paid attention to and not being taken for granted. "People appreciate knowing that

I care about them," explained Judith Wiencke, an engineering manager at Australia's Telecom, "and they seem to care more about what they're doing as a result." Indeed, Peter Birgbauer remembers, when he was working as an investment banking analyst, how the CEO made "everyone he interacted with feel important and valued, regardless of their title or role in the company." And he still recalls the impact that receiving a handwritten note of appreciation from the CEO had on him: "It would have been very easy for him to send me an email or thank me in person when we ran into one another, but he personalized his gratitude, showing that he cared, and this made a significant impression on me. I felt valued, and it made me want to work harder for the company."

One of the most significant ways in which leaders show others that they care is to be there with them. Thank-you notes and emails expressing your appreciation are important, but being visible makes you more real, more genuine, more approachable, and more human. You show you care when you attend meetings, visit customers, tour the plants or service centers, drop in on the labs, make presentations at association gatherings, attend organizational events (even when you're not on the program), recruit at local universities, hold roundtable discussions, speak to analysts, or just drop by your constituents' cubicles to say hello. Being there also helps you stay in touch, almost literally, with what's really going on. And it shows that you walk the talk about the values you and your constituents share. Believability goes up when leaders are personally involved.

For instance, when news of a possible physical move (with potential layoff implications) leaked to employees, Kurt Richarz dropped what he was doing, got on a plane, and flew halfway across the country to speak with the potentially affected team.[20] He began the lunchtime conversation very honestly and plainly, in his signature Texan accent: "I didn't know whether I should come out or not, but I decided that I wanted to make sure I had the chance to talk with y'all and set the record straight. I want to talk about what's going on, and hear what's on your minds, too." Kurt went on to paint a more detailed picture, in the hopes of allaying fears and letting people know the truth about what was really going on. He expressed his belief in their capabilities, and his desire to help them get more satisfaction out of their jobs. For some, this additional information was a breath of fresh air; others left the lunch just as concerned, but better educated on the situation.

The important thing was that Kurt not only acknowledged that his support team was upset but actually did something major to show them that they were important to him. Had he just sent an email or scheduled a conference call, his acknowledgment wouldn't have been very impressive; the fact that he made a special trip just for twenty-five support individuals was a monumental demonstration that he cared for his team. What's more, the roundtable lunch was a celebration of sorts, one recognizing the importance of community and their shared value of transparency.

In case you have any doubt that getting personally involved in celebrations has an impact on others or on their assessment of your leadership, take a look at what we consistently find in our research. Those constituents who say that their leaders "almost always" (or at least "very frequently") find ways to celebrate score nearly 25 percent higher on the extent to which "the organization values my work." Ask people if they feel that they are making a difference, and those who say their leaders find ways to celebrate again score 25 percent higher than those who report that their leaders don't often find ways to celebrate. And here's another result you should pay attention to: we ask people how effective, overall, they think their leader is; we then correlate their ratings of their leaders' effectiveness with the extent to which their leaders find ways to celebrate. Once again we see highly significant differences. People who work for leaders who more frequently celebrate rate their leaders' effectiveness nearly one-third higher compared to those who say their leaders celebrate less. Bottom line: showing you care pays big dividends to leaders and constituents alike.

Spread the Stories

Being out and about and getting personally involved in showing that they care give leaders like Kurt the opportunity to both create and find stories that put a human face on values. First-person examples are always more powerful and striking than third-party examples. It's that critical difference between "I saw for myself" and "Someone told me about." Exemplary leaders are constantly on the lookout to "catch people doing things right," and you can't do this very well if you stay behind a desk or counter.[21] You need to see and know firsthand what's being done right so that you can not only let that person know to "keep up the good work" but also tell others about it. That way, you can give "up close and personal" accounts of what it means to put into practice the shared values and aspirations. You create organizational role models to whom everyone can relate. You put the behavior in a real context. Values become more than simply rules; you make them come alive. Stories also quickly translate information about how people are actually supposed to act and make decisions.[22]

Stories by their nature are public forms of communication. Storytelling is how people pass along lessons from generation to generation, culture to culture. Stories aren't meant to be secret; they're meant to be told. And because they're public, they're tailor-made for celebrations. Emory psychology professor Drew Westen argues that "the stories our leaders tell us matter, probably almost as much as the stories our parents tell us as children, because they orient us to what is, what could be, and should be; to the worldviews they hold and to the values they hold sacred."[23] In fact, you can think of stories as celebrations; and celebrations, in turn, are ready-made occasions to tell and share stories.

Leaders find numerous ways to perpetuate the important stories—for instance, by publishing a story in the company newsletter or annual report, relating a story in a public ceremony, or making a video and broadcasting it on the internal television network. Leaders shine the spotlight on someone who's lived out an organizational value—and provide others in the organization with an example they can emulate.

"The stories that resulted from the Cheer Ticket program at Sprint's corporate audit services team," says Justin Brocato, then intermediate financial auditor, "is one of the key reasons why it worked so well." At the start of each year, each employee was given fifty yellow tickets that had a big smiley face on them. Anytime someone helped you out or you wanted to recognize a job well done, you could give them a cheer ticket along with a handwritten personal message to explain what they did to help and how it was connected with one of the seven Sprint values (for example, initiative, adaptability, and leadership, to name three). Clearly this program made some direct connections with the company's core values, and because employees were required to write in a descriptive message, it served as a reminder of organizational and project goals and values. This connection between goals and values helped keep employees focused and energized. It was a simple way to say thank you and give real-time feedback. According to Justin, "the program worked because the stories were all so personal. . . . The employee receiving the ticket knew right away what they did well and who made the observation. This is an important point because I feel that feedback is too often unspecific and untimely. The program also made coming to work fun. Having fun can be a powerful way to motivate individuals."

This "storytelling" program created an interesting dynamic in the group and, Justin felt, "brought out the best in people." People were always aware that they could become "a story" because others were taking note of their behavior, but at the same time, they too were observing their peers. They expected the best in others because they knew others expected the same from them. Many of the stories were told throughout the year, and some were handed down and related from year to year.

By telling stories, you can more effectively accomplish the objectives of teaching, mobilizing, and motivating than you can through bullet points in a PowerPoint presentation or tweets on a mobile device. Listening to and understanding the stories leaders tell do more to inform people about the values and culture of an organization than do company policies or the employee manual. They communicate what really goes on within the organization. Well-told stories reach inside people and pull them along. They simulate the actual experience of being there and give people a compelling way of learning what is really important about the experience. Reinforcing stories through celebrations deepens the connections.

Make Celebrations Part of Organizational Life

You need to put celebrations on your calendar. You probably do this already for birthdays, holidays, and anniversaries, and you should also do it for the important markers in the life of your organization. Giving them a date, time, and place announces to everyone that these things matter to you. It also creates a sense of anticipation. Scheduling celebrations doesn't rule out spontaneous events; it just means that certain occasions are of such significance that everyone needs to pay special attention to them.

In setting up celebrations, you first need to decide which organizational values, events of historical significance, or specific successes are of such importance that they warrant a special ritual, ceremony, or festivity. Perhaps you want to honor the group or team of people who created the year's important innovations, praise those who gave extraordinary customer service, or thank the families of your constituents for their support. Whatever you wish to celebrate, you need to formalize it, announce it, and tell people how they become eligible to participate. At a minimum, you ought to have at least one celebration each year that involves everyone, though not necessarily at the same site, and one that draws attention to each of the key values of your organization.

Leaders make celebrations as much a part of their organization's life as they can. In their book *Corporate Celebration,* professors Terrence Deal and M. K. Key provide a detailed framework for scheduling and anticipating celebrations, and many of their celebration ideas are presented in Table 11.1. Think about what might work for your organization.

Of course celebrations are not always about one achievement or for one person. Each year, the three employees in Sprint's Cheer Ticket program who had the most tickets in a particular values category were nominated for a special award. The management team reviewed the nominees for each value's category, and the overall category winners were revealed at an annual dinner. Justin described the annual awards banquet

as a wonderful way to celebrate our accomplishments and spread that sense of community. Significant others were encouraged to attend, so it was a nice way to get to know

TABLE 11.1 Events, Accomplishments, and Actions to Schedule

Cyclical celebrations. Seasonal themes, key milestones, corporate anniversaries, individual birthdays, marriages, reunions, and other recurring events.

Recognition ceremonies. Public applause and acknowledgment for a job well done, being best in class, attaining specific goals, achieving a special rank, getting a promotion, and other achievements that deserve broad attention.

Celebrations of triumph. Special occasions for accentuating collective accomplishments, such as winning a championship, beating forecasts, beating the competition, launching a new product or strategy, founding a new company, and opening a new office, plant, or store.

Rituals for comfort and letting go. Not all of organization life is about victory; sometimes there's calamity and loss. There's the loss of a contract, layoffs of employees, a death of a colleague, an experiment that failed, and site closings. These occasions can be marked by ceremony and ritual to help people let go and move on.

Personal transitions. Celebrations of entrances and exits, initiations, separations, and other life passages as people come and go in the organization.

Workplace altruism. Celebrations of doing good for others, pulling together to help others, promoting social change, showing appreciation to customers and clients.

Events. Celebrations of the company's anniversary, opening day, holidays, milestones, and articulation of the organization's vision.

Play. Energizing meetings and conventions, spoofing and poking fun, games and sporting events.

Source: T. Deal and M. K. Key, *Corporate Celebration: Play, Purpose, and Profit at Work* (San Francisco: Berrett-Koehler, 1998), 28.

people outside of an office setting and further build upon existing relationships. It was also the perfect forum to publicly recognize all of the contributions of the team and reflect upon what we had accomplished.

Looking at it from the opposite perspective, what if management had just sent out an email to announce and congratulate the winners? How would that affect the impact of the program? Yes, I am sure employees would have appreciated that, but compare that to the roar of applause and whistles when someone goes on stage to accept their award. Then imagine your boss, on stage, telling you and an audience full of your peers why they felt your accomplishments were worthy of recognition. Celebrating in public is so much more memorable, and the impact that it has on the recipient and on the team is longer lasting. People get energized, and suddenly they have a renewed sense of commitment for the year to come.

There really is no shortage of opportunities to bring people together to celebrate your organization's values and victories. In good times or bad, gathering together to acknowledge those who've contributed and the actions that have led to success signals to everyone that their efforts made a difference. Their energy, enthusiasm, and well-being—and yours—will be all the better for it.

TAKE ACTION

Celebrate the Values and Victories

Celebrating together reinforces the fact that extraordinary performance is the result of many people's efforts. By visibly and publicly celebrating people's accomplishments, leaders create community and sustain team spirit. By basing celebrations on consistency with key values and attainment of critical milestones, leaders reinforce and sustain people's focus.

Social interaction increases individuals' commitments to the standards of the group and has a profound effect on people's well-being. Intimacy heals; loneliness depresses. When people are asked to go beyond their comfort zones, the support and encouragement of their colleagues enhance their resistance to the possible debilitating effects of stress. Make sure that your organization is not regarded as the place where "fun goes to die."

Leaders set the example by getting personally involved in celebration and recognition, demonstrating that encouraging the heart is something everyone should do. Telling stories about individuals who have made exceptional efforts and achieved phenomenal successes provides opportunities for leaders to showcase role models for others to emulate. Stories make people's experiences memorable, often even profound in ways that they hadn't envisioned, and serve as a marker for future behaviors. Making personal connections with people in a culture of celebration also builds and sustains credibility. It reduces we-they demarcations between leaders and constituents. Adding vitality and a sense of appreciation to the workplace is essential.

To Encourage the Heart, you must *celebrate the values and victories by creating a spirit of community*. This means you have to

- Find and create occasions to bring people together.
- Be sure to make connections to the fundamental principles when you explain why you are holding a celebration.

- Find out about people's stories—what they are doing to make the organization successful. Write them down in a journal to make sure you capture them.
- Never pass up any opportunity to publicly relate true stories about how people in your organization went above and beyond the call of duty.
- Hallways, elevators, and cafeterias, in addition to meeting rooms, are all acceptable venues for telling and posting good stories.
- Make sure that people understand how they are "part of the whole" and that lots of others are working to make them successful, even if they don't know them.
- Repeat this phrase at every celebration: "We are in this together."
- Plan a festive celebration for even the smaller milestones that your team reaches. Don't wait until the whole project is completed before you celebrate.
- Get personally involved in as many recognitions and celebrations as possible.
- Have fun when you're celebrating—laugh and enjoy yourself, along with others.
- End each of your team meetings with a round of public praise.

Use *The Leadership Challenge Mobile Tool* app to immediately integrate these activities into your life and make this practice an ongoing part of your behavioral repertoire.

CHAPTER 12

Leadership Is Everyone's Business

THROUGHOUT THIS BOOK, we've told stories of ordinary people who've made extraordinary things happen. They are from all over the globe, from all age groups and walks of life. They represent a wide variety of organizations—public and private, governmental and nongovernmental, high-tech and low-tech, small and large, educational and professional. Chances are you haven't heard of most of them. They're not public figures, celebrities, or megastars. They're people who might live next door or work in the next cubicle over. They are people just like you.

We've focused on everyday leaders because leadership is not about position or title. It's not about organizational power or authority. It's not about fame or wealth. It's not about the family you are born into. It's not about being a CEO, president, general, or prime minister. And it's definitely not about being a hero. Leadership is about relationships, about credibility, and about what you *do*. And everything you will ever do as a leader is based on one audacious assumption: that *you matter*.

You don't have to look up for leadership. You don't have to look out for leadership. You only have to look inward. You have the potential to lead others to places they have never been. But before you can lead others, you have to believe that you can have a positive impact on others. You have to believe that what you do counts. You have to believe that your words can inspire and that your actions can move others. And you have to be able to convince others that the same is true for them. In these turbulent times, there is no shortage of opportunities to lead, and the world needs more people who believe they can make a difference and who are willing to act on that belief.

LOOK TO LEADERS EVERYWHERE

For a long time now, we've been asking people of all ages and backgrounds about the leaders in their own lives who are role models. Not well-known historical leaders, but leaders with whom they've had personal experience. We've asked them to identify the person they'd select as their most important role model for leadership, and then we've given them a list of eight possible categories from which these leaders might come.[1] They can choose from business leader, community or religious leader, entertainer or cinema star, family member, political leader, professional athlete, teacher or coach, or other/none/not sure. Take a look at the results in Table 12.1.

When thinking back over their lives and selecting their most important leader role models, people of all ages are more likely to choose a family member than anyone else. It turns out that relatives are the most influential leaders. In second place, for respondents thirty years of age and under, is a teacher or coach. For the over-thirty crowd, a business leader is number two. But when we

Role Model Category	Respondent Age Category	
	18–30 years old	Over 30 years old
Family member	40%	46%
Teacher or coach	26%	14%
Community or religious leader	11%	8%
Business leader	7%	23%
Political leader	4%	4%
Professional athlete	3%	0%
Entertainer	2%	0%
None/not sure/other	7%	4%

TABLE 12.1 Who Are Role Models for Leadership?

probe further, people tell us that "business leader" really refers to the person who was an immediate supervisor at work, not someone in the C-suite; for those in the workplace, these leaders are their teachers and coaches.

What do you notice about the top groups on the list? You should notice that they're the people you know well and who know you well. They're the leaders you are closest to and who are closest to you. They're the ones with whom you have the closest contact. Leader role models are local. You find them close to where you live and work.

Our research clearly demonstrates that the experience of leadership is not something that happens only at the very top of organizations or that is confined to formal organizations at all. It's experienced everywhere. In other words, *Leadership is everyone's business.*

KNOW HOW IMPORTANT YOU ARE

Here's something else the data show. People are watching you, regardless of whether you know it or not. And you are having an impact on them, regardless of whether you intend to or not.

If you're a manager in an organization, to your direct reports *you* are the *most important* leader in your organization. *You* are more likely than any other leader to influence their desire to stay or leave, the trajectory of their careers, their ethical behavior, their ability to perform at their best, their drive to wow customers, their satisfaction with their jobs, and their motivation to share the organization's vision and values.

If you're a parent, teacher, coach, or community leader *you* are the person that's setting the leadership example for young people. It's not hip-hop artists, movie stars, or professional athletes they seek guidance from. *You* are the one they are most likely going to look to for the example of how a leader responds to competitive situations, handles crises, deals with loss, or resolves ethical dilemmas. It's not someone else. It's you.

These data challenge further the myth that leadership is about position and power. And they support the notion that leadership is about the actions you take. That's certainly what Yukari Huguenard, solutions product manager at KANA Software, learned when she examined her assumptions about the origins of leadership: "I used to think leaders had to be at the top level of a large organization. With that view of leadership, the chasm between where I am and being a leader was uncrossable. Now, I see leaders leading a group of people of any size and leading at any level. You are a leader if you employ the five leadership practices because people around you want to follow. In that sense, I feel that I'm already a leader."

There's no escape. No matter what your position is, you have to take responsibility for the quality of leadership your constituents' experience. You are accountable for the leadership you demonstrate. And because you are the most important leader to those closest to you, you have to decide how good a leader you want to be.

There's little debate that leaders make a difference. The only real question is what kind of difference they make. Consider what people report when we ask them to think about the worst leader they have ever worked for and then to write down a number representing the percentage of their talents that this leader utilized. Our research results (displayed in Figure 12.1) show that people report that their worst leaders generally use only about a third of their available energy and talents. Those few who reported a higher percentage than the average, when referring to their worst leader, clearly noted and

FIGURE 12.1 The Best Leaders Bring Out the Talents in Others

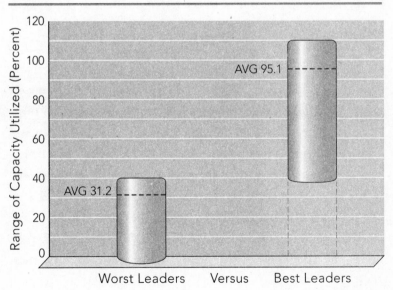

voiced their resentment about how they had to do so much more than was really necessary because of their boss's ineptitude.

This percentage is in sharp contrast to what people report when they think about their most admired leader. For these folks, the bottom of the range is typically *higher* than the top of the range for the former group. Many people indicate over 100 percent, and the average is around 95 percent. Bottom line: the best leaders elicit nearly three times the amount of energy, drive, commitment, and productivity from their constituents compared to their counterparts at the other end of the spectrum. When people reflect on their own experience, it becomes crystal clear that, to repeat, *leaders make a difference.*

We're certain that you want to become the best leader you can be, not just for your own sake, but also for the sake of others and for the success of the endeavors you are pursuing. After all, it's unlikely that you'd be reading this book if you didn't. But how can you learn to lead better than you do now?

PRACTICE

Nearly every time we give a speech or conduct a workshop, someone asks, "Are leaders born or made?" Whenever we're asked this question, our answer, always offered with a smile, is this: "We've never met a leader who wasn't born. We've also never met an accountant, artist, athlete, engineer, lawyer, physician, writer, or zoologist who wasn't born. We're all born. That's a given. It's what you do with what you have before you die that makes the difference."

Let's get something straight. Leadership is not preordained. It's not a gene, and it's not a trait. There is no hard evidence to support the assertion that leadership is imprinted in the DNA of only some individuals and that everyone else missed out and is doomed to be clueless.

Leadership can be learned. It's an *observable pattern of practices and behaviors* and a definable set of skills and abilities. And any skill can be learned, strengthened, honed, and enhanced, given the motivation and desire, along with practice, feedback, and coaching. When we track the progress of people who participate in leadership development programs, for example, the research demonstrates that they improve over time.[2] They learn to be better leaders.

But here's the rub. Although leadership can be learned, not everyone wants to learn it, and not all those who learn about leadership master it. Why? Because becoming the very best requires having a strong desire to excel, a strong belief that new skills and abilities can be learned, and a willing devotion to deliberate practice and continuous learning. No matter how good you are, you have to always want to be better. *The truth is that the best leaders are the best learners.*

One midcareer executive told us about an address he still remembers by General Colin Powell, given at the Naval Academy in 1992: "He told the assembled brigade of midshipmen that one of the tenets of a good leader is to never stop learning. He stressed that we must use every experience, good or bad, to strengthen our leadership identity." He went on to say that "among the leadership lessons I learned, the impact of making time for practicing good leadership strikes me as the most significant." You can't learn to be a good leader without putting in the time and practice.

Florida State University professor and noted authority on expertise K. Anders Ericsson made this same point when he said, "Until most individuals recognize that sustained training and effort is a prerequisite for reaching expert levels of performance, they will continue to misattribute lesser achievement to the lack of natural gifts, and will thus fail to reach their own potential."[3] Anders and his colleagues have found, over the thirty years of their research, that raw talent is not all there is to becoming a top performer. It doesn't matter whether it's in sports, music, medicine, computer programming, mathematics, or other fields; talent is not the key that unlocks excellence.

Staggeringly high IQs don't characterize the great performers, either. Sometimes world-class performers are really brilliant, but in many instances they possess just average intelligence. Similarly, years of experience don't necessarily make someone a high performer, let alone the greatest performer. And as startling as it might sound, sometimes more years of experience can mean poorer performance compared to those newly graduated in a specialty.

What truly differentiates the expert performers from the good performers is hours of deliberate *practice.* You've got to work at becoming the best, and it sure doesn't happen over a weekend. If you want a rough metric of what it takes to achieve the highest level of expertise, the estimate is about 10,000 hours of deliberate practice over a period of ten years.[4] That's about 2.7 hours a day, every day, for ten years!

In other words, you have to have a passion for learning in order to become the best leader you can be. You have to be open to new experiences and open to honestly examining how you and others perform, especially under conditions of uncertainty. You have to be willing to learn quickly from your failures as well as your successes, and find ways to try out new behaviors without hesitation. You won't always be right or do things perfectly, but you will get the chance to grow.

REFLECT

Engineers have computers; painters, canvas and brushes; musicians, instruments. Leaders have only themselves. The instrument of leadership is the self, and mastery of the art of leadership comes from mastery of the self. Leadership development is self-development, and self-development is not about stuffing in a whole bunch of new information or trying out the latest technique. It's about leading out of what is already in your soul. It's about liberating the leader within you. And it starts with taking a look inside.

Your ability to excel as a leader depends on how well you know yourself. The better you know yourself, the better you can make sense of the often incomprehensible and conflicting messages you receive daily. Do this, do that. Support this, support that. Decide this, decide that. Change this, change that. You need internal guidance to navigate the turmoil in today's highly uncertain environment.

Harry Kraemer Jr., Northwestern University's Kellogg School of Management professor and former chairman and CEO of Baxter International, strongly affirms that self-reflection is indispensible for leaders. "The more you self-reflect," he says, "the better you know yourself: your strengths, weaknesses, abilities, and areas to be developed. Being self-aware, you know what you stand for and what is important to you. With this clarity, you are able to connect and communicate with others more effectively. Grounded in self-knowledge, your leadership becomes more authentic."[5]

For Harry, self-reflection is a personal discipline he's cultivated over many years. It all started when he was dating his then girlfriend and now wife, Julie, and was invited on a weekend retreat by his prospective father-in-law. Of course Harry accepted, but he didn't know until he arrived that it would be a "silent retreat." Harry asked what this meant, and he was told, "Harry, I have already noticed that you can't shut up for three minutes. This is going to be a challenge, because you are not going to say anything for three days." Harry was intrigued, and learned that you can't really reflect—can't actually think through what's important—unless you shut up and listen to your inner self.

Every single day, usually at the end of the day when the work is done and it's quiet, Harry spends fifteen to thirty minutes reflecting on "the day that is coming to a close, the impact I have made, and the impact that others have made on me." He asks himself a number of questions about what he said, what he actually did, what went well, what didn't, what he'd do differently, what he learned that had an impact on how he lives going forward, and so on. This practice of self-reflection is something every leader should adopt.

As you begin and continue your journey toward exemplary leadership, you must wrestle with some difficult questions:

What are the values that should guide my decisions and actions?

What are my beliefs about how people ought to conduct the affairs of our organization?

What are my leadership strengths and weaknesses?

How consistent is my view of my leadership with how others see me?

What do I need to do to improve my abilities to move the organization forward?

Where do I think the organization should be headed over the next ten years?

How clear are others about our shared vision of the future?

How much do I understand about what is going on in the organization and the world in which it operates?

What are the challenges we face, and how prepared are we to deal with them?

How prepared am I to handle the complex problems that now confront my organization?

What gives me the courage to continue in the face of uncertainty and adversity?

How will I handle disappointments, mistakes, and setbacks?

What keeps me from giving up?

How solid are my relationships with my constituents?

How much do my constituents trust me and trust each other?

How can I keep myself motivated and encouraged?

How am I doing at sharing the credit and saying thank you?

What can I do to keep hope alive—in myself and others?

Am I the right one to be leading at this very moment? Why?

All exemplary leaders have wrestled with questions like these. Such personal searching is essential in the development of leaders. You can't lead others until you've first led yourself on a journey of self-discovery.

As Harry said, "Turn the spotlight on yourself. The glare will not be more than you can handle. Rather, let it illuminate your life and your choices—personal and professional—and help you see how you are affecting the course of your life and your leadership."[6] If you are to become the leader you aspire to be, you will have to take the time to step back and reflect on your past, your present, and your future.

REMAIN HUMBLE AND HUMAN

We need to add, however, that there's a messy reality all leaders have to face: you can do everything we talk about in this book perfectly and still fail! As a leader, you quickly learn what it feels like to be squeezed between lofty expectations and your own limitations. Sometimes, in spite of your best efforts and your very best intentions, you don't succeed. Perhaps we should have told you this sooner, but it's our guess that you knew it already. You knew it from your personal experience, or you knew it from the experience of those close to you. You knew it because no one can ever be *that* good.

There is no get-rich-quick, instant-weight-loss program for leaders. There's absolutely no way that we can say that The Five Practices of Exemplary Leadership will always work, all the time or with everyone. We do know for certain that these leadership practices will make a significant difference, but there's no ironclad, money-back guarantee. In addition, you will never find, in historic or present times, even one example of a leader who controlled every variable in the environment. And you'll never find an example of a leader who enlisted 100 percent of the possible constituency in even the most compelling of future possibilities.

And there's still another reality to confront: the treachery of hubris is far more insidious than any of the other potential problems a leader might encounter. It's fun to be a leader, gratifying to have influence, and exhilarating to have scores of people cheering your every word. In many all-too-subtle ways, it's easy to be seduced by power and importance. It's possible for any leader to get infected with the disease of arrogance and pride, becoming bloated with an exaggerated sense of self and pursuing one's own ends. How then can you avoid this?

Humility is the only way to resolve the conflicts and contradictions of leadership. "Dig a hole, throw your ego into it, and pour concrete on top. Find humility instead," advises Dave Balter, founder of BzzAgent, the leading word-of-mouth marketing company.[7] Dave knows what he's talking about. His ego, which gave him the confidence to be an entrepreneur and leader, almost destroyed his business.

BzzAgent was Dave's fourth start-up, and it was a hit. Venture capitalists came knocking, he was featured on the cover of the *New York Times Magazine,* and Harvard Business School wrote two cases on the company. He was heralded as a genius, and confesses that he believed all the positive press. He thought he was the reason for the business's success, and said that his "entire style evolved from confident to cocky." He dismissed comments from others around him as "shortsighted," and the only voices he really heard, he later realized, "were the ones in my head."[8]

Then the recession hit, and in 2009, reality struck. It was a hard time for every business, but it was particularly hard on BzzAgent because of "my outsized ego and the way I was leading the company," as Dave himself observed. The chairman of the board eventually took Dave aside and told him that it was his attitude that was the problem. Fortunately, that encounter awakened him from his ego-induced slumber. He took action to make some changes. "I was forced to grasp that I didn't have all the answers," he said. "In fact, I had to face the fact that I was pretty lousy at some things. . . . Humbled, I started to change my mindset. I became a student and a sponge."

Humility is the antidote for hubris. You can avoid excessive pride only when you recognize that you're human and need the help of others. Exemplary leaders know that "you can't do it alone," and they act accordingly. They lack the pride and pretense displayed by many leaders who succeed in the short term but leave behind a weak organization that fails to remain viable after their departure. Instead, with self-effacing humor, deep listening to those around them, and generous and sincere credit to others, humble leaders realize higher and higher levels of performance.

The word *human* and the word *humble* both derive from the Latin *humus,* meaning "earth." To be human and humble is to be down-to-earth, with your feet planted firmly on the ground. Interesting, isn't it, how as you climb the ranks you often climb to a higher floor in the building, getting farther and farther away from the ground? Is it any wonder that the higher you go, the harder it gets to keep your footing?[9]

You have to have the courage to be human and the courage to be humble. It takes a lot of courage to admit that you aren't always right, that you can't always anticipate every possibility, that you can't envision every future, that you can't solve every problem, that you can't control every variable, that you aren't always congenial, that you make mistakes, and that you are, well, human. It takes courage to admit all these things to yourself, but it may take even more courage to admit them to others. If you can find the humility to do that, you invite others into a courageous conversation. When you let down your guard and open yourself up to others, you invite them to join you in the creation of something that you could not create alone. When you become more modest and unpretentious, others have the chance themselves to become visible and noticed.[10]

Nothing in the research hints that leaders should be perfect. Leaders aren't saints. They're human beings, full of flaws and failings like everyone else. They make mistakes. Perhaps the very best advice for all aspiring leaders is to remain humble and unassuming—to always remain open and full of wonder.

SEIZE THE MOMENT

Sometimes leadership is imagined to be something majestic and awe inspiring. Grand visions, world-changing initiatives, transforming the lives of millions—all are noble possibilities, but real leadership is in the daily moments. Sergey Nikiforov, country manager, Russia and CIS, for CA Technologies, one of the world's largest independent software companies, put it to us this way:

> Where do I start becoming a better leader? This question has been nagging me for some time. Naively I assumed that to become a better leader meant to perform formidable tasks: moving mountains, saving lives, changing the world for the better. As you pointed out, these noble, grandiose tasks are often insurmountable for a single person.
>
> Then it occurred to me—I was thinking selfishly. What I envisioned was instant gratification, recognition for my skills and talent. Although the issues at work matched well with your book's materials, the way I dealt with them was far from ideal. In most cases, I used wrong tools and methods.
>
> I found that every day I had an opportunity to make a small difference. I could have coached someone better, I could have listened better, I could have been more positive toward people, I could have said thank you more often, I could have . . . the list just went on.
>
> At first, I was a bit overwhelmed with the discovery of how many opportunities I had in a single day to act as a better leader. But as I have gotten to put these ideas into practice I have been pleasantly surprised by how much improvement I have been able to make by being more conscientious and intentional about acting as a leader.

Sergey is right on point. Each day provides countless chances to make a difference. The chance might come in a private conversation with a direct report or in a meeting with colleagues. It might come while you're sitting at the family dinner table. It might come when you're speaking at a conference on the future of your business, or it might come when you're listening to a friend talk about a current conflict with a peer.

Leadership is in the moment. There are many moments each day when you can choose to lead, and many moments each day when you can choose to make a difference. Each of these moments serves up the prospect of contributing to a lasting legacy.

REMEMBER THE SECRET TO SUCCESS IN LIFE

There's one final leadership lesson that we'd like to pass along. It's the secret to success in life.

When we began our study of leadership bests, we were fortunate to cross paths with then U.S. Army Major General John H. Stanford. We knew that he had grown up poor, that he failed sixth grade but went on to graduate from Penn State University on an ROTC scholarship, that he survived multiple military tours in both Korea and Vietnam, that he was highly decorated, and that the loyalty of his troops was extraordinary. John headed up the Military Traffic Management Command for the U.S. Army during the Persian Gulf War. When he retired from the Army, he became county manager of Fulton County, Georgia, when Atlanta was gearing up to host the 1996 Summer Olympics, and then he became superintendent of the Seattle Public Schools, where he sparked a revolution in public education.

All that we learned of John's public service was impressive, but it was his answer to one of our interview questions that most influenced our own understanding of leadership. We asked John how he'd go about developing leaders, whether in colleges and universities, in the military, in government, in the nonprofit sector, or in private business. He replied,

> When anyone asks me that question, I tell them I have the secret to success in life. The secret to success is to stay in love. Staying in love gives you the fire to ignite other people, to see inside other people, to have a greater desire to get things done than other people. A person who is not in love doesn't really feel the kind of excitement that helps them to get ahead and to lead others and to achieve. I don't know any other fire, any other thing in life that is more exhilarating and is more positive a feeling than love is.

"Staying in love" isn't the answer we expected to get—at least not when we began our study of leadership. But after researching leadership for over thirty years, through thousands of interviews and case analyses, we are constantly reminded of how many leaders use the word *love* freely when talking about their own motivations to lead.

Of all the things that sustain a leader over time, love is the most lasting. It's hard to imagine leaders getting up day after day, putting in the long hours and hard work it takes to get extraordinary things done, without having their hearts in it. The best-kept secret of successful leaders is love: staying in love with leading, with the people who do the work, with what their organizations produce, and with those who honor the organization by using its products and services.

Leadership is not an affair of the head. Leadership is an affair of the heart.

Notes

Making Extraordinary Things Happen in Organizations
Chapter 1: When Leaders Are at Their Best

1. Unless otherwise noted, all quotations are taken from personal interviews or from Personal-Best Leadership Experience case studies written by the respondent leaders. The titles and affiliations of the leaders may be different today from what they were at the time of their case study or publication of this volume. We expect that many have moved on to other leadership adventures while we were writing, or will do so by the time you read this. It is also interesting to note that many of the leaders we interviewed were not always comfortable talking about themselves as "leaders," preferring to give credit for any of their accomplishments to the "great people" they were blessed to be working with. Barby Siegel is a good case in point.

2. For detailed information on our research methodology, the theory and evidence behind The Five Practices of Exemplary Leadership, our Personal-Best Leadership Experience questionnaire, the psychometric properties of the Leadership Practices Inventory (LPI), and reports on the analyses of our data, please see the research section of our Web site: http://www.leadershipchallenge.com/WileyCDA/Section/id-131060.html.

3. J. M. Kouzes and B. Z. Posner, *The Truth About Leadership: The No-Fads, Heart-of-the-Matter Facts You Need to Know* (San Francisco: Jossey-Bass, 2010).

4. Throughout this book, we use *cooperate* and *collaborate* synonymously. Their dictionary definitions are very similar. In *Merriam-Webster's Collegiate*

Dictionary, 10th ed. (2001), the first definition of *cooperate* is "To act or work with another or others: act together" (p. 254). The first definition of *collaborate* is "To work jointly with others or together esp. in an intellectual endeavor" (p. 224).

5. B. Kowitt, "Full-Time Motivation for Part-Time Employees," *Fortune*, October 17, 2011, 58.

6. See B. Posner, "Leadership Practices Inventory (LPI) Data Analysis," accessible on our Web site at http://media.wiley.com/assets/2260/07/LPIData AnalysisSept2010.pdf. The LPI is also available for review at http://www .leadershipchallenge.com/WileyCDA/LCTitle/productCd-PCOL52.html.

7. Respondents identify their age, gender, educational level, ethnicity (U.S. respondents only), nationality (or country of origin), hierarchical (organizational) level, functional field or discipline, industry, time with their current organization, and organization size (number of employees).

8. These ten statements were used to measure workplace engagement and commitment: (1) This person's work group has a strong sense of team spirit; (2) People who are part of this person's work group are proud to tell others that they work for their organization; (3) People who are part of this person's work group are committed to the organization's success; (4) People who are part of this person's work group would work harder and for longer hours if the job demanded it; (5) People who are part of this person's work group are highly productive in their job; (6) People who are part of this person's work group are clear about what is expected of them in their job: (7) People who are part of this person's work group feel that the organization values their work; (8) People who are part of this person's work group are effective in meeting the demands of their job; (9) People who are part of this person's work group seem to trust the management; and (10) People who are part of this person's work group feel like they are making a difference in the organization.

A 5-point response scale (with 1 indicating strongly disagree; 2, disagree; 3, neither agree nor disagree; 4, agree; and 5, strongly agree) is used for each statement; the leader is the "person" referred to in each item. The measure is completed by the leader's manager(s), coworkers (colleagues), direct reports, and "others" (people not in one of the previous three categories). The results do not vary systematically on the basis of these distinctions in the relationship with the leader.

9. Ann Rhoades quotes a 2009 study by the Gallup Organization that "companies in the top decile for employee engagement boosted earnings per share at nearly four times the rate of companies with lower scores." A. Rhoades, "Passionate People = A Profitable Company," *Fortune*, September 5, 2011, 22.

10. Abstracts of more than 500 studies using the Five Practices of Exemplary Leadership framework and the Leadership Practices Inventory (LPI) can be found at www.theleadershipchallenge.com/research.

11. R. Roi, *Leadership Practices, Corporate Culture, and Company Financial Performance: 2005 Study Results* (Palo Alto, CA: Crawford & Associates International, 2006). Downloadable copy available from www.hr.com.

12. For a more in-depth discussion about leadership being a relationship, what people look for in their leaders, and the actions leaders need to take to strengthen that relationship, see J. M. Kouzes and B. Z. Posner, *Credibility: How Leaders Gain and Lose It, Why People Demand It*, 2nd ed. (San Francisco: Jossey-Bass, 2011).

13. For more information about the original studies, see B. Z. Posner and W. H. Schmidt, "Values and the American Manager: An Update," *California Management Review* 26, no. 3 (1984): 202–216; and B. Z. Posner and W. H. Schmidt, "Values and Expectations of Federal Service Executives," *Public Administration Review* 46, no. 5 (1986): 447–454.

14. See Kouzes and Posner, *Credibility*, 9.

15. A point that respondents often make about the checklist is that leadership is not about following a person per se but about following a person who embodies for them a purpose (vision) that they believe is worthy and makes it possible for them to be leaders themselves.

16. The classic study on credibility goes back to C. I. Hovland, I. L. Janis, and H. H. Kelley, *Communication and Persuasion* (New Haven, CT: Yale University Press, 1953); early measurement studies include J. C. McCroskey, "Scales for the Measurement of Ethos," *Speech Monographs* 33 (1966): 65–72; and D. K. Berlo, J. B. Lemert, and R. J. Mertz, "Dimensions for Evaluating the Acceptability of Message Sources," *Public Opinion Quarterly* 3 (1969): 563–576. However, even further back, Aristotle (384–322 BC), writing in the *Rhetoric*, suggested that ethos, the trust of a speaker by the listener, or what some have referred to as "source credibility," was based on the listener's perception of three characteristics of the speaker: the intelligence of the speaker (correctness of opinions, or competence), the character of the speaker (reliability, a competence factor; and honesty, a measure of intentions), and the good will of the speaker (positive energy and favorable intentions toward the listener). These three characteristics (competence, honesty, and inspiration) have consistently emerged in factor-analytic investigations of communicator credibility; see D. J. O'Keefe, *Persuasion: Theory and Research* (Thousand Oaks, CA: Sage, 2002). Another contemporary perspective is provided in R. Cialdini, *Influence: The Psychology of Persuasion* (New York: Collins, 2007).

17. See, for example, B. Z. Posner and J. M. Kouzes, "Relating Leadership and Credibility," *Psychological Reports* 63 (1988): 527–530.

18. P. J. Sweeney, V. Thompson, and H. Blanton, "Trust and Influence in Combat: An Interdependence Model," *Journal of Applied Social Psychology* 39, no. 1 (2009): 235–264. Influence was defined as the willingness to allow another group member to change one's motivation, attitudes, values, thoughts, or behaviors. A sample statement: "Motivates you to push yourself to achieve excellence."

Model the Way
Chapter 2: Clarify Values

1. This example was provided by Gautam Aggarwal.
2. M. Rokeach, *The Nature of Human Values* (New York: Free Press, 1973), 5.
3. B. Z. Posner, "Values and the American Manager: A Three-Decade Perspective," *Journal of Business Ethics* 91, no. 4 (2010): 457–465.
4. B. Z. Posner and W. H. Schmidt, "Values Congruence and Differences Between the Interplay of Personal and Organizational Value Systems," *Journal of Business Ethics* 12 (1992): 171–177. See also B. Z. Posner, "Another Look at the Impact of Personal and Organizational Values Congruency," *Journal of Business Ethics* 97, no. 4 (2010): 535–541.
5. Posner, "Another Look."
6. C. Daniels, "Developing Organizational Values in Others," in *Leadership Lessons from West Point*, ed. D. Crandall (San Francisco: Jossey-Bass, 2007), 62–87.
7. See, for example, A. Rhoads and N. Shepherdson, *Build on Values: Creating an Enviable Culture That Outperforms the Competition* (San Francisco: Jossey-Bass, 2011); R. C. Roi, *Leadership, Corporate Culture and Financial Performance*, doctoral dissertation, University of San Francisco, 2006; and J. P. Kotter and J. L. Heskett, *Corporate Culture and Performance* (New York: Free Press, 1992).
8. See, for example, B. Z. Posner, W. H. Schmidt, and J. M. Kouzes, "Shared Values Make a Difference: An Empirical Test of Corporate Culture," *Human Resource Management* 24, no. 3 (1985): 293–310; B. Z. Posner, W. A. Randolph, and W. H. Schmidt, "Managerial Values Across Functions: A Source of Organizational Problems," *Group & Organization Management* 12, no. 4 (1987): 373–385; B. Z. Posner and W. H. Schmidt, "Demographic Characteristics and Shared Values," *International Journal of Value-Based Management* 5, no. 1 (1992): 77–87; B. Z. Posner, "Person-Organization Values Congruence: No Support for Individual Differences as a Moderating Influence," *Human Relations* 45, no. 2 (1992): 351–361; and B. Z. Posner and R. I. Westwood, "A Cross-Cultural Investigation of the Shared Values Relationship," *International Journal of Value-Based Management* 11, no. 4 (1995): 1–10.
9. Posner, "Another Look."
10. Posner, "Values and the American Manager."
11. This example was provided by Jo Bell and Renee Harness.
12. R. A. Stevenson, "Clarifying Behavioral Expectations Associated with Espoused Organizational Values," doctoral dissertation, Fielding Institute, 1995.

Chapter 3: Set the Example

1. This example was provided by Craig Haptonstall.
2. T. Yaffe and R. Kark, "Leading by Example: The Case of Leader OCB," *Journal of Applied Psychology* 96, no. 4 (July 2011): 806–826.

3. T. Simons, "The High Cost of Lost Trust," *Harvard Business Review* 80, no. 9 (September 2002): 19. See also T. Simons, *The Integrity Dividend* (San Francisco: Jossey-Bass, 2008).

4. Ed Schein has written extensively on how leaders help shape the culture of organizations; see E. Schein, *Organizational Culture and Leadership*, 4th ed. (San Francisco: Jossey-Bass, 2010), 197–298, and also E. Schein, *The Corporate Culture Survival Guide* (San Francisco: Jossey-Bass, 2009).

5. This example was provided by Nick Fan.

6. For a discussion of how language influences our behavior in organizations, see S. Zuboff, *In the Age of the Smart Machine: The Future of Work and Power* (New York: Basic Books, 1988). See also S. Zuboff and J. Maxim, *The Support Economy: Why Corporations Are Failing Individuals and the Next Episode of Capitalism* (New York: Penguin, 2004). Gary Hamel points out that "the goals of management are usually described in words like 'efficiency,' 'advantage,' 'value,' 'superiority,' 'focus,' and 'differentiation.' Important as these objectives are, they lack the power to rouse human hearts . . . [and leaders] must find ways to infuse mundane business activities with deeper, soul-stirring ideals, such as honor, truth, love, justice, and beauty." See G. Hamel, "Moon Shots for Management," *Harvard Business Review*, February 2009, 91.

7. Additional information on DaVita's culture and language can be found in J. Pfeffer, "Kent Thiry and DaVita: Leadership Challenges in Building and Growing a Great Company," Stanford Graduate School of Business, Case OB-54 (February 23, 2006).

8. F. A. Blanchard, T. Lilly, and L. A. Vaughn, "Reducing the Expression of Racial Prejudice," *Psychological Science* 2, no. 2 (1991): 101–105.

9. For in-depth examination of the importance of self-awareness and leadership effectiveness, see the landmark book: D. Goleman, *Emotional Intelligence: Why It Can Matter More Than IQ* (New York: Bantam, 1995). See also D. Goleman, *Leadership: The Power of Emotional Intelligence—Selected Writings* (Northampton, MA: More Than Sound, 2011); D. Goleman, *Social Intelligence: The New Science of Human Relationships* (New York: Bantam, 2006); D. Goleman, *Working with Emotional Intelligence* (New York: Bantam, 1998); and D. Goleman, A. McKee, and R. E. Boyatzis, *Primal Leadership: Realizing the Power of Emotional Intelligence* (Boston: Harvard Business School Press, 2002).

10. R. W. Eichinger, M. M. Lombardo, and D. Ulrich, *100 Things You Need to Know: Best Practices for Managers & HR* (Minneapolis, MN: Lominger, 2004), 492.

11. More information about the Leadership Practices Inventory (LPI), including its psychometric properties and use, can be found on our Web site: http://www.leadershipchallenge.com/WileyCDA/Section/id-131362.html.

12. One final source of feedback is yourself. Take a few moments each day, on a regular basis, to review, reflect, and look ahead. Casey Harbin, account manager at Apple, sets aside a few minutes each day "to reflect on something that bothered me or that I did well, so that I can both move on and move

forward. Reflecting in this manner also helps me learn about other people and appreciate the impact that I have on them, and vice versa."

13. We'll have more to say about this in Chapter Nine, Strengthen Others.

14. D. G. Kolb, "Seeking Continuity Amidst Organizational Change: A Storytelling Approach," *Journal of Management Inquiry* 12 (2003): 180–183.

15. S. Denning, *The Springboard: How Storytelling Ignites Action in Knowledge-Era Organizations* (Boston: Butterworth-Heinemann, 2001), xiii. For the best ways to tell and use stories to communicate vision and values, see S. Denning, *The Secret Language of Leadership: How Leaders Inspire Action Through Narrative* (San Francisco: Jossey-Bass, 2007).

16. J. Martin and M. E. Power, "Organizational Stories: More Vivid and Persuasive Than Quantitative Data," in *Psychological Foundations of Organizational Behavior*, ed. B. M. Staw (Glenview, IL: Scott, Foresman, 1982), 161–168. For additional evidence that storytelling improves a leader's ability to communicate, see also M. Bennett, *Once upon a Time in Leadership: Inspiring a Shared Vision Through Storytelling*, master's thesis, College of Business and Public Management, University of La Verne, March 2005. For more about being a storyteller, see C. Wortmann, *What's Your Story? Using Stories to Ignite Performance and Be More Successful* (Chicago: Kaplan, 2006).

17. A. L. Wilkens, "Organizational Stories as Symbols Which Control the Organization," in *Organizational Symbolism*, ed. L. R. Pondy, P. J. Frost, G. Morgan, and T. C. Dandridge (Greenwich, CT: JAI Press, 1983), 81–92; also Kolb, "Seeking Continuity."

18. For a detailed blueprint you can use to create and reinforce a culture that is based on shared values, see A. Rhoades, *Built on Values: Creating a Culture That Outperforms the Competition* (San Francisco: Jossey-Bass, 2011).

19. We'll say a lot more about reward and recognition in Chapters Ten and Eleven.

Inspire a Shared Vision
Chapter 4: Envision the Future

1. D. Gilbert, *Stumbling on Happiness* (New York: Knopf, 2006), 5–6.

2. G. Hamel and C. K. Prahalad, *Competing for the Future* (Boston: Mass.: Harvard Business Press, 1996).

3. For extensive research on intuitive decision making under conditions of extreme uncertainty, see G. Klein, *The Sources of Power: How People Make Decisions* (Cambridge, MA: MIT Press, 1998). Envisioning and intuiting aren't logical activities, and they're extremely difficult to explain and quantify. Alden M. Hayashi, a senior editor of *Harvard Business Review* who has studied executive decision making, reports, "In my interviews with top executives known for their shrewd business instincts, none could articulate precisely how they routinely made important decisions that defied any logical analysis. To describe that vague feeling of knowing something without knowing exactly how or why, they used words like professional judgment, intuition, gut instinct, inner voice, and hunch, but they couldn't describe the process much

beyond that." Yet, as he points out, the leaders he studied agreed that these hard-to-describe abilities were crucial to effectiveness. They even went so far as to say that it was the "X-Factor" that separated the best from the mediocre. See A. M. Hayashi, "When to Trust Your Gut," *Harvard Business Review* 79, no. 2 (February 2001): 59–65. In fact, by definition, intuition and vision are directly connected. Intuition has as its root the Latin word meaning "to look at"; see E. Partridge, *A Short Etymological Dictionary of Modern English* (New York: Macmillan, 1977), 359, 742.

4. J. P. Schuster, *The Power of Your Past: The Art of Recalling, Recasting, and Reclaiming* (San Francisco: Berrett-Koehler, 2011).

5. O. A. El Sawy, "Temporal Perspective and Managerial Attention: A Study of Chief Executive Strategic Behavior," unpublished doctoral dissertation, Stanford University, 1983. See also O. A. El Sawy, "Temporal Biases in Strategic Attention," research paper, November 1988, Marshall School of Business, University of Southern California.

6. Bob Rodriguez is the managing director and CEO of the $17 billion value investing firm First Pacific Advisors, which under his twenty-five year leadership has never had an annual loss. Bob tells the story that in 1974 when he was taking a portfolio management investment class at the University of Southern California, he asked Charlie Munger, when he was giving a guest lecture, if there was one thing that he could do that would make him a better investment professional. "His answer was, 'Read history, read history, read history.' And so I became a good historian, reading both economic and financial history as well as general history." Reflecting on the past definitely helps you see into the future and understand more about what is going on in the present. As told by E. Florian, "The Best Advice I Ever Got," *Fortune*, February 6, 2012, 14.

7. Gary Hamel observes, "One of the reasons many people fail to fully appreciate what's changing is because they're down at ground level, lost in the thicket of confusing, conflicting data. You have to make time to step back and ask yourself, 'What's the big story that cuts across all these little facts?'" See G. Hamel, *Leading the Revolution* (Boston: Harvard Business School Press, 2000), 128.

8. Elliot Jaques has written extensively about future orientation. See, for example, E. Jaques, *Requisite Organization: The CEO's Guide to Creative Structure and Leadership*, 2nd rev. ed. (Arlington, VA: Cason Hall, 2006), 15–32.

9. Einstein went on to say, "For knowledge is limited to all we know and understand, while imagination embraces the entire world, and all there ever will be to know and understand."

10. This was precisely the viewpoint advocated by the late Bill Walsh, who coached the San Francisco 49ers to three Super Bowl championships. See B. Walsh, S. Jamison, and C. Walsh, *The Score Takes Care of Itself: My Philosophy of Leadership* (New York: Penguin Group, 2009).

11. N. Halevy, Y. Berson, and A. D. Galinsky, "The Mainstream Is Not Electable: When Vision Trumps Over Representativeness in Leader Emergence and

Effectiveness," *Personality and Social Psychology Bulletin* 37, no. 7 (2011): 893–904; J. E. Bono and T. A. Judge, "Self-Concordance at Work: Toward Understanding the Motivational Effects of Transformational Leaders," *Academy of Management Journal* 46 (2003): 554–571; D. A. Waldman, G. G. Ramirez, R. J. House, and P. Puranam, "Does Leadership Matter? CEO Leadership Attributes and Profitability Under Conditions of Perceived Environmental Uncertainty," *Academy of Management Journal* 44 (2001): 134–143; B. Shamir, E. Zakay, E. Breinin, and M. Popper, "Correlates of Charismatic Leader Behavior in Military Units: Subordinates' Attitudes, Unit Characteristics and Superiors' Appraisals of Leader Performance," *Academy of Management Journal* 41 (1998): 387–409; and K. B. Lowe, K. Kroeck, and N. Sivasubramaniam, "Effectiveness Correlates of Transformation and Transactional Leadership: A Meta-Analytic Review of the MLQ Literature," *Leadership Quarterly* 7 (1996): 385–425.

12. See E. L. Deci with R. Flaste, *Why We Do What We Do: Understanding Self-Motivation* (New York: Penguin, 1995). For another excellent treatment of this subject, see K. W. Thomas, *Intrinsic Motivation at Work: Building Energy and Commitment,* 2nd ed. (San Francisco: Berrett-Koehler, 2009); and for an extensive academic treatment, see C. Sansone and J. M. Harackiewicz (eds.), *Intrinsic and Extrinsic Motivation: The Search for Optimal Motivation and Performance* (New York: Academic Press, 2000).

13. D. Pink, *Drive: The Surprising Truth About What Motivates Us* (New York: Penguin Group, 2009); L. Freifeld, "Why Cash Doesn't Motivate," *Training* 48, no. 4 (July–August 2011): 17–22.

14. Deci with Flaste, *Why We Do What We Do,* 25.

15. J. M. Kouzes and B. Z. Posner, "To Lead, Create a Shared Vision," *Harvard Business Review,* January 2009, 20–21.

16. J. Selby, *Listening with Empathy: Creating Genuine Connections with Customers and Colleagues* (Charlottesville, VA: Hampton Roads, 2007); D. Patnaik, *Wired to Care: How Companies Prosper When They Create Widespread Empathy* (Upper Saddle River, NJ: FT Press, 2009).

17. B. L. Kaye and S. Jordon-Evans, *Love 'em or Lose 'em: Getting Good People to Stay,* 4th ed. (San Francisco: Berrett-Koehler, 2008).

18. This particular list was originally shared with us in a telephone interview with Dave Berlew, November 14, 1994, based on his research. See D. E. Berlew, "Leadership and Organizational Excitement," *California Management Review* 17, no. 2 (1974): 21–30. Others have reported similar findings about what employees want most at work. For example, a survey of more than ninety thousand workers worldwide by the management consulting firm Towers Perrin found that 84 percent wanted challenging work that broadened their skills, and 83 percent wanted opportunities to develop new knowledge skills (*Towers Perrin Global Workforce Study,* 2007–2008); according to one popular Web site, the key factors are to be respected, to be members of the in-crowd, to impact decision making about their jobs, to have the opportunity to grow

and develop, and access to reasonable leadership (http://humanresources
.about.com/od/managementtips/qt/four_factors_b4.htm); and the list provided by Kelly Services, a global workforce recruiting and staffing organization, begins with the opportunity to make a difference (purpose), followed
by clear goals and objectives, responsibility, autonomy, and job flexibility
(http://www.kellyservices.us/web/us/services/en/pages/careertips_oct10
_what_employees_want.html).

19. In their studies of "great workplaces," the authors note that although the
context in which people have responded since the 1980s has changed quite
a bit, their answers "point to strikingly consistent experiences: Specifically,
they believe their leaders to be credible, respectful, and fair—they trust them.
They also take pride in what they do, and they share a sense of camaraderie
with their coworkers." M. Burchell and J. Robin, *The Great Workplace: How
to Build It, How to Keep It, and Why It Matters* (San Francisco: Jossey-Bass,
2011), 7.

20. Researchers have challenged the assumption that giving people more money—
providing or increasing financial incentives—improves performance. In fact,
current thinking is that contingent rewards (for example, pay for performance) may be a losing proposition. See, for example, D. Ariely, *Predictably
Irrational: The Hidden Forces That Shape Our Decisions* (New York: Harper-
Collins, 2009); and "LSE: When Performance-Related Pay Backfires," *Financial*, June 25, 2009.

21. See, for example, Pink, *Drive*; M. Novak, *Business as a Calling: Work and the
Examined Life* (New York: Free Press, 1996); R. J. Leider and D. A. Shapiro,
Whistle While You Work: Heeding Your Life's Calling (San Francisco: Berrett-
Koehler, 2001); P. J. Palmer, *Let Your Life Speak* (San Francisco: Jossey-Bass,
2000); D. Zohar and I. Marshall, *Spiritual Capital* (San Francisco: Berrett-
Koehler, 2004); and R. Barrett, *Building a Values-Driven Organization* (Bur-
lington, MA: Butterworth-Heinemann, 2006).

22. See, for example, H. Mintzberg and R. A. Norman, *Reframing Business: When
the Map Changes the Landscape* (Hoboken, NJ: Wiley, 2001); C. Handy, *The
Hungry Spirit: Beyond Capitalism* (New York: Broadway Books, 1999); and
G. Hamel, *Leading the Revolution* (Boston: Harvard Business School Press,
2000).

23. H. Mintzberg, "The Rise and Fall of Strategic Planning," *Harvard Business
Review* 72, no. 1 (January–February 1994): 109.

24. As quoted in L. Ioannou, "Make Your Company an Idea Factory," *Fortune*,
June 12, 2000, F264N–F264R.

Chapter 5: Enlist Others

1. This example was provided by Pierfrancesco Ronzi. Their achievements
reached far beyond the results in the race. Shosholoza became a "hope genera-
tor" for many South Africans, who identified in this success with pride.
Thanks to the creation of the Izivunguvungu MSC Foundation for Youth, a

sailing center based in Simonstown near Cape Town, disadvantaged youths and street children are taught life skills through sail training.

2. "Portraits of Team Shosholoza," http://www.teamshosholoza.com/cms/index .php?id=310&tx_ttnews%5Btt_news%5D=425&tx_ttnews%5BbackPid%5 D=310&cHash=de77148e29.

3. For more on the role of meaning and purpose in work, see S. Sinek, *Start with Why: How Great Leaders Inspire Everyone to Take Action* (New York: Portfolio, 2010); R. M. Spence, *It's Not What You Sell, It's What You Stand For: Why Every Extraordinary Business Is Driven by Purpose* (New York: Portfolio, 2010); and D. Ulrich and W. Ulrich, *The Why of Work: How Great Leaders Build Abundant Organizations That Win* (New York: McGraw-Hill, 2010).

4. M. Burchell and J. Robin, *The Great Workplace: How to Build It, How to Keep It, and Why It Matters* (San Francisco: Jossey-Bass, 2011), 127–128. The Great Place to Work Institute, where Burchell and Robin work, does the research that each year selects the Fortune 100 Best Companies to Work For.

5. Market researcher and author Doug Hall has found that "dramatically different" levels of distinctiveness in a new product or service increase the idea's probability of success in the marketplace from 15 percent to 53 percent. That's a 353 percent greater chance of success. The same is true for a vision; the more unique it is, the higher the probability of success in getting people to buy in. See D. Hall, *Jump Start Your Business Brain: Win More, Lose Less, and Make More Money with Your New Products, Services, Sales and Advertising* (Cincinnati: Clerisy Books, 2005), 126.

6. Researchers Michael Burchell and Jennifer Robin find that "pride" is one of the five dimensions of a great workplace, and scoring high on this dimension is one of the things that qualify a company as a Fortune 100 Best Companies to Work For. See their discussion of pride in Burchell and Robin, *Great Workplace*, 127–154.

7. When we did this on March 1, 2012, for "leadership books," an Amazon.com search returned 82,803 choices, and a Google search returned 205 million hits in 0.28 seconds.

8. "'I Have a Dream' Leads Top 100 Speeches of the Century," press release from the University of Wisconsin, December 15, 1999. Available online at www .news.wisc.edu/releases/3504.html or at http://www.americanrhetoric.com /top100speechesall.html. See also S. E. Lucas and M. J. Medhurst, *Words of a Century: The Top 100 American Speeches, 1900–1999* (New York: Oxford University Press, 2008). Other leaders often seen on international lists of great speakers from recent history are Winston Churchill, Charles de Gaulle, Mahatma Gandhi, Vaclav Havel, Robert Kennedy, Nelson Mandela, Jawaharlal Nehru, Barack Obama, Ronald Reagan, Eleanor Roosevelt, Gloria Steinem, Mother Teresa, Margaret Thatcher, and Lech Walesa.

9. The audio version of the "I Have a Dream" speech that we have found to be most instructive is the six-minute, eleven-second version that contains the most famous passages. It is in the collection *Greatest Speeches of All Time, Vol. 1*. You can download it from Amazon.com: http://www.amazon.com

/Greatest-Speeches-All-Time-Vol/dp/B001L0RONE/ref=sr_1
_cc_3?ie=UTF8&qid=1301516046&sr=1-3-catcorr. A printed version of
this portion of the speech is in C. S. King (ed.), *The Words of Martin Luther
King, Jr.* (New York: Newmarket Press, 1983), 95–98. A video can be viewed
on YouTube at http://www.youtube.com/watch?v=z4qrGWRbUng&feature=
related.

10. This example was provided by Steve Coats.

11. This example was provided by Terri Armstrong Welch. It also appears in
J. M. Kouzes and B. Z. Posner, *The Five Practices of Exemplary Leadership:
Nursing* (San Francisco: Pfeiffer, 2011).

12. J. Geary, *I Is an Other: The Secret Life of Metaphor and How It Shapes the Way
We See the World* (New York: Harper, 2011), 5.

13. V. Lieberman, S. M. Samuels, and L. Ross, "The Name of the Game: Predictive Power of Reputations Versus Situational Labels in Determining Prisoner's
Dilemma Game Moves," *Personality and Social Psychology Bulletin* 30 (2004):
1175–1185. See also Y. Benkler, "The Unselfish Gene," *Harvard Business
Review*, July–August 2011, 78.

14. For a discussion of the role of images, stories, and emotions in creating
memorable ideas, see C. Heath and D. Heath, *Made to Stick: Why Some Ideas
Survive and Others Die* (New York: Random House, 2007).

15. Those who are more auditory by nature talk about this as a "calling."

16. D. Goleman, *Social Intelligence: The New Science of Human Relationships* (New
York: Bantam, 2006).

17. Barbara L. Fredrickson, *Positivity: Groundbreaking Research Reveals How to
Embrace the Hidden Strengths of Positive Emotions, Overcome Negativity, and
Thrive* (New York: Crown, 2009), 21.

18. Fredrickson, *Positivity*, 60–65.

19. See, for example, H. S. Friedman, L. M. Prince, R. E. Riggio, and M. R.
DiMatteo, "Understanding and Assessing Nonverbal Expressiveness: The
Affective Communication Test," *Journal of Personality and Social Psychology*
39, no. 2 (1980): 333–351; D. Goleman, R. Boyatzis, and A. McKee, *Primal
Leadership: Realizing the Power of Emotional Intelligence* (Boston: Harvard
Business School Press, 2002); J. Conger, *Winning 'em Over: A New Model for
Management in the Age of Persuasion* (New York: Simon & Schuster, 1998);
and M. Greer, "The Science of Savoir Faire," *APA Monitor* 36, no. 1 (2005):
28.

20. B. L. Halpren and K. Lubar, *Leadership Presence: Dramatic Techniques to Reach
Out, Motivate, and Inspire* (New York: Gotham Books, 2003), 141.

21. J. L. McGaugh, *Memory and Emotion* (New York: Columbia University Press,
2003), 90. See also R. Maxwell and R. Dickman, *The Elements of Persuasion:
Use Storytelling to Pitch Better Ideas, Sell Faster, & Win More Business* (New
York: HarperCollins, 2007), especially "Sticky Stories: Memory, Emotions
and Markets," 122–150.

22. McGaugh, *Memory and Emotion*, 93.

23. McGaugh, *Memory and Emotion*, 92.

24. See C. Heath and D. Heath, *Switch: How to Change Things When Change Is Hard* (New York: Broadway Books, 2010), 101–123.

25. This example was provided by John Wang. For more information, see J. Udell, "An Unforgettable Lesson," http://blog.jonudell.net/2010/10/27/an-unforgettable-lesson/.

26. This example was provided by Terri Armstrong Welch and Dick Heller. It also appears in J. M. Kouzes and B. Z. Posner, *The Five Practices of Exemplary Leadership: Non-Profit* (San Francisco: Pfeiffer, 2011) and in J. M. Kouzes and B. Z. Posner, *The Leadership Challenge Workshop Facilitator's Guide Set*, 4th ed. (San Francisco: Pfeiffer, 2010).

Challenge the Process
Chapter 6: Search for Opportunities

1. R. M. Kanter, *The Change Masters: Innovation for Productivity in the American Corporation* (New York: Simon & Schuster, 1983), 125.

2. J. M. Crant and T. S. Bateman, "Charismatic Leadership Viewed from Above: The Impact of Proactive Personality," *Journal of Organizational Behavior* 21, no. 1 (2000): 63–75.

3. T. S. Bateman and J. M. Crant, "The Proactive Component of Organizational Behavior: Measures and Correlates," *Journal of Organizational Behavior* 14 (1993): 103–118; T. S. Bateman and J. M. Crant, "Proactive Behavior: Meaning, Impact, Recommendations," *Business Horizons* 42, no. 3 (May–June 1999): 63–70; and J. M. Crant, "Proactive Behavior in Organizations," *Journal of Management* 26, no. 3 (2000): 435–463.

4. See, for example, J. M. Crant, "The Proactive Personality Scale and Objective Job Performance Among Real Estate Agents," *Journal of Applied Psychology* 80, no. 4 (August 1995): 532–537; J. A. Thompson, "Proactive Personality and Job Performance: A Social Capital Perspective," *Journal of Applied Psychology* 90, no. 5 (2005): 1011–1017. See also S. E. Seibert and M. L. Braimer, "What Do Proactive People Do? A Longitudinal Model Linking Proactive Personality and Career Success," *Personnel Psychology* 54 (2001): 845–875; D. Goetsch, *Effective Leadership: Ten Steps for Technical Professions* (Englewood Cliffs, NJ: Prentice-Hall, 2004); and D. J. Brown, R. T. Cober, K. Kane, P. E. Levy, and J. Shalhoop, "Proactive Personality and the Successful Job Search: A Field Investigation of College Graduates," *Journal of Applied Psychology* 91, no. 3 (2006): 717–726.

5. Our sample involved managers from both the United States and Switzerland. See B. Z. Posner and J. W. Harder, "The Proactive Personality, Leadership, Gender and National Culture" (paper presented to the Western Academy of Management Conference, Santa Fe, New Mexico, April 2002).

6. H. Schultz and D. J. Yang, *Pour Your Heart into It* (New York: Hyperion, 1999), 210.

7. For detailed information on mental simulation, see G. Klein, *Sources of Power: How People Make Decisions* (Cambridge, MA: MIT Press, 1999), 45–77; see

also G. Klein, *The Power of Intuition: How to Use Your Gut Feelings to Make Better Decisions at Work* (New York: Currency, 2004).

8. The finding that how we deal with challenge comes from the inside was dramatically related by V. E. Frankl in *Man's Search for Meaning: An Introduction to Logotherapy* (New York: Touchstone, 1984; originally published in 1946).

9. See E. L. Deci with R. Flaste, *Why We Do What We Do: Understanding Self-Motivation* (New York: Penguin, 1995). See also D. Pink, *Drive: The Surprising Truth About What Motivates You* (New York: Riverhead Press, 2011); and K. W. Thomas, *Intrinsic Motivation at Work: What Really Drives Employee Engagement*, 2nd ed. (San Francisco: Berrett-Koehler, 2009).

10. A. Blum, *Annapurna: A Woman's Place*, Twentieth Anniversary Edition (San Francisco: Sierra Club Books, 1998), 3.

11. P. LaBarre, "How to Make It to the Top," *Fast Company*, September 1998, 72.

12. For a discussion of myths and truths about financial incentives, see J. Pfeiffer and R. I. Sutton, *Hard Facts, Dangerous Half-Truths, and Total Nonsense: Profiting from Evidence-Based Management* (Boston: Harvard Business School Press, 2006), 109–134. See also A. Kohn, *Punished by Rewards* (New York: Houghton Mifflin, 1993).

13. See R. Foster and S. Kaplan, *Creative Destruction: Why Companies That Are Built to Last Underperform the Market—and How to Successfully Transform Them* (New York: Currency Doubleday, 2001); C. M. Christensen, *The Innovator's Dilemma: When New Technologies Cause Great Firms to Fail* (Boston: Harvard Business School Press, 1997); C. M. Christensen, S. D. Anthony, and E. A. Roth, *Seeing What's Next: Using the Theories of Innovation to Predict Industry Change* (Boston: Harvard Business School Press, 2004); and G. Hamel, *The Future of Management* (Boston: Harvard Business School Press, 2007).

14. See, for example, S. Johnson, *Where Good Ideas Come From: The Natural History of Innovation* (New York: Riverhead, 2010); J. Ettlie, *Managing Innovation*, 2nd ed. (Burlington, MA: Butterworth-Heineman, 2004); E. von Hippel, *Democratizing Innovation* (Cambridge, MA: MIT Press, 2005); and T. Davila, M. J. Epstein, and R. Shelton, *Making Innovation Work: How to Manage It, Measure It, and Profit from It* (Upper Saddle River, NJ: Wharton School Publishing, 2006).

15. IBM, *Expanding the Innovation Horizons: The Global CEO Study 2006* (Somers, NY: IBM Global Services, 2006).

16. G. Berns, *Iconoclast: A Neuroscientist Reveals How to Think Differently* (Cambridge, MA: Harvard Business School Press, 2008).

17. M. M. Capozzi, R. Dye, and A. Howe, "Sparking Creativity in Teams: An Executive's Guide," *McKinsey Quarterly*, April 2011.

18. Capozzi, Dye, and Howe, "Sparking Creativity."

19. This example was provided by Alex Jukl.

20. R. Katz, "The Influence of Group Longevity: High Performance Research Teams," *Wharton Magazine* 6, no. 3 (1982): 28–34; and R. Katz and T. J. Allen, "Investigating the Not Invented Here (NIH) Syndrome: A Look at the Performance, Tenure, and Communication Patterns of 50 R&D Project Groups," in *Readings in the Management of Innovation*, 2nd ed., ed. M. L. Tushman and W. L. Moore (Cambridge, MA: Ballinger, 1988), 293–309.

21. Katz, "The Influence of Group Longevity," 31.

22. L. Huston and N. Sakkab, "Connect and Develop: Inside Procter & Gamble's New Model for Innovation," *Harvard Business Review* 84, no. 2 (March 2006): 60.

23. C. Christensen, J. Dyer, and H. Gregersen, "The Innovator's DNA," *Harvard Business Review* 87, no. 12 (December 2009): 60–67.

24. Capozzi, Dye, and Howe, "Sparking Creativity."

25. On February 7, 2010, the CBS television series *Undercover Boss* premiered to a staggering 38.6 million viewers, the most watched premiere episode of any reality series in the history of television. It was the most popular new show of the 2009–2010 television season.

26. Quoted in S. Lambert and E. Holzman, *Undercover Boss* (San Francisco: Jossey-Bass, 2011), 41.

Chapter 7: Experiment and Take Risks

1. K. E. Weick, "Small Wins: Redefining the Scale of Social Problems," *American Psychologist* 39, no. 1 (1984): 43. Karl attributes the concept of small wins to author Tom Peters, who wrote about it in his doctoral dissertation at Stanford University. For a related treatment of this topic, see P. Sims, *Little Bets: How Breakthrough Ideas Emerge from Small Discoveries* (New York: Free Press, 2011), 141–152.

2. This example was provided by Dan Schwab.

3. The initial discoveries of psychological hardiness came from a twelve-year longitudinal study of executives at Illinois Bell Telephone as that organization experienced the firestorm of changes produced by the federal antitrust case against the Bell system and the resulting breakup of the company. Some executives were undermined by the mounting stresses of this upheaval; they had high stress scores along with high rates of illness. Yet another group of executives with equally high stress scores thrived and were below average on incidence of illness. As the researchers predicted, there was a clear attitudinal difference between the high-stress and high-illness group and the high-stress and low-illness group. For a history of the research, see S. R. Salvatore, "The Story of Hardiness: Twenty Years of Theorizing, Research, and Practice," *Consulting Psychology Journal: Practices and Research* 54, no. 3 (2002): 175–185. See also S. R. Maddi and S. C. Kobasa, *The Hardy Executive: Health Under Stress* (Chicago: Dorsey Press, 1984); S. R. Maddi and D. M. Khoshaba, "Hardiness and Mental Health," *Journal of Personality Assessment* 67 (1994): 265–274; and S. R. Maddi and D. M. Khoshaba, *Resilience at Work: How to Succeed No Matter What Life Throws at You* (New York: AMACOM, 2005).

4. See R. A. Bruce and R. F. Sinclair, "Exploring the Psychological Hardiness of Entrepreneurs," *Frontiers of Entrepreneurship Research* 29, no. 6 (2009): 5; P. T. Bartone, R. R. Roland, J. J. Picano, and T. J. Williams, "Psychological Hardiness Predicts Success in US Army Special Forces Candidates," *International Journal of Selection and Assessment* 16, no. 1 (2008): 78–81; and P. T. Bartone, "Resilience Under Military Operational Stress: Can Leaders Influence Hardiness?" *Military Psychology* 18 (2006): S141–S148.

5. "Too Many Interruptions at Work?" interview with Gloria Mark, *Gallup Management Journal*, June 8, 2006, 1. Available online at http://gmj.gallup .com/content/23146/Too-Many-Interruptions-at-Work.aspx. See also G. Mark, V. Gonzalez, and J. Harris, "No Task Left Behind? Examining the Nature of Fragmented Work," *Proceedings of ACM CHI'05*, Portland, OR, April 2005, 321–330. See also the classic study on the subject of how managers spend their time: H. Mintzberg, *The Nature of Managerial Work* (New York: Prentice Hall, 1980).

6. T. A. Amabile and S. J. Kramer, "The Power of Small Wins," *Harvard Business Review*, May 2011, 73; see also their book *The Progress Principle: Using Small Wins to Ignite Joy, Engagement, and Creativity at Work* (Boston: Harvard Business Review Press, 2011).

7. Amabile and Kramer, "Power of Small Wins," 75.

8. Amabile and Kramer, "Power of Small Wins," 75.

9. S. Hollander, *The Success of Increased Efficiency: A Study of DuPont Rayon Plants* (Cambridge, MA: MIT Press, 1965). See also D. Ulrich, S. Kerr, and R. Ashkenas, *The GE Work-Out* (New York: McGraw-Hill, 2002).

10. H. Mintzberg, *The Rise and Fall of Strategic Planning* (New York: Free Press, 1994), 134.

11. K. M. Eisenstadt and B. N. Tabrizi, "Accelerating Adaptive Processes: Product Innovation in the Global Computer Industry," *Administrative Science Quarterly* 40 (1995): 84–110.

12. M. Maidique, "Why Products Succeed and Why Products Fail," presentation to the Executive Seminar in Corporate Excellence, Santa Clara University, May 29, 1985; see also M. Maidique and B. J. Zinger, "The New Product Learning Cycle," *Research Policy* 14 (1985): 299–313; G. A. Moore, *Crossing the Chasm: Marketing and Selling High-Tech Products to Mainstream Customers* (New York: Harper Business, 1999); and C. M. Christensen, S. D. Anthony, and E. A. Roth, *Seeing What's Next: Using the Theories of Innovation to Predict Industry Change* (Boston: Harvard Business School Press, 2004). See also J. McGregor, "How Failure Breeds Success," *Business Week*, July 10, 2006, 42–50. McGregor writes, "The best companies embrace their mistakes and learn from them."

13. T. L. O'Brien, "Are U.S. Innovators Losing Their Competitive Edge?" *New York Times*, November 13, 2005, 3.

14. M. Jordan, "Failure" (Nike commercial), accessed on YouTube March 6, 2012, http://www.youtube.com/watch?v=m-EMOb3ATJ0.

15. P. J. Schoemaker and R. E. Cunther, "The Wisdom of Deliberate Mistakes," *Harvard Business Review* 84, no. 6 (June 2006): 108–115. *Harvard Business Review* devotes the entire April 2011 issue to a discussion of failure and its role in business. You can access it online at http://hbr.org/archive-toc /BR1104?conversationId=1855599.

16. L. M. Brown and B. Z. Posner, "Exploring the Relationship Between Learning and Leadership," *Leadership & Organization Development Journal*, May 2001, 274–280. See also J. M. Kouzes and B. Z. Posner, *The Truth About Leadership: The No-Fads, Heart-of-the-Matter Facts You Need to Know* (San Francisco: Jossey-Bass, 2010), 119–135.

17. R. W. Eichinger, M. M. Lombardo, and D. Ulrich, *100 Things You Need to Know: Best Practices for Managers & HR* (Minneapolis, MN: Lominger, 2004), 492.

18. Eichinger, Lombardo, and Ulrich, *100 Things*, 495.

19. A. G. Lafley, "I Think of Failure as a Gift," *Harvard Business Review*, April 2011, 89.

20. For the role of humility in leadership effectiveness, see, for example, J. Collins, *Good to Great: Why Some Companies Make the Leap . . . and Others Don't* (New York: HarperBusiness, 2001), 27–30.

21. C. S. Dweck, *Mindset: The New Psychology of Success* (New York: Random House, 2006), 6–7.

22. A. Bandura and R. E. Wood, "Effects of Perceived Controllability and Performance Standards on Self-Regulation of Complex Decision Making," *Journal of Personality and Social Psychology* 56 (1989): 805–814. Also see Dweck, *Mindset*, for a discussion of numerous research studies in these and other domains.

23. A. Carmeli, D. Brueller, and J. E. Dutton, "Learning Behaviours in the Workplace: The Role of High-Quality Interpersonal Relationships and Psychological Safety," *Systems Research and Behavioral Science Systems Research* 26 (2009): 81–98.

24. This example was provided by Jo Bell and Renee Harness.

25. The feedback instrument used in this instance was J. M. Kouzes and B. Z. Posner, *The Leadership Practices Inventory*, 3rd ed. (San Francisco: Pfeiffer, 2007).

26. To read more about Pat Williams's thoughts on leadership and his personal experience as a ballplayer and sports executive, see P. Williams with J. Denney, *Leadership Excellence: The Seven Sides of Leadership for the 21st Century* (Uhrichsville, OH: Barbour Books, 2012).

27. A. L. Duckworth, C. Peterson, M. D. Matthews, and D. R. Kelly, "Grit: Perseverance and Passion for Long-Term Goals," *Journal of Personality and Social Psychology* 92, no. 6 (2007): 1087–1101.

28. M.E.P. Seligman, "Building Resilience," *Harvard Business Review*, April 2011, 101–106. For a more complete treatment of this subject, see M.E.P. Seligman, *Flourish: A Visionary New Understanding of Happiness and Well-Being* (New York: Free Press, 2011).

29. Seligman, "Building Resilience," 102.
30. It may be difficult to overcome a habitual pattern of avoidance, but it is possible to learn to cope assertively with stressful events through counseling and educational programs. For example, see Maddi and Kobasa, *Hardy Executive*; D. M. Khoshaba and S. R. Maddi, "Early Experiences in Hardiness Development," *Consulting Psychology Journal* 51 (1999): 106–116; S. R. Maddi, S. Kahn, and K. L. Maddi, "The Effectiveness of Hardiness Training," *Consulting Psychology Journal* 50 (1998): 78–86; Maddi and Khoshaba, *Resilience at Work*; K. Reivish and A. Shatte, *The Resilience Factor: 7 Keys to Finding Your Inner Strength and Overcoming Life's Hurdles* (New York: Broadway Books, 2003); and J. D. Margolis and P. G. Stoltz, "How to Bounce Back from Adversity," *Harvard Business Review* 88, no. 1 (January–February 2010): 86–92.

Enable Others to Act
Chapter 8: Foster Collaboration
1. For detailed analyses of alliances and partnerships in the competitive marketplace, see Y. L. Doz and G. Hamel, *Alliance Advantage: The Art of Creating Value Through Partnering* (Boston: Harvard Business School Press, 1998); J. K. Conlon and M. Giovagnoli, *The Power of Two: How Companies of All Sizes Can Build Networks That Generate Business Opportunities* (San Francisco: Jossey-Bass, 1998); and W. C. Kim and R. Mauborgne, *Blue Ocean Strategy* (Boston: Harvard Business School Press, 2005). For a discussion of collaboration and its importance to innovation, see IBM, *Expanding the Innovation Horizons: The Global CEO Study 2006* (Somers, NY: IBM Global Services, 2006). For a discussion of good and bad collaboration, see M. T. Hansen, *Collaboration: How Leaders Avoid the Traps, Create Unity, and Reap Big Results* (Boston: Harvard Business School Press, 2009).
2. For example, see R. F. Hurley, *The Decision to Trust: How Leaders Create High-Trust Organizations* (San Francisco: Jossey-Bass, 2012); P. S. Shockley-Zalabak, S. Morreale, and M. Hackman, *Building the High-Trust Organization: Strategies for Supporting Five Key Dimensions of Trust* (San Francisco: Jossey-Bass, 2010); R. S. Sloyman and J. D. Ludema, "That's Not How I See It: How Trust in the Organization, Leadership, Process, and Outcome Influence Individual Responses to Organizational Change," *Organizational Change and Development* 18 (2010): 233–276; S.M.R. Covey, *The Speed of Trust: The One Thing That Changes Everything* (New York: Free Press, 2008); M. P. Wulandari and J. Burgess, "Trust and Its Relationship to the Quality of Communication and Satisfaction in a Large Indonesian Workplace: A Case Study," *International Journal of Business and Management Studies* 2, no. 2 (2010): 49–55; K. T. Dirks, "Trust in Leadership and Team Performance: Evidence from NCAA Basketball," *Journal of Applied Psychology* 8, no. 6 (2009): 1004–1012; P. J. Sweeney, V. Thompson, and H. Blanton, "Trust and Influence in Combat: An Interdependence Model," *Journal of Applied Social Psychology* 39, no. 1 (2009): 235–264; N. Gillespie and L. Mann, "How Trustworthy Is Your

364

NOTES

Leader? Implications for Leadership, Team Climate, and Outcomes in R&D Teams," in *Leadership, Management, and Innovation in R&D Teams*, ed. L. Mann (New York: Praeger, 2005); K. T. Dirks and D. L. Ferrin, "Trust in Leadership: Meta-Analytic Findings and Implications for Research and Practice," *Journal of Applied Psychology* 87, no. 4 (2002): 611–628; K. T. Dirks, "The Effects of Interpersonal Trust on Work Group Performance," *Journal of Applied Psychology* 84, no. 3 (1999): 445–455; R. B. Shaw, *Trust in the Balance: Building Successful Organizations on Results, Integrity, and Concern* (San Francisco: Jossey-Bass, 1997); and R. M. Kramer, "Trust and Distrust in Organizations: Emerging Perspectives, Enduring Questions," *Annual Review of Psychology* 50 (1999): 569–598.

3. Shockley-Zalabak, Morreale, and Hackman, *Building the High-Trust Organization*.
4. *Innovation Survey* (London: PricewaterhouseCoopers, 1999), 3.
5. See M. B. Gurtman, "Trust, Distrust, and Interpersonal Problems: A Circumplex Analysis," *Journal of Personality and Social Psychology* 62 (1992): 989–1002. See also G. D. Grace and T. Schill, "Social Support and Coping Style Differences in Subjects High and Low in Interpersonal Trust," *Psychological Reports* 59 (1986): 584–586.
6. W. R. Boss, "Trust and Managerial Problem Solving Revisited," *Group & Organization Studies* 3, no. 3 (1978): 331–342.
7. Boss, "Trust and Managerial Problem Solving Revisited," 338.
8. Boss, "Trust and Managerial Problem Solving Revisited," 338.
9. Y. Benkler, "The Unselfish Gene," *Harvard Business Review*, July–August 2011, 77–85. See also P. J. Zak, "The Neurobiology of Trust," *Scientific American*, June 2008, 88–95; F. Fukuyama, *Trust: The Social Virtues and the Creation of Prosperity* (New York: Free Press, 1996).
10. See, for example, Shockley-Zalabak, Morreale, and Hackman, *Building the High-Trust Organization*.
11. This example was provided by Kelly Ann McKnight.
12. M. Mortesen and T. Beyene, "Being There: Firsthand Experience and the Subsequent Role of Reflected Knowledge in Cultivating Trust in Global Collaboration," MIT Sloan School Working Paper 4735-09, April 27, 2009. Available online at http://ssrn.com/abstract=1395732.
13 T. Rath, *Vital Friends: The People You Can't Afford to Live Without* (New York: Gallup Press, 2006).
14. D. E. Zand, "Trust and Managerial Problem Solving," *Administrative Science Quarterly* 17, no. 2 (1972): 229–239; and J. W. Driscoll, "Trust and Participation in Organizational Decision Making as Predictors of Satisfaction," *Academy of Management Journal* 21, no. 1 (1978): 44–56.
15. P. Lee, N. Gillespie, L. Mann, and A. Wearing, "Leadership and Trust: Their Effect on Knowledge Sharing and Team Performance," *Management Learning* 41, no. 4 (2010): 473–491.
16. C. A. O'Reilly and K. H. Roberts, "Information Filtration in Organizations: Three Experiments," *Organizational Behavior and Human Performance* 11

(1974): 253–265; and Boss, "Trust and Managerial Problem Solving Revisited."

17. The breakthrough experiment on group interdependence, and one of the most cited in social psychology, was conducted by Muzafer and Carolyn Sherif. It took place at a Boy Scouts of America camp between two rival groups of kids, the Rattlers and the Eagles. Conditions at the camp required that they cooperate in order to get water flowing to both camps. You can read the story in M. Sherif, O. J. Harvey, W. R. Hood, and C. W. Sherif, *The Robbers Cave Experiment: Intergroup Conflict and Cooperation* (Middletown, CT: Wesleyan, 1988).

18. Another important ingredient in creating common purpose is identity. If you want people to collaborate, there can't be any in-group or out-group, any "us" and "them," or competition for attention among members. People have to identify with the group they are part of in order to work together. Sports teams create identity with uniform colors, mascots, unique gestures, and fight songs. Project teams do it with special names for product versions, insider jokes, badges, and the like. Fraternities and sororities do it with Greek letters, handshakes, secret words, ceremonies, and rituals.

19. R. Axelrod, *The Evolution of Cooperation: Revised Edition* (New York: Basic Books, 2006). See also W. Poundstone, *Prisoner's Dilemma: John Von Neumann, Game Theory, and the Puzzle of the Bomb* (New York: Anchor, 1993).

20. Axelrod, *Evolution of Cooperation*, 20, 190.

21. R. B. Cialdini, "Harnessing the Science of Persuasion," *Harvard Business Review*, October 2001, 72–79. For a discussion of the principle of reciprocity, see R. B. Cialdini, *Influence: Science and Practice*, 4th ed. (Needham Heights, MA: Allyn & Bacon, 2001), 19–51; J. K. Butler Jr. "Behaviors, Trust, and Goal Achievement in a Win-Win Negotiating Role Play," *Group & Organization Management* 20, no. 4 (1995): 486–501; and W.E.D. Creed and R. E. Miles, "Trust in Organizations: A Conceptual Framework Linking Organizational Forms, Managerial Philosophies, and the Opportunity Costs of Controls," in *Trust in Organizations: Frontiers of Theory and Research*, ed. R. M. Kramer and T. R. Tyler (Thousand Oaks, CA: Sage, 1996), 16–39. See also G. Kohlrieser, *Hostage at the Table: How Leaders Can Overcome Conflict, Influence Others, and Raise Performance* (San Francisco: Jossey-Bass, 2006).

22. R. Putnam, *Bowling Alone: The Collapse and Revival of American Community* (New York: Touchstone, 2001), 134.

23. For a discussion of the competencies of collaborative leaders, see H. Ibarra and M. T. Hansen, "Are You a Collaborative Leader?" *Harvard Business Review*, July–August 2011, 69–74. For a variety of examples from organizations ranging from the U.S. Marine Corps to the Montreal-based Cirque du Soleil, see the "Secrets of Greatness: Teamwork!" *Fortune*, June 12, 2006, 64–152. See also A. M. Brandenburger and B. J. Nalebuff, *Co-Opetition: A Revolution Mindset That Combines Competition and Cooperation: The Game Theory Strategy That's Changing the Game of Business* (New York: Currency, 1997); R. Wright, *The Logic of Human Destiny* (New York: Vintage, 2000); Kim and Mauborgne, *Blue Ocean Strategy*; and D. W. Johnson and

R. T. Johnson, *Cooperation and Competition: Theory and Research* (Edina, MN: Interaction, 1989).

24. This latter was clearly revealed in the 2011 NBA championships when the Dallas Mavericks prevailed over the individual superstars on the Miami Heat team.

25. J. Vesterman, "From Wharton to War," *Fortune*, June 12, 2006, 106.

26. Vesterman, "From Wharton to War."

27. Mortesen and Beyene, "Being There." See also A. Van de Ven, A. L. Delbecq, and R. J. Koenig, "Determinants of Coordination Modes Within Organizations," *American Sociological Review* 41, no. 2 (1976): 322–338.

28. Mortesen and Beyene, "Being There." See also D. Cohen and L. Prusak, *In Good Company: How Social Capital Makes Organizations Work* (Boston: Harvard Business School Press, 2001), 20.

29. D. Brooks, *The Social Animal: Hidden Sources of Love, Character, and Achievement* (New York: Random House, 2011).

Chapter 9: Strengthen Others

1. R. M. Kanter, *The Change Masters: Innovation for Productivity in the American Corporation* (New York: Simon & Schuster, 1983). Also see R. M. Kanter, *When Giants Learn to Dance: Mastering the Challenges of Strategy, Management, and Careers in the 1990s* (New York: Simon & Schuster, 1989); and R. M. Kanter, *e-Volve! Succeeding in the Digital Culture of Tomorrow* (Boston: Harvard Business School Press, 2001). For a study of how organizations create a culture of employee confidence, see R. M. Kanter, *Confidence: How Winning Streaks & Losing Streaks Begin and End* (New York: Crown Business, 2004).

2. L. Wiseman, *Multipliers: How the Best Leaders Make Everyone Smarter* (New York: HarperCollins, 2010), 20.

3. A. Bandura, *Self-Efficacy: The Exercise of Control* (New York: Freeman, 1997); K. A. Karl, A. M. Leary-Kelly, and J. J. Martocchio, "The Impact of Feedback and Self-Efficacy on Performance in Training," *Journal of Organizational Behavior* 14, no. 4 (1993): 379–394; C. M. Shea and J. M. Howell, "Charismatic Leadership and Task Feedback: A Laboratory Study of Their Effects on Self-Efficacy and Task Performance," *Leadership Quarterly* 10, no. 3 (1999): 375–396; and A. Bandura, "Social Cognitive Theory: An Agentic Perspective," *Annual Review of Psychology* 52 (2001): 1–26.

4. T. Yaffe and R. Kark, "Leading by Example: The Case of Leader OCB," *Journal of Applied Psychology* 96, no. 4 (July 2011): 806–826.

5. This example was provided by Nicole Matouk.

6. A. Bryant, "Yes, Everyone Can Be Stupid for a Minute," *New York Times*, May 7, 2011, http://www.nytimes.com/2011/05/08/business/08corner.html ?pagewanted=1&_r=1&emc=eta1.

7. A. Wrzeniewski and J. Dutton, "Crafting a Job: Revisioning Employees as Active Crafters of Their Work," *Academy of Management Review* 26, no. 2 (2001): 179–201, and M. S. Christian, A. S. Garza, and J. E. Slaugher, "Work Engagement: A Quantitative Review and Test of Its Relations with Task and Conceptual Performance," *Personnel Psychology* 64 (2011): 89–136.

8. "Winners," *Sibson & Company* 1, no. 7 (October 1991): 2.

9. Evolutionary psychology demonstrates that in ecosystems, collaboration is what assists species to survive rather than become extinct; the group ends up eradicating bad or inefficient behavior. See R. Wright, *The Moral Animal: Why We Are the Way We Are: The New Science of Evolutionary Psychology* (New York: Vintage, 1995). For another interesting look at the origins of social cooperation, see A. Fields, *Altruistically Inclined? The Behavioral Sciences, Evolutionary Theory, and the Origins of Reciprocity* (Ann Arbor: University of Michigan Press, 2004).

10. M. Csikszentmihalyi, *Finding Flow: The Psychology of Engagement with Everyday Life* (New York: Basic Books, 1997), 30.

11. M. Burchell and J. Robin, *The Great Workplace: How to Build It, How to Keep It, and Why It Matters* (San Francisco: Jossey-Bass, 2011), 66.

12. See, for example, MICA Management Resources, "Training Impact on Corporate Competitiveness" (Toronto: MICA Management Resources, April 1991); *America and the New Economy* (Alexandria, VA: ASTD, 1990); and B. Sugrue and R. J. Rivera, *State of the Industry 2005* (Alexandria, VA: ASTD, 2005).

13. N. Merchant, *The New How: Creating Business Solutions Through Collaborative Strategy* (San Francisco: O'Reilly Media, 2010), 63.

14. These are the kinds of questions that successful CEOs also think about. See A. Bryant, *The Corner Office: Indispensable and Unexpected Lessons from CEOs on How to Lead and Succeed* (New York: Times Books, 2011). For another look at this issue, see W. Bennis, D. Goleman, and J. O'Toole, *Transparency: How Leaders Create a Culture of Candor* (San Francisco: Jossey-Bass, 2008).

15. Psychologists often refer to this as self-efficacy. See, for example, Bandura, *Self-Efficacy*; and R. M. Steers, L. W. Porter, and N. Branden, *Self-Esteem at Work: How Confident People Make Powerful Companies* (San Francisco: Jossey-Bass, 1998).

16. R. E. Wood and A. Bandura, "Impact of Conceptions of Ability on Self-Regulatory Mechanisms and Complex Decision Making," *Journal of Personality and Social Psychology* 56 (1989): 407–415. Managers in this study who lost confidence in their own judgments tended to find fault with their people. Indeed, they were quite uncharitable about their employees, regarding them as unable to be motivated and unworthy of supervisory effort; given the option, they would have fired many of them.

17. A. Bandura and R. E. Wood, "Effects of Perceived Controllability and Performance Standards on Self-Regulation of Complex Decision Making," *Journal of Personality and Social Psychology* 56 (1989): 805–814.

18. A. M. Saks, "Longitudinal Field Investigation of the Moderating and Mediating Effects of Self-Efficacy on the Relationship Between Training and Newcomer Adjustment," *Journal of Applied Psychology* 80 (1995): 211–225.

19. See, for example, Wiseman, *Multipliers*; C. Dweck, *Mindset: The New Psychology of Success* (New York: Ballantine Books, 2007); and J. Hagel and J. S. Brown, "Do You Have a Growth Mindset?" Harvard Business School blog,

posted November 23, 2010, http://blogs.hbr.org/bigshift/2010/11/do-you
-have-a-growth-mindset.html.

20. See K. A. Ericsson, M. J. Prietula, and E. T. Cokely, "The Making of an
Expert," *Harvard Business Review*, July–August 2007, 114–121.

21. L. M. Spencer Jr. and S. M. Spencer, *Competence at Work: Models for Superior
Performance* (Hoboken, NJ: Wiley, 1993). See also R. Boyatzis and A. McKee,
Resonant Leadership (Boston: Harvard Business School Press, 2004); M. M.
Hughes, L. B. Patterson, and J. B. Terrell, *Emotional Intelligence in Action:
Training and Coaching Activities for Leaders and Managers* (San Francisco:
Jossey-Bass, 2005); V. U. Druskat, G. Mount, and F. Sala (eds.), *Linking
Emotional Intelligence and Performance at Work: Current Research Evidence with
Individuals and Groups* (Mahwah, NJ: Erlbaum, 2005); and D. Goleman,
Social Intelligence: The New Science of Human Relationships (New York: Bantam
Books, 2006).

22. P. Leone, "Take Your ROI to Level 6," *Training Industry Quarterly*, Spring
2008, 14–18, http://www.nxtbook.com/nxtbooks/trainingindustry/tiq_2008
spring/.

23. An interesting study of this involved 320 soldiers serving in a combat zone
in Iraq. Researchers found that the level of trust that subordinates (soldiers)
had in their leaders determined the amount of influence they willingly
accepted. See P. Sweeny, V. Thomson, and H. Blanton, "Trust and Influence
in Combat: An Interdependence Model," *Journal of Applied Social Psychology*
39, no. 1 (2009): 235–264.

24. F. Hesselbein, "Bright Future," *Leader to Leader*, no. 60, Spring 2011, 4.

Encourage the Heart
Chapter 10: Recognize Contributions

1. Hundreds of research studies have since been conducted to test this notion,
and they all clearly demonstrate that people tend to act in ways that are
consistent with the expectations they perceive. See, for example, D. Eden,
Pygmalion in Management: Productivity as a Self-Fulfilling Prophecy (Lexing-
ton, MA: Lexington Books, 1990); D. Eden, "Leadership and Expectations:
Pygmalion Effects and Other Self-Fulfilling Prophecies in Organizations,"
Leadership Quarterly 3, no. 4 (1992): 271–305; and A. Smith, L. Jussim, J.
Eccles, M. Van Noy, S. Madon, and P. Palumbo, "Self-Fulfilling Prophecies,
Perceptual Biases, and Accuracy at the Individual and Group Levels," *Journal
of Experimental Social Psychology* 34, no. 6 (1998): 530–561.

2. K. S. Cameron, *Positive Leadership: Strategies for Extraordinary Performance*
(San Francisco: Berrett-Koehler, 2008). Fostering virtuousness, according to
Kim, is about facilitating the best of the human condition. He argues that
this is based on an eudaemonic assumption that an inclination exists in all
human systems toward goodness for its own intrinsic value.

3. See, for example, J. E. Dutton, R. E. Quinn, and K. S. Cameron, *Positive
Organizational Scholarship: Foundations of a New Discipline* (San Francisco:

Berrett-Koehler, 2003); K. S. Cameron, *Positive Leadership*; D. Whitney and A. Trosten-Bloom, *The Power of Appreciative Inquiry: A Practical Guide to Positive Change*, 2nd ed. (San Francisco: Berrett-Koehler, 2010); and M. E. Seligman, *Flourish: A Visionary New Understanding of Happiness and Well-Being* (New York: Free Press, 2011).

4. For a classic empirical study of such situations, see D. Eden and G. Ravid, "Pygmalion vs. Self-Expectancy: Effects of Instructor and Self-Expectancy on Trainee Performance," *Organizational Behavior and Human Performance* 30 (1982): 351–364; and D. Eden and A. B. Shani, "Pygmalion Goes to Boot Camp: Expectancy, Leadership and Trainee Performance," *Journal of Applied Psychology* 67 (1982): 194–199.

5. But what happens in organizations when leaders have low expectations of others? And what happens when managers are constantly on the lookout for problems? Three things: they get a distorted view of reality; over time, production declines; and their personal credibility hits bottom. Wandering around with an eye for trouble is likely to get you just that: more trouble. There is other intriguing research which suggests that leaders can set others up to fail. This can happen when managers micromanage and control poor performers, weakening self-confidence and performance, which can in turn lead to living down to expectations rather than living up to them. See J.-F. Manzoni and J.-L. Barsoux, *The Set-Up-to-Fail Syndrome: How Good Managers Cause Great People to Fail* (Boston: Harvard Business Press, 2002).

6. For a discussion of both the research on goal setting and its practical applications, see H. G. Halvorson, *Succeed: How We Can Reach Our Goals* (New York: Hudson Street Press, 2010).

7. For a discussion of flow, see M. Csikszentmihalyi, *Finding Flow: The Psychology of Engagement with Everyday Life* (New York: Basic Books, 1997).

8. See, for example, J. E. Sawyer, W. R. Latham, R. D. Pritchard, and W. R. Bennett Jr., "Analysis of Work Group Productivity in an Applied Setting: Application of a Time Series Panel Design," *Personnel Psychology* 52 (1999): 927–967; and A. Gostick and C. Elton, *Managing with Carrots: Using Recognition to Attract and Retain the Best People* (Layton, UT: Gibbs Smith, 2001).

9. This example was provided by Bilal Burak Ersan.

10. P. A. McCarty, "Effects of Feedback on the Self-Confidence of Men and Women," *Academy of Management Journal* 20 (1986): 840–847. See also Halvorson, *Succeed*.

11. K. A. Ericsson, M. J. Prietula, and E. T. Cokely, "The Making of an Expert," *Harvard Business Review*, July–August 2007, 114–121.

12. For more on this topic, see Truth Nine in J. M. Kouzes and B. Z. Posner, *The Truth About Leadership: The No-Fads, Heart-of-the-Matter Facts You Need to Know* (San Francisco: Jossey-Bass, 2010).

13. B. Nelson, *1001 Ways to Reward Employees*, 2nd ed. (New York: Workman, 2005).

14. See, for example, J. M. Kouzes and B. Z. Posner, *A Leader's Legacy* (San Francisco: Jossey-Bass, 2006), especially chap. 7, "Leaders *Should* Want to Be Liked," 56–61.

15. J. A. Ross, "Does Friendship Improve Job Performance?" *Harvard Business Review* 54, no. 2 (March–April 1977): 8–9. See also K. A. Jehn and P. P. Shah, "Interpersonal Relationships and Task Performance: An Examination of Mediating Processes in Friendship and Acquaintance Groups," *Journal of Personality and Social Psychology* 72, no. 4 (1997): 775–790. There is an important caveat, however. Friends have to be strongly committed to the group's goals. If not, then friends may not do better. This is precisely why we said earlier that it is absolutely necessary for leaders to be clear about standards and to create a condition of shared goals and values. When it comes to performance, commitment to standards and good relations between people go together.

16. T. Rath, *Vital Friends: The People You Cannot Afford to Live Without* (New York: Gallup Press, 2006).

17. As used in this publication, "Deloitte" means Deloitte Consulting LLP, a subsidiary of Deloitte LLP. Please see www.deloitte.com/us/about for a detailed description of the legal structure of Deloitte LLP and its subsidiaries.

18. This example was provided by Steve Coats.

19. J. L. Hall, B. Z. Posner, and J. W. Harder, "Performance Appraisal Systems: Matching Theory with Practice," *Group and Management Studies* 14, no. 1 (1989): 51–69.

20. J. Pfeffer and R. I. Sutton, *Hard Facts, Dangerous Half-Truths, and Total Nonsense: Profiting from Evidence-Based Management* (Boston: Harvard Business School Publishing, 2006).

21. Eric Harvey suggests lots and lots of creative ways to recognize people in his handbook *180 Ways to Walk the Recognition Talk* (Dallas: Walk the Talk Company, 2000). See also Nelson, *1001 Ways to Reward Employees*; L. Yerkes, *Fun Works: Creative Places Where People Love to Work* (San Francisco: Berrett-Koehler, 2001); J. W. Umlas, *The Power of Acknowledgment* (New York: International Institute for Learning, 2007); B. Kaye and S. Jordan-Evans, *Love 'em or Lose 'em: Getting Good People to Stay*, 4th ed. (San Francisco: Berrett-Koehler, 2008).

22. See, for example, J. T. Bond, E. Galinsky, and J. E. Swanberg, *The 1997 National Study of the Changing Workforce* (New York: Families and Work Institute, 1998); F. L. Branham, *Keeping the People Who Keep You in Business* (New York: AMACOM, 2000); B. N. Pfau and I. T. Kay, *The Human Capital Edge* (New York: McGraw-Hill, 2001); and K. Thomas, *Intrinsic Motivation at Work: What Really Drives Employee Engagement*, 2nd ed. (San Francisco: Berrett-Koehler, 2009).

23. L. K. Thaler and R. Koyal, "The Power of 'Thanks,'" the Power of Small blog, posted January 17, 2011, http://www.thepowerofsmallbook.com/index.php/pos/comments/601/.

24. B. Nelson, "The Power of Rewards and Recognition," presentation to the Consortium on Executive Education, Leavey School of Business, Santa Clara University, September 20, 1996; A. M. Grant and F. Gino, "A Little Thanks Goes a Long Way: Explaining Why Gratitude Expressions Motivate Prosocial Behavior," *Journal of Personality and Social Psychology* 98, no. 6 (June 2010): 946–955.

25. R. M. Kanter, *The Changemasters: Innovation and Entrepreneurship in the American Corporation* (New York: Free Press, 1985). See also R. M. Kanter, *SuperCorp: How Vanguard Companies Create Innovation, Profits, Growth and Social Good* (New York: Crown Books, 2009).

26. M. Buckingham and D. O. Clifton, *Now, Discover Your Strengths* (New York: Free Press, 2001). You can go overboard, however. At a thirteen-to-one ratio, productivity declines. Most people don't have to worry about this upper limit; it's meeting the three-to-one ratio that's usually problematic for most people.

27. See T. Rath and D. O. Clifton, *How Full Is Your Bucket? Positive Strategies for Work and Life* (New York: Gallup Press, 2004), 57. Original research: M. Losada, "The Complex Dynamics of High Performance Teams," *Mathematical and Computer Modeling* (1999): 30.

Chapter 11: Celebrate the Values and Victories

1. In writing on this important subject, *New York Times* writer David Brooks combines the most recent research on neuroscience with a fascinating narrative story. See D. Brooks, *The Social Animal: The Hidden Sources of Love, Character, and Achievement* (New York: Random House, 2011). Social psychologist Elliot Aronson has written the most widely read and most accessible textbook on the dynamics of human behavior in social settings. See E. Aronson, *The Social Animal*, 11th ed. (New York: Worth, 2011).

2. For a detailed discussion of, and extensive data on, social capital, see R. Putnam, *Bowling Alone: The Collapse and Revival of American Community* (New York: Touchstone, 2001). For a practical application of social capital research to the business world, see W. Baker, *Achieving Success Through Social Capital: Tapping the Hidden Resources in Your Personal and Business Networks* (San Francisco: Jossey-Bass, 2000).

3. Source: "List of Social Networking Websites," *Wikipedia*, http://en.wikipedia .org/wiki/List_of_social_networking_websites.

4. K. N. Hampton, L. S. Goulet, L. Rainie, and K. Purcell, "Social Networking Sites and Our Lives," *Pew Internet & American Life Project*, June 16, 2011, 22. Available at http://pewinternet.org/Reports/2011/Technology-and-social -networks.aspx.

5. T. Deal and M. K. Key, *Corporate Celebration: Play, Purpose, and Profit at Work* (San Francisco: Berrett-Koehler, 1998), 5.

6. This example was provided by Alex Jukl.

7. D. Campbell, *If I'm in Charge Here, Why Is Everybody Laughing?* (Greensboro, NC: Center for Creative Leadership, 1984), 64.

8. This was precisely the point that our Russian colleague Alexey Astafev made in the previous chapter.

9. This example was provided by Michael Bunting.

10. See, for example, K. J. Fenlason and T. A. Beehr, "Social Support and Occupational Stress: Effects of Talking to Others," *Journal of Organizational Behavior* 15, no. 2 (1994): 157–175; and J. S. Mulbert, "Social Networks, Social Circles, and Job Satisfaction," *Work & Occupations* 18, no. 4 (1991): 415–430.

11. L. L. Berry, A. Parasuraman, and V. A. Zeithaml, "Improving Service Quality in America: Lessons Learned," *Academy of Management Executive* 8, no. 2 (1994): 32–45.

12. S. Achor, *The Happiness Advantage: The Seven Principles of Positive Psychology That Fuel Success and Performance at Work* (New York: Crown Books, 2010), 176.

13. See J. Cacioppo, *Loneliness: Human Nature and the Need for Social Connection* (New York: Norton, 2008). See also L. F. Berkman and S. L. Syme, "Social Networks, Host Resistance, and Mortality: A Nine-Year Follow-Up Study of Alameda County Residents," *American Journal of Epidemiology* 109, no. 2 (1979): 186–204; and S. Cohen, "Psychosocial Models of the Role of Social Support in the Etiology of Physical Disease," *Health Psychology* 7 (1988): 269–297.

14. J. W. Shenk, "What Makes Us Happy?" *Atlantic*, June 2009, http://www .theatlantic.com/magazine/print/2009/06/what-makes-us-happy/7439/.

15. R. D. Cotton, Y. Shen, and R. Livne-Tarandach, "On Becoming Extraordinary: The Content and Structure of the Developmental Networks of Major League Baseball Hall of Famers," *Academy of Management Journal* 54, no. 1 (2011): 15–46.

16. T. Rath, *Vital Friends: The People You Can't Afford to Live Without* (New York: Gallup Press, 2006), 52. See also T. Rath and J. Harter, *Well Being: The Five Essential Elements* (New York: Gallup Press, 2010), 40–43, for an update on this research. See also R. Wagner and J. K. Harter, *12: The Elements of Great Managing* (New York: Simon & Schuster, 2006) for a follow-up report on the Gallup engagement research, including a discussion of the importance of having friends in the workplace.

17. Rath, *Vital Friends*, 51.

18. R. F. Baumeister and M. R. Leary, "The Need to Belong: Desire for Interpersonal Attachment as a Fundamental Human Motivation," *Psychological Bulletin* 117 (1995): 497–529; H. W. Perkins, "Religious Commitment, Yuppie Values, and Well-Being in a Post-Collegiate Life," *Review of Religious Research* 32 (1991): 244–251; D. G. Myers, "The Funds, Friends, and Faith of Happy People," *American Psychologist* 55, no. 1 (2000): 56–67; and S. Crabtree, "Getting Personal in the Workplace: Are Negative Relationships Squelching Productivity in Your Company?" *Gallup Management Journal*, June 10, 2004, available online at www.govleaders.org/gallup_article_getting _personal.htm.

19. See, for example, Myers, "Funds, Friends, and Faith of Happy People"; M. Csikszentmihalyi, "If We Are So Rich, Why Aren't We Happy?" *American Psychologist* 54 (1999): 821–827; D. G. Myers and E. Diener, "The Pursuit of Happiness," *Scientific American* 274 (1996): 54–56; and D. Gilbert, *Stumbling on Happiness* (New York: Knopf, 2006).

20. This example was provided by Alex Jukl.

21. K. Blanchard and S. Johnson, *The One-Minute Manager* (New York: Morrow, 1982). See also K. Blanchard and R. Lorber, *Putting the One Minute Manager to Work: How to Turn the 3 Secrets into Skills* (New York: Morrow, 2006).

22. G. Klein, *The Sources of Power: How People Make Decisions* (Cambridge, MA: MIT Press, 1998). For more on the importance of storytelling and decision making, see G. Klein, *The Power of Intuition: How to Use Your Gut Feelings to Make Better Decisions at Work* (New York: Crown Business, 2004); and G. Klein, *Streetlights and Shadows: Searching for the Keys to Adaptive Decision Making* (Cambridge, MA: MIT Press, 2009). After studying professionals in life-and-death situations, Klein concludes that "the method we found most powerful for eliciting knowledge is to use stories."

23. D. Westen, *The Political Brain: The Role of Emotion in Deciding the Fate of the Nation* (New York: Public Affairs, 2008), 28.

Chapter 12: Leadership Is Everyone's Business

1. This survey was first conducted for Public Allies, now a part of AmeriCorps, in 1998 to those eighteen to thirty-two years old. We adapted the survey and have administered it to a wider range of ages over the past decade.

2. B. Z. Posner, "A Longitudinal Study Examining Changes in Students' Leadership Behavior," *Journal of College Student Development* 50, no. 5 (2009): 551–563.

3. K. A. Ericsson, "The Influence of Experience and Deliberate Practice on the Development of Superior Expert Performance," in *The Cambridge Handbook of Expertise and Expert Performance*, ed. K. A. Ericsson, N. Charness, P. J. Feltovich, and R. R. Hoffman (New York: Cambridge University Press, 2006), 699.

4. See Ericsson, "Influence of Experience," 692. Others have also written about this metric. See, for example, G. Colvin, *Talent Is Overrated: What Really Separates World-Class Performers from Everybody Else* (New York: Portfolio, 2008); D. Coyle, *The Talent Code: Greatness Isn't Born. It's Grown. Here's How* (New York: Bantam Books, 2009); and M. Gladwell, *Outliers: The Story of Success* (New York: Little, Brown, 2008).

5. H.M.J. Kraemer Jr., *From Values to Action: The Four Principles of Values-Based Leadership* (San Francisco: Jossey-Bass, 2011), 15. We interviewed him on November 11, 2011. Noted leadership scholar Warren Bennis has also pointed out that becoming a leader requires you to know your inner self, and he calls that "the most difficult task any of us faces. But until you truly know yourself, strengths and weaknesses, know what you want to do and why you want to do it, you cannot succeed in any but the most superficial sense of the word."

NOTES

W. Bennis, *On Becoming a Leader*, 4th ed. (Philadelphia: Basic Books, 2009), 40.

6. Kraemer, *From Values to Action*, 26.

7. D. Balter, "The Humility Imperative: CEOs, Keep Your Arrogance in Check," *Inc.*, June 23, 2011, http://inc.com/articles/201106/the-humility-imperative -ceos-keep-your-arrogance-in-check.html. Balter became so motivated by his own transformational experience that he instigated a movement called "The Humility Imperative"; see his Web site (www.humilityimperative.com) devoted to spreading the message about the importance of humility in leaders.

8. Balter, "Humility Imperative."

9. For more on the importance of humility in organizational success, see J. Collins, *Good to Great: Why Some Companies Make the Leap . . . and Others Don't* (New York: Harper Audio, 2005), 17–40. See also Kraemer, *From Values to Action*, 59–76. Another interesting perspective is F. Kofman, *Conscious Business: How to Build Value Through Values* (Boulder, CO: Sounds True, 2006).

10. We write more about the importance of courage in *A Leader's Legacy* (San Francisco: Jossey-Bass, 2006).

Acknowledgments

People often ask us how we've managed to work together for such a long time, and one important reason is that we both recognize that you can't do anything great all by yourself! With this in mind, we pay tribute to all those who have helped us over these many years to make this book possible (from the first edition onward).

We gratefully acknowledge the millions of people around the world who have read our books and used our materials. We hear from individuals nearly every week about how they are applying these ideas—not just in their workplaces but in their homes and with their families, communities, and congregations. You give us reason, and encouragement, to continue to do our part in liberating the leader within each and every person, and making extraordinary things possible.

We thank our collaborators in the research—those who participated in our classes, workshops, and seminars; who completed our

375

surveys; and who were gracious in sharing their case studies with us. You are the heart and soul of this book. Your stories and examples bring the numbers and qualities to life. We learned years ago that experience is the best teacher of leadership; your histories reinforce this axiom.

We also give a "shout-out" to all those who made previous editions of this book possible through their generous help, able assistance, and gracious support: Julianne Balmain, Myra Cake, Brian and Anne Carroll, Paul Cohen, Cedric Crocker, Kathy Dalle-Molle, Ray Dallin, Marcella Friel, Bill Hicks, Jerry Hunt, Jan Hunter, JoAnn Johnson, Peter Jordan, Steve Katten, Sarah Kidd, Andre and Barbara Morkel, Trish O'Hare, Lynne Parode, Tom Peters, Debra Scates, Natalie Sibert, Laura Simonds, Tracey Taylor, Janice Van Collie, Francessa Webb, Terri Armstrong Welch, and Barbara Wheeler.

Hats off to the terrific team at Jossey-Bass and Wiley. You have all been first-rate in your support and encouragement—prodding, nudging, and challenging us to think deeply and address a broad set of issues, circumstances, and audiences. This edition has benefited, in particular, from the overall craftsmanship and gentle guidance of Byron Schneider, senior development editor, and Karen Murphy, senior editor. We especially want to thank our developmental editor, Leslie Stephen, who brought clarity and focus to our writing, challenged our thinking, and willingly broke ties when we got ourselves bogged down. Others at Jossey-Bass/Wiley who helped us bring this book into and through production and onto bookshelves who deserve special recognition include Mary Garrett, senior production editor; Michele D. Jones, copyeditor; John Maas, senior editorial assistant; Carolyn Carlstroem, associate marketing director; and Amy Packard, publicity manager. Special notes of thanks for their continuing support, encouragement, sense of humor, and leadership go out to Lisa Shannon, associate publisher, and Marisa Kelly, associate editor.

We dedicated this twenty-fifth anniversary edition to our spouses, Tae Moon Kouzes and Jackie Schmidt-Posner, and we add a final note of appreciation for their ongoing patience, understanding, wise counsel, and love. Many thanks for sticking with us through this project and so many other adventures (and those still to come!).

About the Authors

Jim Kouzes and Barry Posner have been working together for more than thirty years, studying leaders, researching leadership, conducting leadership development seminars, and serving as leaders themselves in various capacities. They are coauthors of the award-winning, best-selling book *The Leadership Challenge*. Since its first edition in 1987, *The Leadership Challenge* has sold more than two million copies worldwide and is available in more than twenty-two languages. It has won numerous awards, including the Critics' Choice Award from the nation's book review editors and the James A. Hamilton Hospital Administrators' Book of the Year Award, and was selected as one of the top ten books on leadership in Covert and Sattersten's *The 100 Best Business Books of All Time*.

Jim and Barry have coauthored more than a dozen other award-winning leadership books, including *Credibility: How Leaders Gain and Lose It, Why People Demand It; The Truth About Leadership: The*

No-Fads, Heart-of-the-Matter Facts You Need to Know; A Leader's Legacy; Encouraging the Heart: A Leader's Guide to Rewarding and Recognizing Others; The Student Leadership Challenge; and *The Academic Administrator's Guide to Exemplary Leadership.* They also developed the highly acclaimed Leadership Practices Inventory (LPI), a 360-degree questionnaire for assessing leadership behavior, which is one of the most widely used leadership assessment instruments in the world, along with The Student LPI. More than five hundred doctoral dissertations and academic papers have been based on their The Five Practices of Exemplary Leadership model.

Among the honors and awards that Jim and Barry have received is the American Society for Training and Development's highest award for their Distinguished Contribution to Workplace Learning and Performance. They have been named Management/Leadership Educators of the Year by the International Management Council; ranked by *Leadership Excellence* magazine in the top twenty on its list of the Top 100 Thought Leaders; named among the 50 Top Coaches in the nation (according to *Coaching for Leadership*); and listed among *HR Magazine*'s Most Influential International Thinkers.

Jim and Barry are frequent keynote speakers, and each has conducted leadership development programs for hundreds of organizations, including Alberta Health Services, Apple, Applied Materials, ARCO, AT&T, Australia Institute of Management, Australia Post, Bank of America, Bose, Charles Schwab, Chevron, Cisco Systems, Clorox, Community Leadership Association, Conference Board of Canada, Consumers Energy, Deloitte Touche, Dorothy Wylie Nursing and Health Leaders Institute, Dow Chemical, Egon Zehnder International, Federal Express, Genentech, Google, Gymboree, HP, IBM, Jobs DR-Singapore, Johnson & Johnson, Kaiser Foundation Health Plans and Hospitals, Intel, Itau Unibanco, L. L. Bean, Lawrence Livermore National Labs, Lucile Packard Children's Hospital, Merck, Motorola, NetApp, Northrop Grumman, Novartis, Oakwood

Temporary Housing, Oracle, Petronas, Roche Bioscience, Siemens, 3M, Toyota, United Way, USAA, Verizon, VISA, the Walt Disney Company, and Westpac. They have lectured at over sixty college and university campuses.

Jim Kouzes is the Dean's Executive Fellow of Leadership, Leavey School of Business at Santa Clara University, and lectures on leadership around the world to corporations, governments, and nonprofits. He is a highly regarded leadership scholar and an experienced executive; the *Wall Street Journal* cited him as one of the twelve best executive educators in the United States. In 2010, Jim received the Thought Leadership Award from the Instructional Systems Association, the most prestigious award given by the trade association of training and development industry providers. He was listed as one of *HR Magazine*'s Most Influential International Thinkers for 2010 and 2011, named one of the 2010 and 2011 Top 100 Thought Leaders in Trustworthy Business Behavior by *Trust Across America,* and ranked by *Leadership Excellence* magazine as number sixteen on its list of the Top 100 Thought Leaders. In 2006, Jim was presented with the Golden Gavel, the highest honor awarded by Toastmasters International. Jim served as president, CEO, and chairman of the Tom Peters Company from 1988 through 1999, and prior to that led the Executive Development Center at Santa Clara University (1981–1987). Jim founded the Joint Center for Human Services Development at San Jose State University (1972–1980) and was on the staff of the School of Social Work, University of Texas. His career in training and development began in 1969 when he conducted seminars for Community Action Agency staff and volunteers in the war on poverty. Following graduation from Michigan State University (BA degree with honors in political science), he served as a Peace Corps volunteer (1967–1969). Jim can be reached at jim@ kouzes.com.

ABOUT THE AUTHORS

Barry Posner is Accolti Professor of Leadership at the Leavey School of Business, Santa Clara University, where he served as dean of the school for twelve years (1997–2009). He has been a distinguished visiting professor at Hong Kong University of Science and Technology, Sabanci University (Istanbul), and the University of Western Australia. At Santa Clara he has received the President's Distinguished Faculty Award, the School's Extraordinary Faculty Award, and several other teaching and academic honors. An internationally renowned scholar and educator, Barry is author or coauthor of more than a hundred research and practitioner-focused articles. He currently serves on the editorial review boards for *Leadership and Organizational Development* and the *International Journal of Servant-Leadership*. In 2011, he received the Outstanding Scholar Award for Career Achievement from the *Journal of Management Inquiry*.

Barry received his BA with honors in political science from the University of California, Santa Barbara; his MA in public administration from The Ohio State University; and his PhD in organizational behavior and administrative theory from the University of Massachusetts, Amherst. Having consulted with a wide variety of public and private sector organizations around the globe, Barry also works at a strategic level with a number of community-based and professional organizations, currently sitting on the board of directors of EMQ FamiliesFirst. He has served previously on the boards of the American Institute of Architects (AIA), Big Brothers/Big Sisters of Santa Clara County, Center for Excellence in Nonprofits, Junior Achievement of Silicon Valley and Monterey Bay, Public Allies, San Jose Repertory Theater, Sigma Phi Epsilon Fraternity, and both publicly traded and start-up companies. Barry can be reached at bposner@scu.edu.

Index

Critical incidents, 88–91
Csikszentmihalyi, Mihaly, 256, 257

D
DaVita, 79–80
Day, Guy, 273–275
Deal, Terence, 324, 325
Decision making: giving employees power in, 242, 250–252; by groups of friends vs. acquaintances, 289; intuitive, 105–106, 352n3; as latent vs. acquirable skill, 263; sharing information about, 260
Deloitte, 289–290, 370n17
Denning, Steve, 91
Developing competence and confidence, 255–267; by fostering self-confidence, 262–264; need for, 255–258; by organizing work, 261–262; by sharing information., 259–261; through coaching, 264–267; training for, 258–259
DeVry, 302–304
di Bari, Paul, 50–51
Diemer, Ryan, 20
Dirking, Jennifer, 23–24
Disney, Walt, 206
Drucker, Peter, 266
Duckworth, Angela, 207
DuPont, 198
Durrani, Yamin, 31–32
Dweck, Carol, 202–203
DWYSYWD (Do What You Say You Will Do), 40, 74
Dye, Renee, 173
Dyer, Jeffrey, 178

E
Edelman, Richard, 9
Eichinger, Bob, 202

Einstein, Albert, 112, 353n9
Emotions: expressing, 129, 147–150; positive, 146; recognition to replenish, 275, 287
Employees. *See* Constituents
Enabling others to act (practice 4), 21–23, 29, 214. *See also* Fostering collaboration; Strengthening others
Encouraging the heart (practice 5), 23–24, 29, 272. *See also* Celebrating values and victories; Recognizing contributions
Engagement: impact of leadership philosophy clarity on, 47–48; influence of leader's actions on, 25–26, 348n9; personal values and, 55–57; when work matters, 133
Enlisting others, 127–153; actions for, 152–153; by animating vision, 139–151; by appealing to common ideals, 130–139; example of impact of, 127–129
Enthusiasm, 141, 147, 315
Envisioning the future, 101–126; actions for, 125–126; by finding common purpose, 116–124; by imagining possibilities, 104–115; importance of, 101–103
Ericsson, K. Anders, 335–336
Expectations: constituents', of leaders, 33–36; living up to, 276–279, 368n1, 369n5
Expecting the best, 276–285; by clarifying goals and rules, 280–281; by giving regular feedback, 282–285; impact of, 276–277, 368nn1–2; by showing that you believe, 277–279
Experimenting and taking risks, 185–211; actions for, 209–211; example of results of, 185–187; by generating small wins, 189–199; by

U
Ulrich, Dave, 202
Undercover Boss, 180, 360n25

V
Vacation policy, 249
Vaillant, George, 311
Values: common, of workers, 120, 354n18, 355nn19–20; communicated by leader, 43–44; defined, 48; as guide for actions, 48–51; how time spent as indicator of, 76–78; language as reflecting, 79–81, 351n6; means and ends classification of, 48; organizational systems to reinforce, 93–95; personal, and commitment, 55–57; questions for reflecting on, 81–84; stated in your own words, 51–54; teaching modeling of, 87–95. *See also* Celebrating values and victories; Clarifying values; Shared values
Vesterman, Jim, 235–236
Virtuousness, 277, 368n2
Vision: animating, 139–151; and appealing to ideals, 130–131; as ends value, 48–49; finding shared, 116–124; inspiring shared, 17–19, 29, 100; origin of, 105–106, 352n3
Vitale, Jessica, 12
Voice. *See* Finding your voice
Vy, MT, 308

W
Walker, Taryn, 18
Walsh, Alison, 10–11
Walsh, Bill, 353n10
Wang, Caroline, 26
Wang, John, 166–167
Wang, Justina, 197
Web site, leadership challenge, 6, 347n2, 351n11
Weick, Karl, 190
West, James E., 200
Westen, Drew, 321–322
Wiencke, Judith, 319
Williams, Pat, 206–207
Wilson, Donna, 291–292
Winkel, Katherine, 19
Winkler, Heidi, 22
Wiseman, Liz, 246–247
Wong, Bert, 93–95
Wong, Jacqueline, 118–119, 293–294
Workplaces: great, 133, 258–259, 356nn4, 6; impact of trust in, 219–222. *See also* Job structure

Y
Yaffe, Tal, 75
Yang, Geoff, 122

Z
Zeno Group, 9–13
Zor, Ferhat, 310

MORE ON *THE LEADERSHIP CHALLENGE* . . .

If you are looking for opportunities to make a difference in your world or tools to keep your community inspired, we can help. Whether you would like to read more works by Jim Kouzes and Barry Posner, gather feedback on your own leadership style, or implement a leadership development program within your organization, we offer abundant resources for *The Leadership Challenge* to help you begin or continue your leadership journey. These include

- **Books**—Jim and Barry's bestselling, award-winning books include *The Truth About Leadership, Credibility, A Leader's Legacy, Encouraging the Heart, The Student Leadership Challenge,* and *The Academic Administrator's Guide to Exemplary Leadership.*
- **Workbooks**—*The Leadership Challenge Workbook, The Encouraging the Heart Workbook,* and *Strengthening Credibility* help you put TLC's teachings into practice. These interactive tools are designed to apply Jim and Barry's framework to productively resolving the problems and situations you face.
- **Assessments**—The Leadership Practices Inventory—LPI is the 360-degree assessment instrument designed by Jim and Barry that has recorded responses from over three million individuals worldwide. Find out more at www.lpionline.com. The Student LPI is also available for high school and undergraduate students. In addition, The Encouragement Index is now available as a stand-alone product.
- **Digital Offerings**—The Leadership Challenge DVD (Revised) is an approximately 90-minute film in which Jim and Barry introduce The Five Practices of Exemplary Leadership® to

viewers through commentary and case studies. It includes a guide for screening and discussion. The Leadership Challenge eLearning Program is a two-hour self-paced course intended to build awareness around the model. It is an excellent introduction to Jim and Barry's work and has many applications, such as pre-work for assessment administration or as a way to cascade the model through an organization. The Leadership Challenge Mobile App helps individuals integrate the leadership practices presented in this book into their lives and daily routines. It includes content from the book and on The Five Practices, as well as features and functionality to help users make plans, take action on recommended activities, and obtain feedback.

- **Workshops**—The Leadership Challenge® Workshop is a unique, intensive program that has served as a catalyst for profound leadership transformations in organizations of all sizes and in all industries. In this highly interactive workshop, participants experience and apply Jim and Barry's leadership model through video cases, workbook exercises, group problem-solving tasks, lectures, and outdoor action learning. For those looking to follow up a workshop experience with a deep-dive into the fifth practice, The Encouraging the Heart Workshop is an excellent solution. The Challenge Continues offers in-person and virtual solutions to refresh leaders on the model and provides opportunities to put the learning into practice.

These offerings represent the authoritative breadth and broad applicability of the ideas that make Jim and Barry the most trusted sources on becoming a better leader. To find out more about these products, and others by the authors, please visit www .leadershipchallenge.com. If you would like to speak to a leadership consultant about bringing *The Leadership Challenge* to your organization or team, call toll free (866) 888-5159 or email leadership@ wiley.com.